SELECTED PAPERS ON
ECONOMIC THEORY

KNUT WICKSELL AT ABOUT SIXTY-FIVE

KNUT WICKSELL

SELECTED PAPERS
ON
ECONOMIC THEORY

Edited with an Introduction
by
ERIK LINDAHL

REPRINTS OF ECONOMIC CLASSICS

Augustus M. Kelley · Publishers
NEW YORK 1969

First Edition 1958

(London: George Allen & Unwin, 1958)

Reprinted 1969 by

AUGUSTUS M. KELLEY · PUBLISHERS

New York New York 10010

By Arrangement With GEORGE ALLEN & UNWIN

Library of Congress Catalogue Card Number

68 - 58667

PREFACE

KNUT WICKSELL'S most important works in economic theory—the earlier German publications *Value, Capital and Rent* (1893) and *Interest and Prices* (1898) and the later *Lectures on Political Economy*, published in Swedish (1901–4)—have been translated into English and thus make it possible for English readers to study his main contributions. The object of the present volume is to supplement these works with a selection of various articles, mostly published in the Swedish *Ekonomisk Tidskrift* during the first quarter of this century, and hitherto not available to the English-speaking public. In this way the reader may obtain a fuller picture of Wicksell as an economist than is possible merely by reading his major works.

The collection includes only articles that have not previously been available in English. I have also excluded articles which deal with problems of more domestic or temporary importance, and which therefore cannot be fully appreciated without a fairly detailed knowledge of their background. This selection thus contains articles of a more general interest that can be read with profit even now, half a century after their first publication.

The papers have been divided into four groups. The first contains two early lectures, one explaining Wicksell's views on Economics in general, the other giving a summary of his monetary theory. The second group consists of three papers containing the kernel of Wicksell's contributions to the theory of production and distribution. Wicksell's theories in this field are, of course, more fully developed in the other works mentioned above, especially in his *Lectures*, but the inclusion of these articles here may nevertheless be justified since they give a more readable exposition of his views, and also contain some interesting comments not included in the *Lectures*. Some articles in which Wicksell expresses his opinions on the works of other well-known economists of his time have been put together as a third group. The first two on Pareto and the last one on Bowley seem to be of value from the scientific point of view as they also contain original contributions to economic theory by Wicksell himself. The others, dealing with the Austrian economists Böhm-Bawerk and Carl Menger, are of interest as throwing light both

5

on these economists and on Wicksell himself. The last group contains some papers on foreign trade problems, written by Wicksell after the end of the First World War. Wicksell had then reached a ripe old age—the last article was written in his seventy-fourth year—but the reader is not conscious of any decrease in the acuteness of his mind.

As an introduction I have used an article on Wicksell's life and work which I wrote in 1951, celebrating the centenary of his birth. In this is presented the personal background to his writings, emphasising the fact that Wicksell was not only a great economist but also a prominent reformer, whose activities have been of great importance for the social development of Sweden. For a more extensive account of Wicksell's life the reader is referred to the excellent biography by Torsten Gårdlund which will be available in English before long.

The translation of most of the articles has been done by Mr. Reginald S. Stedman, B.A. However, the paper on 'The Influence of the Rate of Interest on Commodity Prices' has been translated by Mrs. Sylva Gethin, M.A., and my paper on 'Wicksell's Life and Work' by Mr. Alan Williams, B.Com. Mr. Williams has also given generous help and guidance in the preparation of the whole volume.

The editor also wishes to express his thanks to the Swedish Academy of Science and to the Government Council for Social Science Research for grants covering the cost of translation.

E. L.

Uppsala, August 1956

CONTENTS

INTRODUCTION

WICKSELL'S LIFE AND WORK[1]

by

Erik Lindahl

JOHAN GUSTAF KNUT WICKSELL was born on December 20, 1851, and died on May 3, 1926. Internationally, he is now numbered among the great economists who were at work around the turn of the century. His influence, for a long time rather limited, has in recent years been growing noticeably, and even makes itself felt on the frontiers of economic theory. From the Swedish viewpoint, Wicksell's life-work assumes a special stature. For Wicksell was not only an ingenious scholar, but also a radical political thinker and untiring social reformer of great calibre. Through his contributions to political and cultural debates, he has decisively influenced the development of political ideas in Sweden, and has thereby also played a considerable part in the remarkable remoulding of Swedish society that took place in the last quarter of the nineteenth century and the first quarter of this.

I

Knut Wicksell was a Stockholmer. He said that it was music for him to walk along the streets of Stockholm when, on reaching his retirement, he had the opportunity of living once more in the neighbourhood of the capital. His father, who was descended from a farming family, was a provisions dealer. After five years at the Maria Elementary School, and four at Stockholm Secondary School, Knut Wicksell passed the *mogenhetsexamen* (school-leaving examination) in 1869, and in the autumn went to Uppsala, to study, first of all, Mathematics, in which he had already particularly interested himself at school. He had also learnt Latin and Greek at school, however, and the *fil.-cand.* (B.A.) examination, which he passed at the beginning of 1872, after only five semesters of study, included, besides

[1] Translation of an article 'Till hundraårsminnet av Knut Wicksells födelse' (On the Centenary of the Birth of Knut Wicksell), *Ekonomisk Tidskrift*, 1951, pp. 197–243. Some passages of mainly Scandinavian interest have been omitted.

two *betyg* (honours marks) in Mathematics, one in each of the following subjects: Latin Language and Literature, Scandinavian Languages, History, and Theoretical Philosophy. After this, it was not until 1885 that he was ready for his *fil.-lic.* (M.A.) examination, in which his subjects were Mechanics, Mathematics, and Physics. In the meantime, however, Wicksell had gone through the experiences that brought him over into the social sciences.

'Originating from a religious home, he seems to have gone through a religious crisis, about which he never spoke, however, even with those closest to him. After inner struggles, from the beginning of 1880 he supported the cause of the neo-Malthusians, for which he soon became notorious throughout the country.'[1] In his commemorative article on Wicksell, Sommarin points out that it was the translation into Swedish in 1878 of the work of the English doctor George Drysdale that awakened Wicksell's interest in population problems, from which he was led deeper and deeper into social and economic studies.

Wicksell's first appearance as a social reformer was as discussion leader at a temperance meeting arranged by the 'Hoppets Här' (Band of Hope) branch, in a mission hall in Uppsala on February 19, 1880. The address was repeated afterwards before a more academic audience, and was printed and published by the author, under the title 'A Few Words on the Most Important Cause of Social Misery and its Remedy, with Special Reference to Drunkenness.'[2] In it, Wicksell, in tactful but determined words, gave expression to the opinion that drunkenness was associated with poverty, and poverty was caused by overpopulation, so that it should be a holy duty for all married people to limit the size of the family to two or three children.

The address was a *succès de scandale*. Several thousand copies of the pamphlet were quickly sold, and gave rise to a heated discussion in the newspapers, and a whole series of counterblasts. Wicksell's style of presentation was fascinating—as a literary work the pamphlet is a masterpiece—but the idea of birth control, in spite of the fact that it could hardly have been presented more delicately, was found so repugnant that Wicksell was described as a 'human

---

[1] Emil Sommarin, 'Minnesord över professor Knut Wicksell' (In Memory of Professor Knut Wicksell), *Kungl. Humanistiska Vetenskapssamfundet i Lund, Årsberättelse* 1926–7 (Bulletin de la Société Royale des Lettres de Lund 1926–7), pp. 21–52.

[2] *Några ord om samhällsolyckornas viktigaste orsak och botemedel med särskildt afseende på dryckenskapen*, Uppsala, 1880.

monster.' 'The address was considered so compromising,' says Mrs. Ann Margret Holmgren, 'that practically all doors were closed against the young man, who had previously been so sought after. As far as I remember, ours was the only home that was still open to him after that lecture.'[1] Wicksell, who during the immediately preceding years had played a prominent role in Uppsala's student life—he was Chairman of the Students' Union during the academic year 1878–9—now found himself the subject of disciplinary action by the Council of the University.[2] He soon felt at home in his new role as a radical member of the opposition, however. That he had suddenly become the centre of a great social debate,[3] 'the Wicksell question,' may indeed have appealed to his belligerent temperament. He immediately wrote a reply in which he courteously but crushingly answered his critics,[4] and in Stockholm and Uppsala in the autumn of 1881 he gave a new lecture on the population problem, which was printed in 1882.[5] Wicksell here showed that the great flow of emigrants from Sweden (approximately 50,000 per annum) was a consequence of the high birth rate, and thereby he had another telling argument in favour of his neo-Malthusian ideas: 'if we want to prevent emigration in the future, or at least to reduce it to less alarming proportions, we must cease giving birth to emigrants' (p. 61).

Wicksell's experiences during these years were of decisive significance for his future as a scholar and social reformer. It was his opponents' charge that he expressed himself on economic matters without having the necessary knowledge that led him to study economics seriously. Sommarin has also rightly noted 'that the controversy carried him even more deeply and broadly into the central problems of economics, and forced him from the outset to

[1] Erik Lindorm, *Oscar II och hans tid* (Oscar II and his Time), Stockholm, 1934, p. 117.

[2] According to the Council's protocol, Mr. Knut Wicksell, after first having been called upon for written explanations, appeared before the Council on March 5, 1880, at 5 p.m., and was remonstrated with and warned by the Rector, as the Council had decided. It appears from the protocol that the Council had considered, but not deemed it necessary to apply, some of the more severe disciplinary penalties which otherwise would have been within its powers, since it 'considered Mr. Wicksell's false statements to be occasioned to a significant extent by theoretical confusion, insufficient insight, and thoughtlessness.'

[3] A graphic description of this has been given in Gunnar and Alva Myrdal's book *Kris i befolkningsfrågan* (Crisis in the Population Problem), Stockholm, 1934, pp. 28 *et seq.*

[4] *Svar till mina granskare* (Reply to my Reviewers), Uppsala, 1880.

[5] *Om utvandringen, dess betydelse och orsaker* (On Emigration, its Significance and Causes), Stockholm, 1882.

11

direct his critical vigilance towards the arguments of his opponents and towards the solidity of his own.'[1] One can also find confirmation of this in Wicksell's later, purely scientific, writings, where the positive presentation is nearly always built upon a penetrating examination of other writers' arguments.

Wicksell may also have found that shock tactics, such as those he involuntarily produced on his first appearance as a social reformer, did not hinder the propagation of new ideas, for afterwards it became characteristic of him almost always to shock his opponents, achieving this deliberately by a skilful use of the weapons of irony and satire. During these years in Uppsala, which are remarkable for an unusually great interest in current affairs, Wicksell was characterised by a contemporary biographer as 'the most outstanding champion of the liberal contingent of the Students' Union, whose audacious statements, thrown out during public discussions, are received by the various factions alternately with admiration and dismay.'[2] Even so, on several subsequent occasions, especially in dealing with religious matters, he obviously went too far—in one case the shock was so great that he was sent to prison—though he would probably have defended his way of handling the matter by pointing out that the end justifies the means.[3] Whether, at the same time, he found satisfaction in goading his opponents into anger with his pointed phrases, or whether he found justification for them in the often unfair methods which they used against him, may here be left an open question.

---

[1] Op. cit., p. 24.

[2] Hofberg, *Svenskt Biografiskt Handlexikon* (Swedish Biographical Handbook), Stockholm, 1906, II, p. 720. In this connection it should be mentioned that Wicksell was one of the founders of the liberal student club 'Verdandi' (1882), in which, during the immediately succeeding years, he came to play a leading role.

[3] Wicksell's petition to the Supreme Court, in the blasphemy case referred to above, which will be further touched upon later, concluded in the following way: 'I am not so conceited as to think that I have made the best possible use of this sort of weapon [viz. irony]. A wittier person, or one with a finer literary taste, would perhaps have succeeded in achieving the same effect, or perhaps an even greater one, without having to get people's minds into such a disturbed state. However, this is not the question at issue here, of course, and a literary or aesthetic survey is no affair of the court. On the occasion in question I said what I believed should be said, and I said it in the way which I supposed would have the greatest effect. And since I am conscious of having acted in this matter not out of malice, but, on the contrary, with the utmost goodwill, I still ask to be relieved of all punishment . . .,' etc.

II

In the autumn of 1884 Wicksell left Uppsala, and after he had finished studying mathematics and natural science for the *licentiatexamen* (M.A.) (September 1885), he devoted himself entirely to the social sciences. At that time Economics did not figure very prominently at the universities. In Uppsala, the lawyer and politician C. G. Hammarskjöld was Professor of Political Economy and Fiscal Law, but during his term of office as a Cabinet Minister the duties of the professorship were discharged, as far as economics was concerned, by David Davidson, who was three years younger than Wicksell, and had been appointed Docent (Assistant Professor) in Political Economy in 1879. (He became a full professor in 1890.) In Lund there was a chair in Administrative Law and Political Economy, which since 1862 had been held by Count G. A. K. Hamilton. Academic activity in the subject was limited, and Wicksell decided to transfer his economic studies abroad. On his list of qualifications[1] he himself stated: 'During the years 1885–6 and 1887–90, partly by my own resources, and partly as Lorén Scholar, I resided in England, France, Germany, and Austria for the purpose of studying political economy. During this time I attended lectures by Professors Leroy-Beaulieu and Desmoulins in Paris, Knapp and Brentano in Strasbourg, Wagner in Berlin, and Menger and Singer in Vienna. Where the opportunity arose, I also took part in seminar discussions.'

The second period of resident study abroad was probably financed mainly by the Lorén Foundation, which later also generously supported the publication of Wicksell's three chief works in German, and the working out of his *Lectures*. At this time Wicksell had no support from any Swedish university, and his own meagre resources he probably used up during his first study trip.[2] Viktor Lorén, the

---

[1] See *Handlingar rörande tillsättandet af extra ordinarie professorsämbetet i nationalekonomi och finansrätt vid universitetet i Lund* (Documents concerning the Appointment of an Associate Professor of Political Economy at the University of Lund), Lund, 1901.

[2] During the winter of 1886–7 Wicksell was in Sweden, and apparently supported himself by lecturing on social affairs. The lectures were later published in three volumes during 1887–90: 1. *Om prostitutionen. Huru mildra och motverka detta samhällsonda?* (On Prostitution—how to Alleviate and Counteract this Social Evil). 2. *Om folkökningen i Sverige och de faror den medför för det allmänna välståndet och för sedligheten* (On the Population Increase in Sweden, and the Dangers it Entails for the General Well-being and Morality). 3. *Om äktenskapet och dess framtid* (On Marriage and its Future).

young son of a Gothenburg brewer, who through his Foundation enabled Wicksell to devote himself for a succession of years to undisturbed research into political economy, thereby became a benefactor of economics to a much greater extent than he himself could surely have imagined.[1] On the whole, it is difficult to see how, without this support, Wicksell would have had the opportunity of writing these books, which constitute his lasting contribution to the science.

The foreign economists mentioned above by Wicksell himself are not among those who influenced his thinking most, however. His teachers were first and foremost the English Classicists, especially Malthus, John Stuart Mill, and Ricardo; during his years of study abroad, he was also much impressed by the newer streams of thought in economics represented by the names Walras, Jevons, Menger, and Böhm-Bawerk. In his commemorative article on the latter, Wicksell has himself written how strongly he was influenced by the great work on capital theory published by Böhm-Bawerk in 1889:[2]

I remember as if it were yesterday the day 25 years ago when, in the window of a bookshop in Berlin—where I was at that time holder of the Viktor Lorén scholarship—I first read the book-title *Positive Theorie des Kapitales* by Eugen v. Böhm-Bawerk. . . . I bought a copy of the book and was soon deeply engrossed in it. There was much of it that I only understood incompletely, as my still extant notes in the margin illustrate; the final section, 'The Height of the Rate of Interest,' which I have subsequently come to value above all the rest, at the time I could

[1] Viktor Edvard Lorén (1857–85) was enrolled as a student in Uppsala in 1876, and may, during his period of study there, have been greatly impressed by Wicksell's attempts to improve society. He found himself unable to make any academic contribution of his own, because of an incurable lung disease, so he decided, as early as 1882, to bequeath the main part of his fortune, which, at about 150,000 crowns, was a considerable sum for that time, to a fund whose object was to be to subsidise the investigation of social problems, and to disseminate more widely knowledge of the social sciences. Not only was the capital as well as the interest to be used up within a period of not more than 50 years, but according to verbal directives 'better in 15 than in 50 years.' The board of the fund, which consisted of five specified people, would, under the directives of the testator, especially satisfy Wicksell's needs. Other economists too, e.g. Gustav Cassel, received generous support. The fund further financed the publication of a series of works which included some original inquiries into social history, and also found the money for the purchase of a large collection of social science literature, which was later transferred gratis to the library of the Riksdag and to the University of Stockholm. Seldom has such donated capital been put to a more effective use.

[2] *Ekonomisk Tidskrift*, 1914, p. 322.

only partly assimilate. But the book was, nevertheless, a revelation to me. I had, previously, myself attempted to dissect the phenomenon of interest on capital theoretically, and also the problem of economic distribution in general when it is complicated by the inclusion of capital (as well as labour and natural resources), but with scant success. Even the brilliant ideas in Jevons's *Theory of Political Economy* had not helped me much, although they really contain the same basic thought, expressed too aphoristically. Now, for the first time, I saw before my own eyes the roof being laid on the theoretical construction of which economists since Ricardo's day had only been able to complete the lower storeys, having to content themselves, meanwhile, with accumulating building material of varying degrees of usefulness.

When Wicksell appeared as an economic theorist before an international audience for the first time,[1] it was with the article 'Kapitalzins und Arbeitslohn' (Interest and Wages) in *Conrads Jahrbücher*, December 1892, in which he completed Böhm-Bawerk's reasoning. The next year his first main economic work *Über Wert, Kapital und Rente nach den neueren nationalökonomischen Theorien* (On Value, Capital and Rent in Recent Economic Theory) was published by Fischer at Jena. This work, of about 160 pages in all, in which Wicksell tries to achieve, partly by applying mathematical methods, a synthesis of the Austrian theories of capital and marginal utility and Walras' equilibrium system, on the whole got a rather cool reception, especially from the representatives of the German historical school, who ranged themselves against Wicksell's mathematical method of presentation. Later, however, a remarkable reappraisal of this work took place.[2] As George Stigler in particular pointed out in his well-known history of doctrine, Wicksell, through this book, became one of the founders of the marginal productivity theory.[3]

---

[1] For the Swedish public Wicksell had already, some years earlier, made clear the main features of the modern theory of value and capital, at a lecture in Stockholm.

[2] The book was reprinted in 1933 in the 'Series of Reprints of Scarce Tracts in Economics and Political Science' published by the London School of Economics. In 1954, more than sixty years after its first publication, an English translation of the book, with a Foreword by Professor G. L. S. Shackle, has been published under the title *Value, Capital and Rent*, in the 'Library of Economics,' edited by Allen and Unwin in London.

[3] See Stigler, *Production and Distribution Theories, The Formative Period*, New York, 1941, pp. 293–4: 'Wicksell's mode of presentation in the *Über Wert* unfortunately obscures the fact that he is presenting the first complete mathematical formulation of the marginal productivity theory of distribution. . . . Wicksell must be acknowledged as one of the founders of the general marginal productivity theory of distribution. His own development contains all the essentials of this

15

By the compactness of its composition and the stringency of its reasoning, this book, with its moderate scope, is outstanding even from the technical viewpoint as Wicksell's most thorough scientific performance. As an academic pioneer he undoubtedly achieved more in *Geldzins und Güterpreise* (Interest and Prices), but this later work is written more in the style of an essay, and does not have the same precision and clarity as the former.

To posterity it seems extraordinary that Wicksell did not use this remarkable treatise as a doctoral dissertation. In fact, he did make an application to this effect, but it was rejected, as is evident from the following letter to Davidson (January 1, 1894):[1]

> As you perhaps have heard, some time ago I applied to the Government for permission to defend as a doctor's thesis a treatise on political economy. This has been refused, but according to what the Minister of Education led me to understand, the matter could be arranged so that I requested permission to complete my *licentiatexamen* with this subject instead. Thus he considered that, on sending in such an application, I should provide particulars of a person who has undertaken to serve as examiner. May I therefore ask whether you, as Professor of Political Economy, would be willing to undertake this—on the assumption, of course, that the examination takes place in Uppsala.

In order to understand this, one should remember that in Sweden at that time the subject of political economy belonged to the law faculty, and that Wicksell had passed no law exams. Only after a special dispensation could the *licentiatexamen* in political economy be taken in the philosophy faculty. Requests for such dispensation were sometimes granted, but by no means invariably, and from the faculty's protocols it appears that opinions there were often divided as to whether one should assist in such a *confusio facultatum*. Wicksell, however, got a dispensation to complete his *licentiatexamen* by submitting to a supplementary examination in political economy with public finance. In May 1895 the 43-year-old scholar was examined by the Professor, three years his junior, with whom he then hardly stood on so friendly a footing as in later years.

theory, and he suggests, even though he does not give explicit mathematical statement of, the general theorem: . . . that the shares of product of the various productive factors must be proportional to the partial derivatives of the . . . production function with respect to the factor in question as variable.' Stigler also points out (p. 374) the interesting fact that Wicksell, when he 'rediscovered' the marginal productivity theory around 1900, was obviously unaware that he himself had already presented this theory in his first work, although in a less explicit form.

[1] This and other letters from Wicksell to Davidson are deposited in the University Library in Uppsala.

Davidson had, of course, in the earlier debate on neo-Malthusianism, not shown any great sympathy with Wicksell's viewpoint. The examination seems to have gone off well, however, if one can judge by the grading (the highest). Wicksell was now able to defend his doctoral thesis, and as his doctoral dissertation he used a smaller paper (seventy-five pages) that he had written in the meantime: *Zur Lehre von der Steuerincidenz* (To the Theory of the Incidence of Taxation). The theoretical apparatus that he had presented in *Value, Capital and Rent* was applied here to the problem of tax incidence. The disputation took place in Uppsala on May 29, 1895.

This was by no means the end of Wicksell's difficulties, however. The intention was, of course, to get a docentur (assistant professorship) with the disputation, but an application for this, submitted to the philosophy faculty, was there recommended for rejection by 10 votes to 6, and was not approved by the Chancellor either. In the opinion of the majority, a docentur in political economy should be located in the faculty to which the subject belonged, i.e. the law faculty; moreover, Wicksell had no training in the humanities, and was also unsuited to teaching as he showed in his propaganda on the population question. After that, Wicksell turned to the law faculty, but since he had no law examination he there encountered an even more powerful opposition. Davidson supported him, to be sure, but with such reluctance on matters of principle that he really gave Wicksell no support at all. After this reverse, only one way stood open, if Wicksell wished to carry out his intention of pursuing an academic career. Now 45 years old, and already an internationally esteemed economist, he was compelled to begin a systematic study of law. His energy was, however, equal to that too, and on April 8, 1899, he passed the *Juris utriusque kandidatexamen* (LL.B.) with honours in half the subjects. After that, he was immediately appointed Docent in Political Economy and Fiscal Law at Uppsala University.

On the whole, Wicksell's intellectual activity and creative power seem to have stood at their peak during the 1890's. It was during that period that he made his pioneering contributions as an economist. During the following twenty-five years too he was certainly a prolific writer, and his writings did in many respects enrich the economic science. But broadly speaking his scientific activity during this period can be characterised as a further development, and as a more systematic—even, as a rule, a more popular—presentation of the important ideas he put forward in the 1890's.

After *Value, Capital and Rent* he turned to taxation problems and published in 1896 the sizeable volume *Finanztheoretische Unter-suchungen nebst Darstellung und Kritik des Steuerwesens Schwedens* (Investigations in Public Finance with a Critical Survey of the Swedish Tax System) which included the doctoral thesis as the first section. In a second section, 'Concerning a New Principle of Equit-able Taxation,' Wicksell dealt with the theory of public finance, and on it he based a new interpretation of the 'benefit principle': parlia-mentary decisions in taxation matters should, in principle, be unanimous, so as to give every group of citizens the possibility of ensuring (through their elected representatives) that their tax pay-ments do not become greater than their benefits of the corresponding governmental activity. This treatise stimulated the present writer to produce a doctoral dissertation upon the principles of justice in taxation, but otherwise it does not seem to have attracted a great deal of attention, although its ideas are valuable from a theoretical viewpoint. In the third, and longest, section of the book (approxi-mately 185 pages) Wicksell gave a critical survey of the development of the Swedish tax system during the last two centuries. In it he seeks to apply the theoretical views set out in the second section. The treatise is of interest, in so far as it is an attempt by Wicksell to apply economic theory to the interpretation of an historical course of events. From the strictly historical viewpoint, however, it is considered less satisfactory, because it is based on secondary sources.

On the completion of this great work, Wicksell immediately set about studying monetary theory. In autumn 1896 we find him in Berlin. Now, for the first time, he had got a state grant of 1,000 crowns from a fund for publishing learned works, and could pursue his researches for the next projected work: *Geldzins und Güterpreise* (Interest and Prices). In studying the problem of bimetallism, which at the time was particularly topical, Wicksell had come to the conclusion that the Quantity Theory was lacking, but that there was no other acceptable theory of the value of money, so that economics here showed a suspicious gap. It was now Wicksell's ambition to fill this gap, and the result of two years of persevering mental effort—the book was ready for publication at the beginning of 1898—was his famous theory that the relationship of the money rate of interest to the natural or real rate of interest on capital was of decisive im-portance for changes in the price level and in the value of money. In propounding this theory, which afterwards proved to have con-siderably greater scope than Wicksell himself supposed, and which gave rise to a new treatment of the entire dynamic problem in economics, Wicksell had made his most brilliant contribution to the science.[1]

Beside this activity on a high scholarly plane, Wicksell carried on extensive journalistic activity throughout the 1890's as the correspondent of several Swedish, Norwegian, and Finnish newspapers, wrote a series of booklets of a more popular kind, especially on taxation questions, and continued, in addition, to give lectures on social and political matters. This seems to have happened partly for financial reasons, for Wicksell had no paid position at this time, and the grants that he obtained from the Lorén Fund during the 1890's were probably devoted to the publication of his scientific works.[2] At the same time, he now had a family to support. In 1889, when he was staying in Paris as Lorén Scholar, he had married the talented Norwegian Anna Bugge (1862–1928), who was later to take up a leading position in the movement for the emancipation of women,[3] and their two sons were born at the beginning of the 1890's.[4] Obtaining a livelihood must have been a pressing problem for the Wicksell family. They lived in Stockholm or Djursholm for the most part, but later in the 1890's, when Wicksell had to start studying for the *juris kandidatexamen* (LL.B.), they moved to Uppsala. Above all else, the mystery is how Wicksell, during this period of his life, could find time for so much, for, as has already been mentioned, it was during the 1890's, when he lived under such poverty-stricken conditions and was besieged by troubles and

---

[1] In a more popular form, Wicksell first gave an account of this theory in an article in *Conrads Jahrbücher*, 1897, 'Der Bankzins als Regulator der Wahrenpreise' (The Bankrate as Regulator of Commodity Prices), and later in a lecture to the 'Nationalekonomiska föreningen' (Economic Association) in Stockholm in 1898. (The latter has been included in this volume.) For the English public, the theory was not set forth until 1907, when Wicksell was invited to give a lecture to the Royal Economic Society in London. A summary of this lecture was published in the *Economic Journal* for 1907, under the title 'The Influence of the Rate of Interest on Prices.'

[2] The only assistance Wicksell obtained from the Swedish State was the above-mentioned grant of 1,000 crowns from a fund for the publication of scientific works.

[3] See, *inter alia*, the miniature biography by Gulli Petrini, *Anna Bugge Wicksell*, Stockholm, 1934. Like her husband, Anna Wicksell began law studies at an advanced age, and passed her *juris kandidatexamen* (LL.B.) at Lund in 1911. She took part, as a deputy, in the League of Nations first meeting at Geneva, and in 1921 became the only female member of the League of Nations Mandate Commission.

[4] Sven Dag (1890–1939), afterwards Professor of Statistics at Lund, and Finn Hjalmar (1893–1913), who met with an accidental death during his early student years.

adversities of various kinds, that Wicksell wrote his most important scientific papers.

III

The situation seemed to brighten at the beginning of 1900, when Hamilton's Chair in Administrative Law and Political Economy at the Faculty of Law in Lund was divided up through the creation of a separate chair in Political Economy and Fiscal Law. Wicksell, then newly appointed Docent at Uppsala, accepted the commission of performing the duties of the new position, and gave notice of his intention of applying for it. His rivals were Gustav Cassel, Johan Lembke and Gustaf Steffen. The latter two soon withdrew their applications, and Cassel eventually did so too, but not until after a fierce struggle had taken place between him and Wicksell.

Cassel, who was fifteen years younger than Wicksell, and had only been studying economics for three or four years,[1] had not at this time written any of the works for which he later became so famous. His list of qualifications comprised only a series of essays and the booklet *Das Recht auf den vollen Arbeitsertrag* (The Right to the Full Product of Labour), 1900. It might therefore be expected that Wicksell's superiority in economics would be overwhelming at that time. In addition, Wicksell through his LL.B. degree had qualified himself for a professorship in the law faculty, whereas Cassel completely lacked such qualifications. The evidence was unanimous that Wicksell also showed considerable superiority in the lecturing tests that were undertaken. It is against this background that this matter of promotion, which gradually aroused the interest of the entire country, should be viewed.

The experts, who were appointed to consider the scientific qualifications of the applicants, were Hamilton and Davidson, and Professor Falbe Hansen of the University of Copenhagen. Hamilton wrote a relatively long report, which on the whole breathed more sympathy for Cassel than for Wicksell, but which nevertheless gave Wicksell some precedence.[2] According to Davidson, only Wicksell

[1] Cassel's disputation was held in September 1894 on a thesis in mathematics, and from the Spring Semester of 1894 to the Spring Semester of 1898 (inclusive) he served as upper-school master in Stockholm. Not until the summer of 1898, when as Lorén Scholar he travelled to Germany, was he able to devote himself wholly to economics.

[2] In this connection a matter may be touched upon which might seem to be of secondary importance, but which was actually of great importance to Wicksell himself. In his report Hamilton had taken the liberty of reprimanding Wicksell

was competent to take the Chair in question. If the matter had been one of a Chair in Political Economy within the Philosophy Faculty, Cassel's competence, though less than Wicksell's, would have been indisputable. But for a professorship in a law faculty, with which, in addition, fiscal law was actually combined, the legal insight which Cassel lacked was an absolute necessity. Falbe Hansen eventually declared both men well qualified for the post. He was doubtful about the order of ranking between them, but at the faculty meeting he placed Cassel in first place.[1]

because his application to the King for the professorship was signed 'respectfully' instead of 'humbly,' and because, in the accompanying communication to the Senate, he had omitted 'respectfully.' 'His legal examination notwithstanding, it seems from the form of his applications to His Majesty and to the Senate that he does not yet possess a fully developed sense of legal propriety, a point which is only referred to in passing.' This gave Wicksell the opportunity to explain, in a letter to the Rector and in a communication with the faculty, that he had had no intention of showing himself lacking in proper deference towards the *Senate*, but had been nervous over the wording of the application. He offered *no* apology, on the other hand, for the fact that his communication with the King had not been 'humble.' It appears from his exchange of letters with Davidson that Wicksell found the situation embarrassing. In earlier communication with the King he had replaced 'humbly' by 'respectfully' (in some cases with unpleasant results), and was now wondering whether such a way of writing would make his application legally invalid; 'if the worst comes to the worst I shall surely have to take a bite of the sour apple so as not to make my wife and children destitute, but I'd rather not do so, and if there is any possibility of avoiding it I shall be extremely grateful.' From the correspondence preserved in the Wicksell Archives, it appears that Wicksell's friends, after a considerable effort, believed themselves to have persuaded him not to adhere to such a form of address, but to write 'humbly.' At the last moment, however, Wicksell changed his mind, and signed the communication 'respectfully.'

1 Falbe Hansen's expert report opens with an objection common to both applicants: they came to economics from mathematics. History, law, or even practical business experience are to be preferred as an introduction to the study of economics. This failing was especially noticeable in Wicksell. Cassel is not so original or enterprising as Wicksell, but he is more discreet. He is also better suited to guide the young and to train practical officials. At the faculty meeting he sharpened his criticism of Wicksell: he is somewhat one-sided, and his conspicuous unfamiliarity with the conditions of real life, in conjunction with his boundless self-assurance, leads him astray. Wicksell is now too old to learn, while Cassel is a young man, who can learn by experience. Moreover, Cassel is a promising scholar 'and he is particularly well fitted to set forth other writers' opinions on a subject, an attribute which is, of course, of special importance for a university teacher. On these grounds I think that Dr. Cassel might be recommended as No. 1.' This is quoted here to show how much Falbe Hansen misjudged the situation, both as regards Swedish principles of promotion and the attributes of the two applicants. Even an admirer of Cassel would hardly wish to assert nowadays that the ability to penetrate other authors' reasoning and to set them forth accurately was his strong point.

The ordinary members of the faculty, with the exception of Hamilton, followed Davidson, however, and declared Wicksell fully competent and Cassel incompetent because of his lack of legal knowledge. Cassel was nevertheless supported by a strong minority in the Senate.

Afterwards a more general expression of opinion for and against Wicksell's appointment began in the Press and at meetings.[1] In conservative circles in Sweden Wicksell was looked upon as an extremely dangerous person, who by all means should be kept out from the universities. He had made himself known as an advocate for Birth Control and for wanting even to diminish the Swedish population. He also had expressed a defeatist opinion about Sweden's capacity of defending itself against Russia. Besides this he had deeply offended the religious feeling in the country by his rather ruthless agitation against the dogmas of the Church. Wicksell's activities in these respects were in general deprecated in liberal quarters also. However, the action against his promotion was there regarded as an attack on the Freedom of Science. An important fraction of academic teachers as well as of students strongly emphasised that academic promotions should be settled on the basis of scientific merits only, and without consideration to whether the applicant was supposed to cherish ideas dangerous to Society or not.

Cassel, who at that moment came home from England, found the situation embarrassing and withdrew his application, explaining in a letter to the editor of *Svenska Dagbladet* (September 28, 1901) that he did so because irrelevant considerations had been brought up during the handling of the affair in the Senate.[2] In spite of the fact

[1] The struggle over Wicksell's appointment, and the attitude towards Wicksell in radical quarters in Lund at the time, have recently been depicted in an interesting way by Ernst Wigforss (then a radical student in Lund, later Minister of Finance in the Labour Government 1932–49) in his *Minnen* (Memoirs), I, 1950, pp. 183 ff. About Wicksell he writes, *inter alia* (p. 189): 'His utter freedom from all consideration of his own well-being and pleasure, his irrepressible impulse to speak the truth as he saw it—usually truths unwelcome to public opinion or to those with power and authority—these things were of a kind to get young critics of society to rally to his defence, even if they did not share his opinions.'

[2] In this letter—reproduced in Cassel's autobiography *I förnuftets tjänst* (In the Service of Reason), I, 1940, pp. 35–7—he at the same time took the opportunity to criticise Wicksell as a scientist. After having declared that he did not want to profit from the agitation against Wicksell and therefore had to resign, he added: 'Now being out of the game, I should like to express in a few words my own view of this competition. Wicksell is an adherent of the Austrian School and in all important questions he has acted as a disciple of the leading man of this school, Böhm-Bawerk. W.'s doctrinaire disposition has led him to support these teachings with a bias which often makes strange and incomprehensible to him not only the

that Wicksell was now the only remaining applicant, the Pro-Chancellor, Bishop Gottfrid Billing, opposed his appointment. The Chancellor was in favour, however, and the conflict ended with Wicksell's being appointed on November 1, 1901.

'So deeply had the ideas of freedom of science and freedom of teaching become ingrained in the ancient bourgeois society,' comments Wigforss, and he is obviously right, inasmuch as a person so supposedly dangerous to society as Wicksell would not, under another political system, have obtained a professorship at all. On the other hand, it should also be mentioned that Wicksell's very struggle for promotion, and what preceded it, shows that respect for freedom of science and freedom of teaching was manifestly limited in the Sweden of that time, for it seems evident from the foregoing that it was not Wicksell's superior academic qualifications, but the fact that he had taken the *juris kandidatexamen*, while Cassel had not, that proved decisive in this competition. If Cassel had had any legal qualifications (according to Hamilton even the elementary law examination would have been enough), he would have been given pride of place by two of the experts, after which he would have been declared competent and would perhaps also have been placed as No. 1 by the law faculty, in which case the promotion affair would probably have ended very differently.

In this connection it may also be mentioned that at the time the University of Stockholm had at its disposal two large funds for economic studies—Lars Johan Hierta's of about 300,000 crowns, and

offerings of economists of other persuasions, but also actual economic and social life. From the beginning I have been an opponent of the Austrian School, and especially I have criticised its speculations on Value, as being theoretically meaningless and useless to practical economic investigations. In the theory of Interest W. always gives prominence to Böhm-Bawerk as the "Master," and he makes it his special object to express B-B.'s theory in mathematical formulae. In the course of my work I have gained quite a contrary opinion of the importance of Böhm-Bawerk, and I have had the satisfaction to find some of England's leading economists on my side in this matter. . . . The fight for the professorship at Lund was for me a fight over academic principles. In Sweden a real interest in economic studies is now, at long last, beginning to show itself. I would be very sorry if this interest were to be diverted into such sterile channels as those of the Austrian School, or congealed in an academic discussion about dogma. But attitudes at home seem still to be too narrow for one to be able to get such matters of principle decided before impartial judges without external considerations becoming involved. . . .' It is interesting to note that even at that time, when Wicksell was at the height of his scientific career and Cassel had hardly begun his, Cassel considered himself superior to Wicksell as an economist. Cassel had probably not yet acquainted himself with Wicksell's *Interest and Prices* (1898) to which he later did not deny some merit. See Cassel's *Theory of Social Economy*, II, p. 479.

Söderström's of about 70,000 crowns—which no one dared to touch until 'the dangerous Wicksell' was installed at Lund. Had Wicksell had a more opportunist outlook upon social and political questions, his dream of getting an academic post in the city of his birth would probably have been realised some time during the 1890's, after Wicksell had emerged as a theorist of the first rank.[1] Instead, it was now Cassel who got this chance, though obviously with certain reservations on the part of the University Board, for he too was considered to be rather radical. (He had given lectures on 'social policy' in Gothenburg's Workers' Educational Institute among other places.) Cassel first had to be tried out as Docent for a couple of years, before he was permitted to move up into the professorship in 1904.[2]

The professorship that Wicksell got at the age of 50 was only 'associate,' and did not carry a full professorial salary.[3] In a letter to Davidson, Wicksell complained that it was expensive to live in Lund, and that he had 'to spend much time on the railway at public lecture work every single Sunday plus one weekday or another, time which could be put to better use.' His attempt to become full professor was actively opposed by Hamilton, whose professorship was now limited to special civil law, and not until after the latter's departure did Wicksell become a full professor (on April 22, 1904), this time by the unanimous invitation of the faculty.

Wicksell's activity as an academic teacher was limited to the law faculty. His task was to teach tax law to the young lawyers and to give them elementary training in economics as far as they took the subject in the examinations, after which he had to examine the

[1] In that way too, Wicksell would have avoided having to devote many years of his most productive period to taking the *juris kandidatexamen*. Whereas a law examination was considered necessary in order to obtain a teaching post in economics at Uppsala or Lund, in Stockholm it was counted a point in Cassel's favour that he was not a lawyer when the Board determined his competence for the professorship. It is understood that Wicksell found this 'queer.'

[2] When the Lars Hiertas Chair in Political Economy and Finance was established at the University of Stockholm, Wicksell was advised by his friends to apply for it. He was very tempted, he writes to Davidson, but since he would not profit from it at all financially, and the family had begun to feel at home in Lund, in addition to which he considered that it would be wrong to stand in Cassel's way, he resigned himself: 'I might as well face up to reality and bid the fair temptress a final farewell.' And it was all for the best, for a fresh struggle with Cassel in Stockholm would certainly have gone against Wicksell. Cassel was summoned to this professorship very quickly, in spite of the fact that both Wicksell and Davidson, as invited experts, opposed the summons in order to give the other competitors a chance.

[3] The salary for an associate professor was only three-quarters of that of a full professor.

already large batches of students in both subjects. The Chair was indeed no sinecure. Fiscal law seems especially to have caused him some trouble at the beginning.[1] But even in economics he did not make things easy for himself, for his ambition was to lecture not only in those fields which touched upon his own work, but also to go into the more 'practical' parts of the subject. In the lecture list of the time is thus found such titles as 'industry and raw material production,' 'industry and labour questions,' 'the stock exchange system,' 'trade and consumption,' etc. Presumably he must have had to devote considerable time to preparing such lecture series. According to the custom of the time, he also usually gave two tutorial courses, one in economics and one in fiscal law, for which a charge was made, and which were over and above his obligatory lecturing duties, comprising three lecture hours per week and a (two-hour) seminar each alternate week. This relatively large burden of teaching and examinations must have lain rather heavily on this middle-aged man, especially as he had no help whatever of the kind that is at the disposal of professors nowadays.

As an examiner, Wicksell was friendly but not especially indulgent. At that time fiscal law was a lesser subject than it is now—tax legislation had then not yet become so involved and extensive—but in compensation the students had to read a great deal of the history of the subject. In economics Wicksell made what he considered to be rather few demands, and was fairly benevolently disposed towards the examinees, since it was a matter of an optional subject, though the syllabus was not small by present-day standards.[2] Under strong

---

[1] 'I am now toiling with lectures in fiscal law,' he writes to Davidson in 1904. 'I see, moreover, that you are lecturing in fiscal law: if there were some way of hearing them by telephone, I would immediately join your audience. I have no less than thirty-four (registered students) and I writhe to think that I cannot give them anything that is really worth hearing.'

[2] Wicksell's first contribution to the Law Faculty's study handbook (1904) resulted in a syllabus which stands on a par with what is now required for two *betyg* (honours marks) in the *fil-kand* (B.A.) examination. Afterwards, the syllabus was cut down, and in the study handbook for 1912 the following works were to be digested for the lower 'honours mark': Gide, *Principles of Political Economy*, Wicksell, *Lectures*, Vols. I and II; Scharling, *Bankpolitik* (Banking Policy); Goschen, *The Theory of Foreign Exchanges;* the sections of *Det ekonomiska samhällslivet* (The Economic Life of Society) concerning agriculture, commerce, and industrial labour problems; in addition to which attendance at lectures and courses was required. For higher 'honours marks' it was necessary, besides having thoroughly learnt the earlier course, to be acquainted more extensively with economic literature, especially the classics, represented by Adam Smith, Malthus, Ricardo, and John Stuart Mill, as well as writing a thesis showing exhaustive and independent work.

pressure from the other subjects, economics later occupied a gradually more distressed position in the *juris kandidatexamen* (LL.B.).

At the beginning of the century, when Wicksell became Professor, economics was not a regular subject for study in the philosophy faculty. The subject was only permitted to be included in the philosophy examination by dispensation. The subject did not enjoy any great importance in studies of the humanities until after Sommarin, who had transferred to the study of economics under the influence of Wicksell, became Docent in Economics in the philosophy faculty at the beginning of 1909, and was appointed examiner within that faculty, whereupon the dispensation requirement was dropped. Sommarin was a great admirer of Wicksell, and encouraged his pupils to read the latter's works. In this way Wicksell exerted a dominating influence on all who were reading economics at Lund at that time. But Wicksell had no direct pupils among the juniors, and contacts between the teachers and the more advanced students such as are established nowadays in the licentiat seminar, and in the Students' Economic Associations, did not exist at that time.

There is no doubt that Wicksell would have made a better showing as a teacher if the teaching staff in economics had been larger and more differentiated, as is now the case at the universities. Wicksell would then have been able to concentrate upon guiding the senior students and encouraging the junior ones in the discipline. Those who had the advantage of having their theses reviewed by him can testify to the interested effort he expended upon such a task. It seems that both he and the students would have derived benefit from such a system of teaching.[1]

[1] In spite of the fact that I consider myself to be a pupil of Wicksell, I did not actually have any personal contact with him during my period of study at Lund. From my first student year (after 1910), I remember him as a distinctive and eccentric, but respected, professor. He then lived at Linero, a beautifully situated estate about half an hour's walk out of Lund in the direction of Dalby, and the journey into town which he made for his lectures was combined, as a rule, with various other tasks: fetching the post, buying food, etc. It was not unusual for him to come to the lecture in the morning with a bag filled with groceries and other things he had bought for the household as he passed the market-place. He placed the bag beside the rostrum before beginning to teach the astonished law students what the Austrian Sax or the Italian Mazzola thought about the nature of collective needs. This not very tall and somewhat corpulent man was a well-known feature of the Lund street-scene, where he marched along carrying a net bag (which was used for books as well as merchandise), a black peaked cap over his grey locks, and sometimes wearing an overcoat upon which time had bestowed a grey-green patina. He exerted his greatest influence upon the intellectual life of Lund as a participant in public discussions of political and social questions, where his pungently framed and wittily delivered contributions ensured that there was

During the period at Lund, Wicksell devoted much time to the preparation of his *Föreläsningar i nationalekonomi* (Lectures on Political Economy) which were published in many revised editions and were also translated into German (1913–22).[1] 'I am writing my new book on Money with might and main,' he told Davidson in a letter in 1904.[2] During these years he was also a frequent contributor to *Ekonomisk Tidskrift*, which Davidson had founded in 1899, and afterwards edited single-handed for forty years, in spite of endless troubles; at the outset lack of subscribers, and later lack of contributors. Davidson was grateful to Wicksell for his valuable contributions, and Wicksell was grateful to Davidson for his support in the dispute over his appointment[3] and for his good advice on various matters. Both profited, meanwhile, from the continuing exchange of opinions on scientific matters. The amicable relationship existing between the two men in later life has already been noted by Eli F. Heckscher in a memorial paper on Davidson.[4]

Wicksell's participation in public debates increased rather than diminished after he became a professor. On at least two occasions his utterances were of such a kind that they were regarded as a nation-wide scandal. The first occasion was at the traditional Tegnér Festival in Lund in October 1905, when, after Verner von Heidenstam's patriotic address, Wicksell asked to speak, in order to advocate the adoption of a more conciliatory attitude towards the Norwegians in the current union crisis. How Wicksell was almost manhandled by the incensed students, and how the whole festival had to be abandoned in confusion, has been told many times, both

life in the discussion. Occasionally it happened that both Wicksell and his wife, who had similar views but different interests, took part in the same discussion, and amicably opposed each other. My personal acquaintance with Wicksell is of later date, by which time Wicksell had already left Lund. My doctor's thesis of 1919, *Die Gerechtigkeit der Besteuerung* (Equity in Taxation), was to a large extent based on Wicksell's theories, and for this reason Sommarin let Wicksell read it; at its public disputation Wicksell also officiated as the critic appointed by the faculty.

[1] After Wicksell's death, they were also published in English (1934–5), Spanish (1947) and Italian (1950).

[2] The 'new book on Money' was Volume II of Wicksell's *Lectures*. The first edition of Volume I had been published as early as 1901.

[3] Wicksell found it difficult, however, to forget that Davidson, in his expert report, had declared that Cassel was undoubtedly sufficiently qualified had it been a question of a Chair in the Philosophy Faculty. 'Have you ever heard of anyone in Europe who in such a short time qualified as a professor in a subject such as economics?' Wicksell wrote to Davidson.

[4] Published first in *Ekonomisk Tidskrift*, 1951, and then in English translation in *International Economic Papers*, No. 2, 1952, pp. 111–135.

in novels and memoirs.[1] On the second occasion the immediate reaction was not so violent, but the later consequences for Wicksell himself were far more serious. During a lecture in 'Folkets Hus' (the Socialist Party Headquarters) in Stockholm, on November 2, 1908, called *Tronen, altaret, svärdet och penningpåsen* (The Throne, the Altar, the Sword, and the Money-bag), which, in spite of its provocative title, on the whole maintained a serious tone, Wicksell made some ironical remarks, in passing, on the teaching of the Church concerning the Immaculate Conception. An action was brought for blasphemy, and the result was long-drawn-out legal proceedings, with lengthy defence submissions from Wicksell. The magistrates' court sentenced him to two months' imprisonment, the circuit court of appeal reduced the penalty to a fine, but the High Court upheld the judgment of the magistrates' court. It is true that Wicksell, then nearly 58 years old, does not seem to have suffered any lasting harm from the actual stay in prison, during which he was occupied with academic work,[2] but this whole affair—described by his wife as 'an unforgivable stupidity'—must nevertheless be deeply regretted, for it brought much unpleasantness upon Wicksell, without assisting the cause he was trying to further.

IV

When, at the end of 1916, Wicksell was emeritus, he and his wife moved to Mörby in Stocksund, a garden suburb of Stockholm. A testimonial gift from friends and admirers had made it possible for them to build a small villa there, and there he was able to spend his

[1] See, for example, Sommarin, *Studenter och arbetare* (Students and Workers) Lund, 1947, pp. 132 ff.; and also Gustaf Hellström's novel *Sex veckor i Arkadien* (Six Weeks in Arcady), 1925.

[2] He wrote the Verdandi Pamphlet No. 170, *Läran om befolkningen* (The Theory of Population), which represents a revised edition of Chapter I of Volume I of the *Lectures*, omitted in later editions (also in the English one). The Foreword of this paper is signed 'Ystad Prison, October 1909,' and concludes with the following words: 'Working on this pamphlet has been an agreeable diversion during my enforced idleness. I hope that it may contribute to the dissemination of knowledge of the population problems, the most important of all social problems, and at the same time the most neglected.' Ystad Prison was noted for its humane treatment of prisoners, and after preliminary inspection Wicksell had chosen this prison. From the purely material standpoint Wicksell seems to have had things relatively well arranged during his stay there. (In the Wicksell Archives in Lund there is preserved a letter of this period from Hotel Prins Carl, from which Wicksell obtained his food, with the enquiry 'whether the Professor desires goose and black broth on Michaelmas Eve? If black broth is not desired we will send dessert instead').

last decade, the most peaceful and most carefree of his life. He had now finally come to the milieu, near the capital, where he felt most at ease.

The advent of retirement did not diminish Wicksell's intellectual activity. Right up to his death, which came suddenly after an accidental chill, he was intensively occupied with his writing, which now consisted mostly of shorter works, articles for newspapers and journals, and also of officially commissioned inquiries. Through frequent visits to Stockholm he maintained contact with friends and colleagues. Among the latter he now stood out as the acknowledged and revered master. Wicksell was the focal point of the Economic Club which was formed for the exchange of views between economists in the Stockholm area. In this circle of younger scholars he actually came into his own as a teacher more than he had done at Lund. His stimulating influence undoubtedly had something to do with the liveliness that the Club exhibited at this time, which was never surpassed subsequently.

Wicksell also frequently took part in public discussions, especially in the Economic Association. He was now no longer considered a danger to society, but the respected doyen of the Stockholm economists, whose individualistic contributions to the debate were always worth hearing. That the differences of opinion between Wicksell and society had to some extent been settled did not, however, mean that Wicksell had eventually conformed to the popular view. All through his life he maintained, with remarkable consistency, the view which he had formed during the 1880's concerning the population problem and other social and religious questions. Nor did he cease propagating them. As late as 1924, for instance, he made a contribution to the population question in which are found the same basic views as in his first sensational pamphlet. But now he no longer created any scandal, for in the meantime the popular viewpoint had shifted, and it could probably be shown that Wicksell's own persistent and sensational propaganda played a not unimportant role in this shift. But although much of what Wicksell had striven for had gradually been brought about, that is not to say that Wicksell was satisfied with the current state of society. He remained a rebel to the end. The greater part of his activity as a writer during these ten years can be characterised as a running criticism of current economic policy.

Wicksell's position in the debate on monetary policy which was precipitated by the inflation of the First World War, will only be touched upon briefly here.

All Wicksell's contributions on the subject of inflation—and they

The subsequent course of events proved Wicksell to have been right. The Riksbank's stock of gold and exchange increased to such an extent that in February 1916 the Riksbank requested, and obtained, permission not to have to pay gold at par. Through this 'gold-blockade' the crown was free from gold, and it was consequently possible for the Riksbank to manipulate the exchange rates so that an increase in the domestic price-level could be avoided. Wicksell now asserted forcefully that the Riksbank should exploit this possibility by maintaining a relatively high discount rate, until the price rise was checked. As an alternative to the lowering of exchange rates (appreciation[1]), he proposed a combination of export duties and import premiums. The price rise in Sweden could not, at this time, he maintained, be blamed on the shortage of goods caused by the war, for, since Sweden's terms of trade had improved, if anything, we had the means to maintain, and perhaps even to increase somewhat, our usual level of consumption.

After the all-out submarine warfare began in February 1917, and the full provisioning of the country with necessities became technically impossible, the problems of monetary policy naturally became more difficult. For his part, Wicksell recommended a further raising of the discount rate, combined with the granting by the Riksbank of a corresponding rate to lenders. He also maintained (in *Dagens Nyheter*, December 23, 1917) that the Government should cease borrowing from the Riksbank in order to finance commissions. The Government should either cease borrowing and obtain the necessary funds in some other way, or, if resort must be had to loans, 'better to borrow from commercial banks than from the Riksbank, and best of all direct from the public.' In addition, he considered that rationing of scarce goods should have been applied more widely, to fuel for instance, and that the law regarding requisitioning should have been used more extensively. Had all these measures been taken, including the export duties, import premiums, and also probably the lowering of the exchange rate, the price rise during the two blockade years 1917 and 1918 would undoubtedly have been less marked, although, because of the growing scarcity of goods, it would not wholly have been avoided.

motivation—finds its expression in the Riksbank Committee's famous memorandum (No. 17) that the gold reserves should always be kept at a certain minimum amount, 'not less than 100,000,000 crowns,' seems pretty pointless. It reminds me a little of the parsimonious farmer, who gave each of his sons some money to enjoy himself with at the fair, but with strict instructions that the money was to be brought back home again.'

[1] Cf. footnote *infra*, p. 229.

With this sketch of Wicksell's monetary programme during the First World War I have tried to disprove Östlind's thesis that 'even the most expert economists stood rather nonplussed in the face of the unique fluctuations of the Swedish economy during the war years 1914–18.'[1] Wicksell did not stand nonplussed, but his advice was not followed. Most of what he wrote then has such general validity that it can also be applied under present circumstances, though with certain reservations made necessary by the difference between our present-day society and the more liberal one in which Wicksell lived.[2]

V

Knut Wicksell's contributions, both as a practical and as a theoretical economist, are so extensive and penetrating that an account of them would carry me far beyond the bounds of this commemorative article. Only a few concluding remarks concerning his view of society and his more important contributions to economic theory will be added here.

Wicksell's political position can best be characterised as liberal, with a generous dash of social-radicalism. The demand for liberty, equality, and fraternity awoke deep echoes in him. He set himself up as the advocate of freedom of speech and of religion,[3] as well as of

---

[1] Anders Östlind, *Svensk samhällsekonomi 1914–1922* (The Swedish Economy 1914–1922), Stockholm, 1945, p. 125.

[2] In one respect the situation has changed fundamentally between the two wars. The various classes of society have become more tightly organised, especially as regards the labour market and agriculture. For this reason, the risk of what are called *autonomous* price increases—brought about, for example, by a spontaneous wage increase which is not caused by an increased demand for labour—has become considerably greater than hitherto. To this extent the solution of the problem of stabilising the value of money has come up against a special obstacle of an eminently political kind—namely, that of preventing the various social groups from seeking to improve their economic position at the expense of the value of money—which was only of minor significance in Wicksell's day. Even under these new institutional conditions Wicksell's monetary theory retains its validity as far as it goes, but it has to be extended to include, in addition, the phenomenon just mentioned.

[3] Wicksell did not work for the disestablishment of the State Church, but for the abolition of the *doctrinal discipline* imposed upon priests. He was shocked by the law then in force under which priests who propagate views conflicting with the teaching of the Swedish Church can be admonished, deprived of their livings for a certain period, or in very serious cases may even be unfrocked. In an article on 'The Future of the State Church' in *Tiden*, 1909, No. 3, he propounded the thesis

political and economic equality between classes and between the sexes, which we in Sweden have come to associate with 'the 'eighties.'

In the economic field Wicksell was, in principle, a supporter of free competition, to be applied within each individual country as well as between countries. But he strongly emphasised that certain fundamental conditions must be fulfilled in order that free competition should bring about a favourable result. He maintained too that

that a priest should not be made destitute because of his opinions. His argument developed in the following interesting way:

'But, someone says, if no more is demanded of priests and teachers of religion than of other teachers and functionaries, i.e. sufficient knowledge and seemly conduct, and if they are permitted to follow their consciences and convictions unhampered to the end, what will then be left of the Church and of Christendom, would it not entail the collapse of both? The answer to this is that the Church, as such, will certainly manage as long as, and to the extent that, it is permitted to do so; it will certainly not die as long as it has at least something to live by, in the ordinary, straightforward, material sense. Regarding Christendom, on the other hand, the answer is more involved. I think that the result—the eventual result, that is, for the immediate consequence would certainly not be any sweeping change at all—would be some *broader* sort of Christendom, by which I mean broadened to include *everything* of value in all ancient culture and literature, in which Christendom, take it how one will, would constitute only one small part. That Christendom won its real and most striking victories in the world because of the elements of Greek philosophy and Roman law that it contained, seems nowadays generally acknowledged by the experts in this field; it has carried the bread and wine of good manners and moderate behaviour to the barbarians, though in insufficient quantities, and mixed up, unfortunately, with less edible and more unhealthy matter. In the same way, even today, though with a broader frame of reference, the priests, or their successors, would be able to stand as intermediaries between the culture of ancient times and that of today.'

Such a cultural achievement on the part of the priests, Wicksell continued, would be all the more important, since the consequence of the increasing emphasis upon *practical* education in modern society will, it is feared, be an educated class which will have no first-hand knowledge of the ideas of the ancient world. 'There are, of course, still many educated people, at any rate amongst us of the older generation, in the happy position of being able to take down from our bookshelf our Cicero or Horatius, if all goes well, our Sophocles, Plato, Xenophon, and many other grand old men of the past—the ancient Homer must not be forgotten —and to commune with them *on an intimate footing*, that is to say, in the original tongue. But this will soon be a lost art, and consequently all this literature, *to which the moderns have nothing fully comparable to show*, stands in danger of being lost to us. Only the priests whose training must, of its very nature, include the classical languages, will be in a position to keep it alive; but for this to be brought about successfully, their attitude towards the special part of ancient philosophy which they at present cultivate must be much less narrow. A priest who chose as the text of his sermon a passage from Plato's dialogues, or from the moralistic writings of Cicero or Seneca, or appropriate parts of the poetry and drama of earlier times, would certainly not be debasing himself or his office, and he could freely reached agreements between the parties were often better than unrestrained competition,[1] and also that State intervention would be fully justified in some cases. The latter should, however, 'occur with the greatest circumspection, having regard, *inter alia*, to the likely consequences, both direct and indirect, since an ill-judged regulation of economic affairs must always be expected to lead to worse results than no regulation at all, and regulation by voluntary agreements is as a rule to be preferred to compulsion.'[2]

The original points in Wicksell's economic programme lay in the restrictions he proposed to place upon the *laisser-faire* system:

1. *The population problem* was for him primary. Through birth control, voluntarily applied in marriage, and supported by official policy, the population in each country should be kept at what Wicksell called the 'optimal' size, which was where the national product per head attained its maximum. Wicksell did not, however, pursue the concept 'optimum population' further, since in his opinion there was no room for doubt that the actual size of population in most countries considerably exceeded the optimal one. With his fairly pessimistic view of Sweden's economic prospects—he frequently recalled the excessive exploitation of the forests—he considered it desirable that the number of people in the country be gradually reduced to about three millions. The number of favourable results that Wicksell hoped to attain simply by a rational solution of the population problem is amazing. Material well-being would be considerably increased, and prostitution and other unsatisfactory sexual relationships would almost disappear. In addition to this, peaceful co-operation between peoples would be facilitated, for Wicksell—who was a staunch pacifist and opposed military expendi-

count on as much devotion and edification among his hearers as at present, perhaps a little more. . . . This is not to say, however, that it ought to be them (the priests) or anyone denied to fight for Christendom, even in its most "orthodox" form, so long, and insofar, as each and every one desires, only that no one should be compelled to do so against his convictions. In this, as in other matters, evolution's own laws may perhaps be relied upon, provided that no artificial restraints are placed upon them.'

[1] Cf. the following declaration in Verdandi Pamphlet (No. 109) *Allianser mellan arbetare och arbetsgivare* (Alliances between Workers and Employers), 1902, p. 7: 'Unlimited competition could, to take a quite trivial but rather telling illustration, be likened to a so-called "free for all" supper, where everyone, without regard for his fellows, runs amok amongst the food and tries to get as much as possible for himself. The result, nevertheless, is often that a large amount of food ends up on the tablecloth or on the floor, and no one is really satisfied. It would have been much better if everyone had sat down and tried peacefully to satisfy his neighbour's needs as well as his own.'

[2] Sommarin's reproduction of Wicksell's views in *Minnesord*, p. 49.

ture on principle[1]—considered that it was ultimately the pressure of growing population that occasioned envy and mistrust between peoples, and imperialistic tendencies in certain states. Sometimes he seems vaguely to have considered a stationary population as an ideal, or at all events as a normal phenomenon in the *long* run. If the population ceased growing, welfare would increase inasmuch as the tempo of capital formation could be reduced, and a greater part of the national income would be devoted to the satisfaction of immediate needs.

2. In order that wealth should be distributed as evenly as possible, steps should be taken to eliminate the existing class-differentiation in society. In Wicksell's opinion, the most important step would be a radical *educational reform* to make possible increased general education for the masses and further higher education for all those who had the ability and need for it. It is interesting to note that Wicksell's educational programme—common primary schools, and free education (even at the higher stages), combined with *board*—coincides almost exactly with what is now being carried through almost forty years later.

3. The next step was a levelling out of property distribution by a *high inheritance-tax* or a change in the law of inheritance. Wicksell always maintained that the Government's share in inherited property should be considered as capital, and not squandered on current expenditure. In popular lectures he sometimes stimulated his audience with the idea that the capital which the Government obtains in this way should be shared out amongst the members of society, so that once in his life every citizen—upon attaining the age of 25 years, say—might draw his share of society's inheritance. This small capital sum he could then use to furnish a house or start a business, but he would have the moral obligation to leave behind at

---

[1] In the first place, however, Wicksell gave as the grounds for his demand for disarmament in Sweden 'that the military defence of a state of Sweden's size was, at the present time, impossible and unreasonable, and our entire defence system was therefore a useless, though not harmless, plaything.' In this field too he said that he was requesting 'only realism and honesty. A commission should be appointed, composed not of fanatical militarists exclusively, but of people representing all parties and all strata of society, to investigate impartially the question whether our country still has any actual military mission, and if so, what it is. If, after a thorough investigation, such a body gave a fairly unanimous affirmative answer to the first of these two questions, then for my part I would bow before expert knowledge and surrender on this point—our efforts for the achievement of peace and disarmament would then have to be redirected.' *Tronen, altaret, svärdet, och penningpåsen*, p. 33.

least an equally large capital sum at his death.[1] With this important exception, and the further limitation inherent in it, that certain unearned profits (such as those derived from the trade cycle and from appreciation of property values) should also be taxed, Wicksell respected the right to private property, and considered that it should be protected from the assaults of excessive taxation. In his opinion, the taxation of the various classes of society should, as a matter of principle, be kept within the bounds of what they would voluntarily undertake. In order to protect the rights of the minority, he went so far as to propose that they should have the right of veto on tax decisions in Parliament. On this point he thought that taxes should be voted at the same time as the corresponding expenditure, and in this way a compromise solution could in principle always be reached.

If the structure of society could be changed, in these three ways, everyone would be tolerably equally situated at the start, so that greater faith could then be placed in the principle of free competition.

4. Wicksell also fully appreciated, however, the importance of *free combination*, both in the productive and the distributive trades,[2] as well as in the relationships on the labour market. Wicksell looked upon the trade-union movement with great sympathy, but maintained that the real significance of trade unions lay in the self-realisation they entailed for the working class. They had increased the workers' self-consciousness and sense of dignity and responsibility. Through their activities they had also achieved an improvement in working conditions, but on the wage-front he thought that their importance was over-rated, for he considered that wages were determined by competition between firms according to the marginal

---

[1] To the immediate objection that the net saving of the society would be diminished by such a procedure, Wicksell replied that with a stationary population there was no need for so much capital accumulation. He conceded, however, that the proposal could be shown to be impractical on closer inspection.

[2] The importance of trusts and cartels did not only lie in the striving for self-enrichment at the consumers' expense. 'On the contrary, the fact is that inherent in combination itself there is an efficiency, even in the higher sense used in economics, a cause of lower costs and higher productivity, by which profits may accrue to producers without anyone else suffering, and by which, indeed, other classes of society also share in the gains. A mutual understanding to substitute a peaceful sharing of the market for a wild struggle for customers would, by itself, bring about the elimination of many deadweight production costs, those that might be called competition's *war* expenditure: advertisements, publicity, commercial travelling, and all the humbug of warepuffing, which in itself adds nothing to the quality, or quantity, of the product, but which is, under present conditions, a painful necessity for each producer if he is not to be entirely forgotten, or pushed out by other, more enterprising, competitors.'

37

productivity theory, and that trade unions could not do much about it. He was, therefore, a zealous advocate of peace on the labour front, of mutual understanding, and amicable relationships between workers and employers. The struggle for further increases in the economic standards of the working class should be fought out on another battlefield, namely, the political front.

5. To the extent that the course of economic development tends towards monopoly and cartelisation in various branches of industry, *socialisation* or some other similar form of state control should be considered. The object of this should be to make possible a price policy that is more favourable to the consumers. Price fixing in public companies which served the consumer should be based, in principle, on marginal costs, even if this entails the recovery of part of the fixed costs by taxation. When the marginal costs are negligible, then the public should enjoy the goods or services *gratis*, as is the case, for instance, with roads and streets. It was, therefore, the possibility of achieving such technical gains and improved price policies, rather than the possibility of bringing about a more equal economic distribution, that would justify measures of socialisation in any particular case, for according to Wicksell one could not hope for any important increase in wages themselves once the socialist state had been established. He thought that even there marginal productivity was the simplest and fairest norm for wage-fixing.

6. As regards the Government's economic policy in other matters, Wicksell strongly emphasised that the *monetary policy* should be directed towards the maintenance of a constant value of money. He was one of the first to advocate the freeing of the currency from gold. If, in the face of this, exchange rates were to be kept fixed, it would be necessary for the central banks of the various countries to collaborate. After the fluctuations of the First World War, however, Wicksell became a supporter of free monetary standards (with variable exchange rates) in Sweden. He also asserted that a monetary policy aiming at price-stabilisation would entail a levelling out of cyclical fluctuations. On the other hand, no expression can be found in his writings of the view that fiscal policy should also be used to this end, although such a conclusion follows logically from his own theories.

Much of what Wicksell strove for has gradually been realised since, but in some respects the course of events has run differently from what he would have considered to be desirable. Thus, as far as the monetary system is concerned, it can be maintained that its international organisation on the whole followed the lines he laid down, but that the actual monetary policy took poor advantage of the possibilities created thereby for the achievement of the norm of a constant value of money which he advocated.

VI

When Wicksell came to the University of Lund at the beginning of the century, and thereby got the job, *inter alia*, of teaching economics to the law students, he planned to arrange his lectures so that they formed a coherent course which could be used as the basis of a systematic exposition of all the material in textbook form. This textbook would comprise three parts: a *theoretical* part, treating the 'economic laws,' i.e. the general relationships between economic phenomena; a *practical* part, comprising an application of the theoretical results to the various fields of the concrete economic life of society; and a *social* part, containing, on the one hand, a critical appraisal of the economic ordering of society, from the welfare standpoint, and, on the other, the orientation of an economic policy programme. Wicksell got this framework from his predecessor Léon Walras, who had then just finished his great systematising work on political economy, consisting of the three volumes *Éléments d'économie politique pure*, *Études d'économie politique appliquée*, and *Études d'économie sociale*.

As is well known, Wicksell never fulfilled this plan, but wrote only the first, theoretical, part (divided into two volumes) of his *Lectures on Political Economy*. No one seems to regret this today. On the contrary, it would have been an obvious waste of valuable energy if Wicksell had fulfilled his purpose, and worked out a second, practical, part, on 'The theory of raw material production,' 'The theory of manufacturing industry,' 'The theory of commerce and stock exchange organisation,' etc., which would certainly have given him much trouble, without any corresponding gain for science. Nor is the third, social, part missed, which would presumably have contained a systematic exposition of his ideas on social reform, a brief account of which has been given in the preceding section. If Wicksell had sought to dress his reform programme in scientific clothes by deducing it from some higher welfare postulate, then much of the freshness which characterises the original presentation would probably have been lost, while at the same time its scientific validity would have been brought into question.

The theoretical part of the lectures, which we will now consider, is certainly kept in so easily comprehensible a form that Wicksell's

immediate pupils, the law students, would have been able to read it
with profit, yet it maintains a high level of scholarship, and, as has
been rightly remarked, really has more the character of a 'textbook
for professors.' Wicksell has here fused the theories that he developed
in earlier writings into a unified system of extraordinary logical consistency. The essentials of the system are (1) the determination of
stationary equilibrium, (2) the comparison of various stationary
equilibria (comparative statics), and (3) the introduction of dynamic
theory in the proper sense.

In determining the *stationary equilibrium* Wicksell proceeded as
follows. He first explained price formation in the market for goods,
assuming incomes and quantities of goods to be given. Equilibrium
prices were characterised by the fact that they would be proportional
to the marginal utilities of the various goods for all individuals. In
this price situation, therefore, no individual can increase his total
utility by buying more of one good and less of another. The next task
was to explain incomes and the quantities of goods. To this end,
prices and technical knowledge were assumed to be given, and so
were the amounts of the various sorts of productive factors. How
much of each good to produce, and how to share the proceeds
between the different factors, is then determined according to the
marginal productivity principle. Equilibrium requires that productive
factors be employed where they make the greatest contribution at
the ruling prices. Later, when money and credit are introduced into
the system, two further equilibrium conditions can be stated: the
money rate of interest must coincide with the rate of interest on
capital determined by marginal productivity, and the general price
level must stand in a certain relationship (itself determined by a
multitude of factors) to the actual volume of money.

Wicksell's own contribution to the theoretical construction out-
lined here, can be brought out most clearly by comparing it with the
system that Walras had propounded earlier: (1) Wicksell had replaced Walras' fixed 'technical coefficients' by productivity functions,
and thereby became, as already mentioned, one of the founders of
the marginal productivity theory. (2) The Austrian capital theory
received a rational reformulation in terms of marginal productivity,
so that the net yield of real capital is made to depend upon the higher
marginal productivity of the services of labour and land when invested in real capital; the maximisation of the net yield requires that
the investment period extends in all cases to a point where any
further lengthening would involve an increase in marginal productivity which is less than that which would be achieved by a corre-

40

sponding lengthening elsewhere; in this way the rate of interest ruling on the market is brought into conformity with 'the marginal productivity of time.' (3) By introducing the money rate of interest as a particular variable, it became possible to include credit in the general equilibrium system. (4) Setting out from his theory of money, Wicksell achieved a deeper understanding of the character of stationary equilibrium: the equilibrium is *stable* as far as *relative* prices are concerned, but *unstable* as regards absolute prices, i.e. with respect to the relationship between the total demand for, and total supply of, goods.[1]

The theory of stationary equilibrium has, in the meantime, obviously made some progress in many respects. The theory of marginal utility has generally been replaced by the theory of choice. A great deal of energy has also been devoted to the theoretical treatment of costs, and other problems relating to the economics of individual firms. Wicksell succeeded in avoiding this complex of problems by assuming, unrealistically, that on attaining equilibrium all firms were of optimal size, in the sense that they were at the point where profits ceased rising and began to fall. With this assumption, the total product can everywhere simply be divided among the factors of production according to their marginal productivity, so that the market problem can be treated without any special reference to the structure of the firm. In a more realistic theoretical framework, all the restrictions on free competition which exist in reality must be considered.[2] In other respects Wicksell's theories have been completed

[1] Cf. *Lectures*, II, pp. 196–7: 'Thus the great and decisive difference between *relative* commodity prices on the one hand and the *general* price level on the other is, as I have already explained in my book *Geldzins und Güterpreise* (Interest and Prices), that the equilibrum of the former is usually *stable*, and comparable to a freely suspended pendulum, or a ball at the bottom of a bowl. If by any chance it is disturbed from the position of equilibrum, it tends itself, through the force of gravity, to resume its former position. The general price level, on the other hand, is, assuming an infinitely elastic monetary system, in a position of what might be called *unstable* equilibrium, of the same kind as that of a ball or cylinder on a flat, but rather rough, surface. It will not move of its own accord, but, by inertia and friction, remains wherever it is left; if forces of sufficient strength to disturb it from its position of equilibrum are brought into play, however, it shows no tendency to return; yet, when the forces that set it in motion—in this case the difference between the normal or real rate of interest and the actual loan rate—cease to operate, it will remain in a new, similarly unstable, equilibrium position.' (The original translation has been slightly changed.)

[2] In this connection it should be noted that Wicksell did deal with price formation under restricted competition too, though rather outside his general system, introducing into the discussion several novel points of view. See especially the article 'Matematisk nationalekonomi' (Mathematical Economics), included in this volume, pp. 204 ff.

by later scholars,[1] but hardly superseded. I would especially like to draw attention to the fact that the full significance of Wicksell's definition of the character of stationary equilibrium has not been widely enough realised. As a rule, it can be supposed that a disturbance in any particular market will entail some shift in total demand and total supply, which will give rise to a new general equilibrium or to a dynamic process, before the tendency to return to the original market situation has had time to come into effect. From this the important conclusion may be drawn that stationary equilibrium should generally be considered—except in certain special cases—to be unstable.

In *comparative statics* too, where comparisons are made between different stationary equilibria varying in different respects, Wicksell interested himself above all in the treatment of capital problems. He showed that an increase in capital, other things being equal, would, after a point, involve a fall in the capitalists' relative share of the national product, and later of their absolute share too. In the same way, an increased quantity of capital involves a shift in the structure of real capital, inasmuch as the lower rate of interest increases the profitability of the longer investments, and thus modifies somewhat the change in distribution mentioned above. 'In the peculiarity of capital that, when it grows, it grows, so to say, more in height than in breadth, there consequently lies a counterweight to the tendency of such growth to raise wages and rents.'[2] By this analysis, capital theory was carried far beyond the point reached by Böhm-Bawerk.[3]

It should not be concealed, however, that Wicksell ran into difficulties when he tried to apply this *static* theory (as I conceive of it) to a *dynamic* process. When, for example, as above, the question was raised how an increase of capital influences the economy, the answer

[1] Gustaf Åkerman, in his doctoral dissertation, *Realkapital und Kapitalzins*, I–II, Stockholm, 1923–4, has, of course, completed Wicksell's capital theory by introducing durable capital goods into the system.

[2] *Lectures*, I, p. 163.

[3] Among Wicksell's other contributions in this field, mention may be made of his investigations into the significance of technical inventions for the size of output and its distribution. Refuting Ricardo, Wicksell showed that a technical invention always involved an increase in the total output of society under free competition. If the new technique is more capital-using than the old, or if it increases the profitability of long-term investments, the relative—and in some cases also the absolute—share of the workers in the total product will fall, assuming that this is not counteracted by a simultaneous increase of capital. 'The capitalist-saver is thus fundamentally a friend of the worker; but the inventor is quite often his enemy' is one of Wicksell's better-known utterances on this point.

was really based on a comparison between alternative stationary equilibria, deviating from each other with regard to the amount of capital. Such a comparison does not imply, however, that a corresponding capital increase in any given society would involve precisely these effects. For, in the latter case, saving, and the capital accumulation associated with it, would set in motion a dynamic process, which may, certainly, be thought eventually to end up in a stationary position, but need not lead to the same result that one would expect from a static analysis. To elucidate the effects in this case is a much more involved problem, which can only be treated by dynamic methods. Wicksell did not always observe this distinction. But the relation between dynamic and comparative statics is still one of the questions that await definitive solution in economic theory.

In spite of this sometimes unsatisfactory application of static methods to dynamic problems, it turned out that Wicksell made his greatest contribution precisely by paving the way for *dynamic theory* in the proper sense. This he did by demonstrating that the discrepancy between the real rate of interest on capital and the money rate, so long as it persisted, gave rise to a cumulative process which, amongst other things, included a continually shifting price level.

Wicksell's first formulation of this theory in *Interest and Prices* was far from perfect. The real rate of interest is, of course, a static concept. It can be determined in a position of stationary equilibrium, but it is not so easily grasped in a developing society. In order that the scope of the theory should not be limited to the rather uninteresting case where a stationary equilibrium situation is disturbed because the previous conformity between the real rate and the money rate of interest ceases, Wicksell had to reformulate it. The presentation in his *Lectures* can, with the use of later terminology, be interpreted so that the concept of 'normal or equilibrium money rate,' defined as the rate of interest that brings *planned* saving and investment into equality, is substituted for the concept of real rate of interest. (When Wicksell talks about 'the savers' *decisions* not to consume a part of their incomes in the near future,' he must obviously have meant planned saving, and not that which came about as a result of developments during the period.) His thesis, therefore, can be formulated so that this normal or equilibrium rate is neutral with respect to the price level. If the actual money rate of interest deviates from this equilibrium rate, the result is a cumulative process. Even in this formulation the theory is certainly not invulnerable, and may certainly still be improved in important respects. But so far, at least, the critics have not touched its actual foundation, namely, that certain price movements may be considered a consequence of an *excess* of *total* demand over *total* supply, or vice-versa. Beside such price-movements, which are caused by a lack of balance of this kind, there are also others, however, which are of a more autonomous character.[1]

With this theory, Wicksell did not only increase our understanding of the mechanism of price movements, he also demonstrated a fruitful method of attacking dynamic problems. Indeed, in pursuing his monetary theory further one is led into more general dynamic theory. He thus made a contribution to science which is of more than historical interest, for it is still a living force and an incentive to further research. The full significance of Wicksell's achievement as an economist can therefore not yet be appreciated.

VII

The brief account of Knut Wicksell's life and work that has been given above can only give a very incomplete impression of his remarkable personality. He was a man of great calibre, combining qualities usually considered incompatible.

Wicksell was both a scholar and a social reformer, the latter on an ideological plane in his capacity as lecturer, debater, and writer of polemical pamphlets on social and political topics. One would think that it would be rather an abrupt switch for him to leave his hyper-theoretical work at the writing table to sally forth and deliver a propagandist speech to a demonstration rally, or to appear on the platform at a socialist youth meeting. But Wicksell was as absorbed in the one task as he was in the other. His time and energy sufficed both for the furthering of science and for participation in the work of removing the anomalies existing in society. And in his case it is clear that the one sphere of activity had a fruitful influence upon the other. As has already been pointed out, it was Wicksell's interest in social affairs that drove him over into economics. For him, therefore, scientific work was not an interesting game of theoretical trickery—although he certainly derived intellectual satisfaction from it—but was justified as a means of furthering our knowledge of the possibilities of increasing general well-being. Wicksell thereby obtained a firm grasp of the essential problems of economic theory, and because he always kept the welfare of the public in mind, his mode of presentation was more lively than is usually the case in scholarly investigations. In the other sphere, his social pronounce-

[1] Cf. above, p. 33, not 2.

ments gained in striking power, because they were founded on logical argument.

As a scientist Wicksell made great use of his mathematical gifts and training. In his days, mathematical economics was not as fashionable as it is now, and, like Marshall, Wicksell practically apologised for occasionally taking the liberty of expressing his economic theories in mathematical form. Nowadays, the pioneering work that he did in this field is considered especially to his credit. But Wicksell was not only a theoretician with mathematical inclinations, he also possessed literary gifts, which does not seem to be so very common among the many mathematical economists of today. That he wrote verse and drama during his student days, some of which was published, is, perhaps, not so unusual, even for an economist. But all his literary work is marked by a finesse which makes his style easily accessible and affords the reader pleasure. It is also worth noting that Wicksell enjoyed refreshing himself in the evening by reading, in the original, the Latin and Greek authors that he had studied in his youth. The experts consider, however, that Wicksell was not much of a success as an historian, on the few occasions when he tackled problems in that field. He seems to have been conscious of his limitations in this respect himself. The combination of theoretical insight and historical vision is more noticeable in Wicksell's colleague Davidson, who was also decidedly superior to Wicksell in legal training.

Among Wicksell's scholarly attributes also belongs the fact that he was both a pioneer and a follower-up. He especially admired the English classics—he seems to have felt a particular spiritual affinity to John Stuart Mill and his liberal ideas—and considered that a thoroughgoing study of them should be part of every economist's training. In the exposition of his own theories he often refers to them, and on the whole he nearly always established a connection with earlier authors in the field. Indeed, he does so to such an extent that the reader cannot always be sure how significant Wicksell's own contributions are.[1] The opposite, and more usual, technique—viz. to emphasise one's own efforts at the expense of one's forerunners— is perhaps more effectively self-assertive in the short run, but Wicksell's own case shows that where an individual scholar is at pains to pick up where his predecessors left off, and to maintain the con-

---

[1] Cf. Stigler's remark quoted above (p. 15) on Wicksell's contribution to the marginal productivity theory. The originality of Wicksell's monetary theory has also sometimes been underestimated, because it is put forward as a modification of the Quantity Theory.

45

tinuity of scientific development, the prospects of his own contribution lasting are greater in the long run.

Linked with this self-effacing attitude towards science is another of Wicksell's characteristics, namely, his personal modesty. He was completely free of vanity, and it is a matter for discussion whether he even had any real personal ambition. Against this may be contrasted the general impression of him in his public capacities. Wicksell became known throughout the country as a dangerous fighter for radical ideas, whose methods were certainly not marked by any great sensibility for the feelings of others. Even so radical a colleague as Bengt Lidforss thought proper to attack Wicksell after the latter's above-mentioned speech at the Tegnér Festival of 1905, and to criticise his excessive political activity, which bore witness to an overweening self-confidence and a lack of discretion. Wicksell's reply[1] to Lidforss's newspaper article has been quoted before, but it may be repeated here, as it clarifies, in a remarkable way, Wicksell's view of himself as a public debater:

> My 'over-weening self-confidence' is perhaps not quite as great as Lidforss supposes, and my fault in the political field is rather that I participate too *little*, not too much. I have espoused the principle never to push myself forward when the things that I think ought to be said on any particular subject have already been said by others; and, conversely, never to remain *silent*, no matter how small and insignificant my contribution may be, when *no one* speaks on a subject that is close to my heart. Clearly, with such a maxim it is easy to give the impression of being paradoxical; it would undoubtedly be better and more effective to support ideas now and again that are already being voiced: but this, for one thing, would require more *time* than I have at my disposal at present. It still remains for Lidforss to show that, with my methods, I have actually damaged the liberal cause on any occasion.
>
> The accusation of lack of *discretion* would have been fully justified if I had been the one to bring up the question of union on an occasion when it was out of place, e.g. at an ordinary Tegnér Festival. But on this occasion the entire festival simply consisted of a glorification of the way in which we had dealt with this very question. If it is permissible to brag, why not also to criticise?

We have now come to another noticeable characteristic of Wicksell: his strong sympathy for liberal ideas. He was an opponent of every form of oppression, and to him the demand for truth and justice was absolute. He tolerated no compromise, and it was for this reason that he so often felt himself compelled to act in an apparently

---

[1] *Arbetet*, October 6, 1905.

impertinent manner. That Wicksell's persistent public activity may be interpreted in this way, and not as the outcome of a desire for self-assertion, becomes more plausible when it is remembered that Wicksell had a basically religious attitude towards life. The crisis that he went through in his youth—diary entries make it likely that it occurred in 1874—resulted in his replacing Christianity, as preached by the Church, by other ethical principles, which he embraced with the same intensity. Even his later ruthless struggle against those aspects of the teaching of the Church which, in his opinion, conflicted with historical reality—a struggle which made him so notorious as an enemy of religion—can be considered as a manifestation of his own religion. What was often taken by the public to be light-hearted mockery was actually the expression of his striving to further the search for truth. That his basic attitude to these questions was extremely serious is shown, *inter alia*, by his very thorough attempt to get to grips with modern Biblical scholarship.

This may also explain another apparent contradiction in Knut Wicksell. As a scholar he was always receptive to new ideas. His own solutions of economic problems were always put forward as hypotheses, which he was prepared to abandon or modify as soon as he got to know of something better. Consequently, he was anything but doctrinaire in this field, even though he demanded good positive reasons for changing his standpoint. In strong contrast to this was his unshakable adherence to what have here been called his ethical principles. The obstinacy with which he refused to make the slightest concession in this field often placed him and his family in an awkward situation. It has already been recounted above how, as a supporter of parliamentary government, and therefore on principle an opponent of the monarchy, he could not bring himself to place the word 'humbly' before his name in addressing the King, even though his livelihood was at stake. When the University of Lund decided to send a wreath to the funeral of Oscar II, Wicksell's dissension aroused unpleasant observations in the University Senate. As an opponent of the Church, he arranged for his children to be excused from religious instruction at school, which was, perhaps, not so remarkable, although it would attract attention. A more marked deviation from bourgeois conventions had occurred earlier, when, at his marriage, he refused to submit to a church ceremony. Since there were no civil marriages at that time, the couple had no choice but to substitute a ceremony of their own arranging. For the bride and her family in particular, this sacrifice for the sake of principle must have been rather trying.

Finally, it may be pointed out that although Wicksell espoused a materialistic and utilitarian philosophy—in this respect he was true to the ''eighties'—he was not much concerned about material advantages of his own. He lived for ideas. The fact that even for a life of this kind there are material prerequisites, certainly occasioned him trouble, but it never occurred to him to depart from his chosen course. In spite of the fact that he met with opposition from academic quarters the whole time instead of with encouragement,[1] and although it was not until he was 50 years old that he succeeded in obtaining a meagre academic livelihood, he pursued his scholarly course with resolute consistency, and thereby laid the foundations of economics as an independent academic discipline in Sweden. At the same time, he continued, inflexibly and undauntedly, to play the still more trying role of social reformer outside the political parties. By these contributions, which were made possible by an unusual combination of brilliant intellect and strong character, he has richly earned the admiration and gratitude of later generations.

[1] Not until he was 70 years old did Wicksell obtain any mark of academic honour in Sweden, when a volume of *Ekonomisk Tidskrift* was devoted to Economic Studies in his honour (1921, Vol. 12). Immediately afterwards he became a Fellow of 'Humanistiska Vetenskapssamfundet' (a learned society in Lund). He was never elected a member of the 'Vetenskapsakademien' (Academy of Science), however, although he would certainly have much appreciated it, and would also have felt quite at home in this gathering, with its strong natural science element. Among the public recognition that came Wicksell's way from *abroad* may be mentioned the honorary Doctor of Laws he received from Oslo University in 1911, and his honorary membership of the American Economic Association in 1923.

I

TWO EARLY LECTURES

ENDS AND MEANS
IN ECONOMICS[1]

WHEN a speaker has the honour, which is now mine, of standing as a representative of one science before an audience interested in science, some of whose members are scientists of high standing—mostly in other sciences, it is true—then it is a good opportunity to choose as the subject of his lecture some of the latest achievements of his science, to take from its treasure-house some precious jewels, so to speak, preferably some of the most recent acquisitions, and to lay them out for all to gaze on and admire. The scientist in question thus experiences a feeling of pride in himself, and one might say he salutes the flag under which he has fought in the past and will fight in the future, and in so doing he hurts no one and arouses no one's jealousy; on the contrary, we usually experience a stimulus of increased interest in our own studies when we hear of the work being done in other branches of knowledge and of the results achieved.

Unhappily, this satisfaction is denied the economist; within the whole of his science, or what he insists on calling science, no generally recognised result is to be found, as is also the case with theology, and for roughly the same reasons; there is no single doctrine taken to be a scientific truth without the diametrically opposed view being similarly upheld by authors of high repute. Of course, it is true that conflicts of opinion take place in other sciences, and indeed to some extent they constitute a real part of scientific life and research; but there is this great difference, that in other fields of science these conflicts usually come to an end, the defenders of the false opinion are defeated and admit themselves beaten; or, as more frequently occurs perhaps, they withdraw from the struggle and no new defenders come forward to take their places.

There have been supporters and opponents of the Copernican view of the universe, of Newton's system, of the theory of the circulation of the blood, of the phlogiston theory in chemistry, of the

1 'Mål och medel i nationalekonomien,' *Ekonomisk Tidskrift*, 1904, pp. 457–74. Inaugural lecture delivered on September 16, 1904, at the University of Lund.

51

corpuscular theory in optics, supporters and opponents of the principle of absolute monarchy in constitutional law, the Roman concept of property in civil law, the principle of retribution in penal law—there *have* been, but scarcely any longer; now there are only supporters *or* opponents, unless in the latter case the whole theory has been forgotten. The theory of biological evolution, the most important subject of controversy in our own day, is all too recent in date for the struggle yet to be fought out to its conclusion; but it would seem that already the principal opponents of this theory may be described as an extinct species, at least, among active natural scientists. Even the comparison I made just now with theology really turns out to the advantage of theology, for theologians are beginning to agree about certain results yielded by research; the crude verbal inspiration which still held sway within theology during my youth seems nowadays to have scarcely a single supporter; there seems to be increasing unanimity that even religious documents should be treated by essentially the same methods and be subject to the same criteria of truth as all other original sources.

It is only in the field of economics that the state of war seems to persist and remain permanent. The Malthusian doctrine of population has been discussed for more than a hundred years, and yet we have come no farther than a situation where there are some economists who regard an uncontrolled growth of population as a country's greatest misfortune, while others regard it as the greatest good fortune and every limitation of the growth of population a great misfortune. The controversy about the best foreign trade policy has an even older ancestry. It actually seemed to have been decided about half a century ago; but no, it has flared up again and while some economists urge the abolition of all national boundaries in an economic sense, so that the whole world's economic resources may be available for everybody, others endeavour—and actually with considerable success—to raise and strengthen these barriers as much as possible, so that every tiny patch of the earth's surface or section of mankind may become a sort of microcosm, a self-perpetuating and self-dependent whole, like the entire universe. The third and most recent theory in this field, neo-mercantilism as it is called, 'the policy of trade and power,' which is at present in fashion in the German universities, expounds, in effect, the view that the way to national prosperity is founded on armour-plate and dynamite, that each nation ought to try to deprive its competitors of life by force of arms, and, one might say, to force other people to consume its dear, inferior goods at the point of the bayonet. In the field of trade cycle theory, there is the well-known contradiction between those who say that the bad times in the economy of a people, as of an individual, are due to the fact that too much has been consumed and too little produced, and those who say the opposite, that too much has been produced and too little consumed. Closely connected with this are the differing opinions about the great problem of distribution: for some it is an axiom that the position of the working class can only be improved at the cost of the owning class, if other circumstances remain unchanged, whereas others with a brighter outlook on life consider that an increase in workers' incomes is all that is required to bring about an increase in purchasing power, an increase in sales, and thereby an increase in the prosperity of all classes of society. And lastly, to take a more specialised though still important field: when it is a matter of finding the cause of general changes in the prices of commodities, and especially the influence on these of credit and of the institutions regulating credit, some maintain that cheap and easy credit, in other words, a low rate of interest, will tend to increase the amount of means of payment in circulation and the demand for goods and thus will tend to increase the general level of prices; while others maintain the contrary, that cheap credit means the same thing as cheaper costs of production and so tends to *lower* the level of prices, not to raise it; and naturally, just as with the cases previously mentioned, there is no lack of more moderate opinions between these two extremes, eclectics who say that the influence of credit on prices is sometimes in one direction, sometimes in another, and is sometimes nil.

It is not for lack of material, but out of consideration for the patience of my audience that I forbear to prolong this list. But I would be quite nonplussed if I were asked to cite any economic proposition other than of merely formal significance, which might be adduced as a scientific result recognised by everyone. Some years ago, my more famous colleague, Professor Gustav Schmoller of Berlin, of whom I will say more later on, on one ceremonial occasion chose as the subject of one of his much admired academic discourses: 'Changing Theories and Lasting Truths in the Field of the Political and Social Sciences'; but he was as eloquent when it came to the changing theories as he was brief in his dispatch of 'the lasting truths'—all he really did was to maintain that there are such things, but he did not quote any of them, and perhaps it is just as well that he did not.

It is not very pleasant to have to confess to such a state of affairs, but, of course, it is no good trying to conceal it. It might be an advantage to have a clear idea of what this characteristically stubborn difference of opinion ultimately depends upon. Is it the innate *difficulty* of economic problems which makes it impossible ever to reach a solution of them which would be convincing for everyone; or is it perhaps that we have not yet hit upon the right *way* to handle them adequately; or, finally, do you think it may be the investigators' individual sympathies and antipathies, their different political ideals, in a word, their conception of the *ends* of practical, social and economic activity, which tends also to colour their treatment of theoretical questions?

It is undoubtedly true that the first of these reasons goes a long way towards explaining the phenomenon in question. Some economic problems—for example, that just mentioned, of the causes and course of economic crises—are so complicated that it may sometimes seem almost hopeless to expect a completely satisfactory solution of them; and it is always true of such problems that they are more difficult than they appear to be. The most common source of error is actually just that treacherous appearance of simplicity and easy comprehensibility which these problems present, due to the fact that we are familiar with similar questions in the field of private economy, and too much inclined to transfer our experiences there to the social economy without further investigation, forgetting that what is true for A or B or C, taken by themselves, is not necessarily true of A, B and C taken together. If *one* farmer succeeds in doubling his harvest by diligent work and improved methods, he becomes extremely wealthy; but if every farmer does the same, they are almost all forced into bankruptcy, for the surplus of farm produce would make its value negligible and the farmers would no longer be able to pay interest or taxes, stipulated in money terms, nor would they be able to make their necessary purchases. For the society as a whole, however, or, to put it more cautiously, for the whole society except the farmers, the result would be a gain, since the unpaid interest and taxes would be more than offset by the cheapness of foodstuffs; and if technical progress occurred harmoniously in all occupations, it might well be that it would be to the advantage of all classes of society without exception. It *might be*, for it is in no way impossible that, because of the altered distribution of products among the propertied and propertyless classes which would follow the other change, and depending on the actual choice of means of exchange and measures of value, the general prosperity might still be accompanied by the economic decline of not a few individuals or families. I have given this little example—which, by the way, has already taken us on to disputed ground—merely in order to show how entirely different and much more complex is the character of an event judged from the viewpoint of the social economy, as compared with a similar one judged from the viewpoint of private economy; for what could be more indisputably certain than that progress in private economic life is to be won by diligence and a progressive attitude? Actually, a considerable degree of practice, or else a more than ordinary acuteness of judgment, is necessary in order to follow the logical thread of an economic argument without a break through all its twistings and turnings. If it is lost even for a moment, it is all too easy to take up a false thread, so that the reasoner, quite unsuspectingly, suddenly comes back to the point from which he started, perhaps unaware of the fact. Circular proofs, circular conclusions, circular definitions, and whatever else such logical capers may be called, would thus hardly seem to occur so frequently in the literature of any other subject as they do in that of economics, and without the necessity of descending to second- or third-rate publications.

Difficulties exist to be conquered, however, and mistakes to be corrected; moreover it is true of the mistakes indicated above that they really belong to the childhood of our science, before it had had time to set due limits to its proper scope; or if, in some exceptional cases, they have found their way into recent writing, that is because of a special circumstance which I will come to later.

It is possible to stray from the truth otherwise than by directly mistaken conclusions, however. It may happen that in seeking the truth the wrong path is taken at the beginning, and by consistently following it one gets farther and farther away from the goal. Perhaps that is the case here? Well, if we are to believe the representatives of the trend which has dominated German economics for more than thirty years—the so-called historical or historico-ethical or historico-ethico-realistical school—that was the case with the whole of classical economics, or, it might even be said, with all researches in economics before 1870.

According to those who go farthest in this opinion, all reasoning from general points of view in economic matters is, on the whole, in vain. For either the assumptions made are purely arbitrary, and only adopted in order to make the reasoning easier, in which case the conclusions drawn are absolutely worthless as far as actual practical problems are concerned, or, at best, the propounder of the argument bases it on the economic environment of his own time and his own country, and, without justification, makes a false extension of his conclusions to other times and other countries. Instead, they say, the most that one can strive for is by a thorough examination of the economic conditions of different periods and different nations, to trace out certain parallels which may serve as indicators for the assessment of the period during which we ourselves are living and developing, and for the period which lies immediately before us. The deductive, abstract, systematic method of procedure is no longer rejected without reservation, however, owing to the gradually increasing influence of the more moderate members of that school, or, it might be better to say, owing to the moderation which is gradually affecting that school. But it is maintained that the classical economists have already carried the method as far as was generally possible with the narrow basis of factual experience which was at their disposal, so that it would be fruitless to continue with it, at least for the present. As Schmoller, the leader of the school, has said somewhere: no useful purpose is served by sifting and resifting the thin substratum of abstractions which has already been sifted ten times by Ricardo and his successors. What is now necessary is to fill the scoop anew with a new and wider selection of facts, gathered by years of patient and specific study, so that at some time in the future it may be possible to build up a theoretical system which is richer and more substantial and, through increased experience, more adequate. Thus the same conclusion is drawn in both cases: away with systems, away with abstractions, definitions and classifications, and every man to the laboratory, to work; salvation lies in special investigations in the fields of statistics, occupational reports, and particularly economic history, fields which have received so little attention in the past.

This is not a suitable occasion to enter into a detailed criticism of the activity of this school, which has lasted more than thirty years, and more than fifty years if we include the old vanguard, Knies, Roscher, Hildebrand, and so on; nor, for that matter, am I the right person to attempt such a criticism. As far as I know, the positive good accomplished by the school has never been denied by its opponents, on the contrary, it has been readily acknowledged, more so even than present-day historians of the subject seem prepared to admit. It is beyond doubt that those members of the school more eminently gifted for historical and statistical investigations—and they are not necessarily its most prominent members—have carried out work of permanent, not to say inestimable, value for the science of economics; and the extent to which academic tuition gains living interest and graphic qualities when economic theories are presented, so to speak, in a gallery of concrete pictures taken from bygone or present-day economic life, will be admitted by anyone who, like me, has had the good fortune to listen to the lectures of G. F. Knapp. The only danger is—and I am not saying that such was the case with Knapp's teaching—that simplicity and clarity are gained only at the expense of thoroughness and that the student will not be required to make contributions of his own, as in the case of excessive illustration of textbooks.

But because of its one-sidedness and the purely negative, harshly deprecatory, even conceited and offensive attitude which it always adopts towards contemporary research of the theorising and systematising sort, this school has, in my opinion, hindered and damaged the development of economics, especially in Germany; and, more than anything else, it has helped to create and maintain the state of affairs with regard to the body of known and recognised truths in the structure of scientific theories which I described at the outset.

I am unfortunately no trained methodician or logician, but it would surprise me if the final outcome of all the conflicts on scientific method, which are often so bitterly contested, were not that all scientific knowledge, in fact, all human knowledge, is ultimately won in the same way. To call one science, or one scientific method (usually one's own scientific method), 'exact,' and another 'empirical' or 'speculative and abstract,' according to the circumstances, is unjustifiable. All real science and every effective method is empirical in so far as it must start from, and end in, reality or experience. That method is exact which leads to the objective, neither more nor less: as Adolf Wagner, with good reason maintains, *exactus* means *finished* or complete, and a science is not finished until it has completed all its tasks; so it is never really exact in the strictest sense of the word. If the objective can be gained by immediate observation of reality, so much the better; for the evidence of the senses, if not infallible, is nevertheless the safest source of knowledge, and, at all events, the most popular. But for most of us, our curiosity and questioning go far beyond the bounds of immediate observation, and there begins that necessary element in almost all scientific activity, which is called speculation, abstraction, hypotheses, or in plain language: guesswork. To use one's eyes as far as they can be used, and then to guess the way forward—the art of science is no more than that; but it is quite enough, nevertheless, because the point is to guess right, that is to say, so that the result may be tested, and confirmed by experience. What guides our guesses and prevents them from going

hopelessly astray is the feeling or conviction of the relative simplicity and interdependence of all things, which is another of the
products of experience. As soon as we discover a similarity between
two phenomena, we at once suspect a closer connection, and tenta-
tively assume that they are also similar in other respects. This method
of proceeding by analogy has not a high place in formal logic, but
it is fundamentally the only one at our disposal apart from immediate perception; it is often deceiving, even usually deceiving, and
it is then called false analogy. The difference between false and
true analogy cannot be seen *a priori*, only *a posteriori* in accordance
with the evidence of experience. The history of science shows conclusively that guesswork has played an immense part in all discoveries, including those in pure mathematics, and that usually it
has only been after a series of false analogies that the correct one has
eventually been found. Error is the mother of truth. And the same
thing applies to the life of the individual doing research; after a
thousand guesses which get no farther than the table drawer, or
perhaps do not even get as far as that because their lack of agreement
with experience was immediately apparent, at last one occurs which
is found to conform to reality, or if the discoverer is not so lucky,
one which at least does not conflict with the reality known to him,
and this may therefore be offered to the scientific world as a
hypothesis to be subjected to further testing, bringing refutation or
confirmation. Thus speculation, abstraction, and hypotheses are not
an escape from reality, but on the contrary, the only way of reaching
that reality which cannot be reached by direct observation. Their
ultimate goal is always a comparison with reality, or *verification*.

Both friends and foes of systematic or theoretical economics,
however, have claimed that it is in general impossible to give a strict
verification of the propositions or rules which we formulate as
hypotheses, as tentative abstractions from experience, because it is
impossible to isolate economic phenomena to the extent necessary
for such verification. Unlike the natural sciences, economics is not
in a position to carry out experiments, they say. It seems to me
that this contention is to a great extent exaggerated; as a matter of
fact, such experiments are constantly being made in the realm of our
science and they are of the most incisive character conceivable,
because one economic element is altered discontinuously while everything else remains the same—and the experimenter is the economic
legislator. These experiments are frequently even direct and quite
deliberate; the measures introduced by the legislation are based upon
the supposition that some abstract economic proposition or other is

valid, and the result is either confirmation or refutation of the proposition in question. The so-called Gresham's Law in monetary theory provides a striking example of this: it says that an inferior currency which is legally valued as high as a better one will tend to force the latter out of circulation. This hypothesis has been confirmed countless times by experience, usually *against* the wishes of the experimenters, and it may now be said to be the basis of the currency policies of all countries. Another example, also from the monetary field, is the old Quantity Theory, which is probably correct in its essentials although still the subject of controversy. This theory says that the function of money is purely formal and that its exchange value is therefore regulated by its quantity and speed of circulation only, and not by its intrinsic properties. This theory has been abstracted from experience: the fall in the value of money during periods of sharply increased production of the precious metals, after the discovery of America for example; the sharp depreciation of the value of paper money not convertible into gold or silver when altogether too much of it is issued; and so on. But, if necessary, it is possible to explain these phenomena in another way: for instance, by the change in the *cost of production* of precious metals in the former case, and in the latter by *lack of confidence* in the Government's ability and intention to back the paper money with hard cash at a subsequent date. But recently, the Austrian Government succeeded over a large number of years in keeping its inconvertible paper money more or less constant in value, and at a value which was even higher than that of the silver into which it was once redeemable. This was done by withdrawing some of the paper money, when necessary, through the sale of interest-yielding paper, the so-called Salinenscheine, or, alternatively, by releasing paper money in turn by repurchasing its Salinenscheine. Similarly, at the beginning of the 'seventies, when silver had already begun to decline in value, Holland raised the value of its main coinage, the silver guilder, not merely to its former gold-parity, but higher than it had ever stood with respect to gold, by the simple expedient of ceasing to mint silver coins on private account. Furthermore the Indian Government used just the same method twenty years later in successfully raising the value of the silver rupee from the 13 pence in gold to which it had fallen, up to an arbitrarily determined maximum value of 16 pence, at which value it has stayed ever since despite the continued fall in the gold-value of silver. When we consider these examples, it is evident that they imply an experimental confirmation of the quantity theory as strong as anyone could really desire. The last-mentioned Indian measure aroused a good deal of attention in the economic world, and many economists regarded it with a good deal of misgiving, as for instance the eminent monetary expert Lexis. The value of the rupee did actually continue to fall during the first years, although not as much as that of metallic silver, and the opponents of the quantity theory were triumphant, but, as was subsequently shown, prematurely.[1]

Verification is not always as striking as in this case; but perhaps that is usually due to the fact that verification is not sought: the necessary steps in order to obtain verification are not taken. It is not infrequently that the real motives for an administrative measure are quite different from those which are given, and in such cases the Government will not be particularly inclined to betray its intentions by gathering statistical data. The history of economic legislation is, regrettably, not without examples where the gathering of such statistics has been *avoided* most carefully, even when the nature of the matter called for such statistics, and where they would certainly have yielded good results in a theoretical sense, and maybe in a practical sense too.

What I have already said will make it sufficiently clear that economic history and statistics have an immense importance for economics. They are really its most important auxiliaries. History has, in particular, the illuminating and exhilarating task of teaching us to understand the existing order of things, and of showing us how certain out-of-date institutions or social customs which now seem completely irrational to us were once fully justified, under a different set of conditions. In this way, it is the best guide for progress, and it rescues us from throwing away, in a rash fit of reforming zeal, things which, although concealed by old forms, may still be full of life and perhaps too precious to lose.

---

[1] Hardly had I uttered these words when I received one of the new issues of *Conrads Jahrbücher*, containing an article by Otto Heyn who sharply *disagrees* with the idea that the Indian coinage experiment in any way confirms the quantity theory, the validity of which he denies. At the time of writing, Heyn's article has not been completed, but it seems that his argument is based on the statement that the value of money with respect to commodities ought to be strictly differentiated from the exchange value with respect to the currencies of other countries, in this case the value of silver with respect to gold. In the former case, the quantity theory should apply, in real terms, at least, but not in the latter. What Heyn really seems to object to is the opinion that a change in the amount of money in a country leads to a corresponding change in its external exchange value, *regardless of the changes which have simultaneously taken place in the value of other countries' money* (in this case, the value of gold with respect to commodities), an opinion which is certainly untenable, but which can scarcely be said to be a consequence of the quantity theory.

But first and foremost it must be questioned whether here, as with all other auxiliary sciences, the actual work of research should not be left to those who devote their whole time to the science. We economists are essentially only dilettanti in the field of historical research, with the usual faults of all dilettantism: over-hasty conclusions, insufficient criticism of sources, tendentious colouring of facts, and even, on occasion, unconscious fabrication of them. An historian of the subject who in a German periodical has recently subjected the work of the historical school in economics to a thorough and penetrating criticism, with special reference to its chief member, Schmoller, pronounces a judgment which I will not repeat here, but which is based precisely on establishing the existence of the above faults. But, secondly, if statistics and history are indispensable aids to systematic economics, it is also equally true that the latter is an aid, an auxiliary science, to the former. It may not be possible to study economic—or even political—history successfully without a proper knowledge of the fundamental concepts and principles of economics, despite the fact that these are to a great extent still only hypothetical in character. The same thing applies in an even higher degree to economic statistics, which run the risk of going astray altogether, thus wasting time, energy, and also expenditure on the collection of useless data, if they are not based on a comprehensive knowledge of the current state or research in systematic economics, which enables the statisticians to decide what the economic problems are which require the help of statistics at the moment. Thus, however much we may deplore the fact that, for instance, at our universities economists-in-the-making have all too little contact with history and statistics—most of our professional economists have, moreover, had to acquire their education independently and without direct help from the universities—it is even more inappropriate that our historians and even our statisticians lack economic training. The way to make good this deficiency in practice is something I cannot enter into here.

Thus, systematic economics cannot be disregarded in the circle of sciences, nor can economics itself disregard the assistance available to it. It would be so if, as Schmoller asserts, it had already, during its classical period a hundred years ago, progressed as far as it could on the whole with the empirical material available; but that is a contention which has very little real basis, and which is decisively disproved by the way in which theoretical economics has begun to flourish during the last few decades in England, America, Italy, Austria, everywhere except in Germany. The classical economists' analysis of economic phenomena, even as they saw them, was certainly far from complete, and their synthesis still more so, because they generally considered no other connection between these pheno-mena than that of cause and effect, while we have now learnt (especi-ally since Walras) to regard them as a whole group of interrelated logical relationships, a system of forces in equilibrium, whether the equilibrium is of the static or dynamic (kinetic) sort. But their *method* was undoubtedly sound and, used in the right way, has proved to be capable of considerable development. It is interesting to learn from Ricardo's correspondence, published in recent years, how little he himself was satisfied with his system, although this is such an extraordinary logical achievement, and how, year after year, he endeavoured to perfect it, without success, and how the very pieces he was groping for were obviously those which, when they were included in the modern theory of value and capital, led for the first time to the construction of an edifice of economic theory whose form is firmly fixed and consistent, although it must still deal with simplifications and abstractions from reality.

Tempting though it would be to do so, time does not permit me to attempt an explanation of how it has come about that such an obviously one-sided school as the historical one should hold exclusive sway for so long a time in a country of such many-sided intelligence as Germany. It seems to me beyond question that the main reason is to be sought in Germany's peculiar political development. While political storms are raging, history provides a refuge for the timid, and for the warlike a phalanx either for attacking or defending the *status quo*. But it is equally certain that the effect of the trend on German politics has not been unreservedly favourable. Basically, it means the dismissal of economics as a living and developing science, the abandonment of its most forward positions, with the result that these are occupied by its enemies, the enemies of truth and science, as soon as it comes into conflict with unenlightened private interests.[1]

---

[1] The direct political influence of the school has been quite small in Germany: the workers' insurance, which is often supposed to be the work of the historical or social-political school, on the contrary, owes its origin, strange to say, to the school's most zealous opponent, the well-known manufacturer von Stumm, who operated the system at his factory in Neunkirchen for a long time before Bismarck adopted it. The adherents of the school also have experienced the ignominy of having their attack on the Manchester doctrine, which was intended for something quite different, taken up by the agrarian party as a substantiation of their protec-tive tariff policy. They now attempt to console themselves (cf. Schmoller, in the speech mentioned earlier) with the strange statement that 'the question of pro-tective tariffs and free trade is not a scientific question.'

With this I come to the third and, in my opinion, deepest cause of the present state of schism in economics: namely, the varying viewpoints, and more or less spirited feelings, on what the *ends* of economic social development should be. Schmoller was quite right when he said, in the academic discourse I have already mentioned, that the theoretical divergences in economics are nowhere near so great as they may appear at first sight, and that among what might be called the inner circle of economists they are regarded as due to different nuances within the same opinion rather than to different opinions. The drastic contradictions I referred to in my introduction really belong more to the popular discussion than to the scientific, but that some are left and allowed to extend into practical and political life is not therefore any less the fault of the science, or rather the scientists, who do not come to the defence of scientific truth with sufficient strength and ardour—obviously because their hearts are not always on the same side as their heads, their sympathies being in conflict with their scientific convictions.

That the goal of economic activity must be the greatest possible social prosperity, individually and collectively, is a thing about which everyone is in formal agreement; but what does 'society' mean in this connection? Are all the individuals of the society to be included, each one to the same extent as all the rest, or is a predominant, perhaps exclusive, place to be accorded to certain families, races, language groups, or faiths? Is the concept of society to extend beyond the more or less temporary geographical boundaries of states, or is a national advantage won at the expense of another nation, and perhaps causing that nation's destruction, still to be regarded as a social gain? Here are questions which we, in our attitude to the problems of practical economics, cannot disregard, and which also in any case make themselves felt in everything which affects the *importance and significance* we attach to our theoretical conclusions, although, strictly speaking, they cannot affect their abstract truth.

We know with what naïveté they went about answering these fundamental questions in the past. For the old mercantilism it was axiomatic that social prosperity *can* only be won at the expense of other nations, since what one gains, they said, another must lose. And then, and for a long time after, *society* meant just the upper propertied classes; the propertyless mass constituted only the low and unworthy earth from which the blossoms of culture, riches and national power grew.[1]

[1] Our enthusiasts for manufacture took it as self-evident during the period of freedom that flourishing factories required the most wretched wages for their

Faced with the progress of the working people in education, maturity and political importance, this way of looking at things could not be maintained. During the past century we therefore find no direct denial of the idea that workers also belong to the society, and that their wishes and interests must also be taken into account, but instead the defenders of the established order devoted all their efforts to showing that the workers' interests already were satisfied, as far as they could be. The classical economists, however, took no part in that work of embellishment, that 'Harmonieduselei'; their scientific sense of honour was much too strong; towards the middle of the century, therefore, the allegation was made that they put wind in the sails of the socialist attack by undermining the fundamental privileges of the owning class. No attempt was made to master the difficulties, to solve and overcome the problem of the conflict between individualism and socialism, by an extended analysis and synthesis of fundamental economic concepts. Instead economic dilettantism was put into the saddle, represented by Carey, Bastiat (I mean Bastiat the harmony economist, not Bastiat the deserving populariser of the doctrine of free trade), and their numerous imitators in all countries, in order to make black white, and to reason away the most glaring anomalies. It seems that even the historical school cannot be absolved from all participation in this, although their general standpoint—they have been called 'teacher's desk socialists'—seems to have been just the opposite to start with. Who could then be surprised if the workers and their leaders were filled with contempt for such a pseudo-science, and on their part set up a system of their own, which, however deficient, survives comparison with that of the harmony economists as far as intrinsic truth is concerned, and who could blame them if, in interpreting history, they preferred their own version to that of the other people. I have always regarded the

continued operation. In order to get them sufficiently low it was advisable to encourage the immigration of foreign labour, 'so that,' as an economic paper of the time put it, 'if possible there may be ten applicants for each vacant situation'; and when the system in practice had the consequence that the children of the factory workers could not be kept alive, and there was the threat that there would be few applicants in the future, a secret committee of the Riksdag in 1756 wanted to establish children's homes for them where they would be looked after until the age of five, after which they were to be set to spinning, winding and the like, under the supervision of the factory (Arnberg). In order not to be unjust, one has to remember in connection with such statements the low level of intellectual and material development which still existed in most countries; there was not much question, or there seems not to have been much question, whether the workers— as we would now express it—ought to partake of the blessings of culture, but the question was rather whether there ought to be any culture at all.

fact that the former derision by the workers' parties of everything concerned with economists has now died down, as an indication that modern theoretical economists are on the right track, although no one has more thoroughly criticised the exaggerations of Marxism than Böhm-Bawerk, probably the most prominent personality in the theoretical school. It seems that the workers instinctively realise that the aim of economics has once again become a search for truth that takes nothing for granted, and they are inspired with the noble consciousness that they and their cause have nothing to fear from the *truth*.

It is easy to understand that many people, even the most ardent well-wishers, may hesitate before the decisive and radical upheaval of the existing state of affairs which would seem to be the inevitable consequence of an unconditional recognition of the complete equality of political, social and economic rights for the workers, those at present without property; but it is only possible to go forwards or backwards in this matter: he who is not prepared to go forward along the road indicated by previous trends must drop back into more reactionary attitudes.

It is certainly rather peculiar to see Schmoller, the former 'teacher's desk socialist,' making his small contribution as a member of the Prussian Senate to what seems to us to be a most reactionary proposal, although the wording he used was not too enthusiastic. The proposal I am referring to is that recently put forward by the Government, according to which a certain class of Prussian subjects, namely workers and small farmers of Polish descent, could be forbidden outright to acquire or own land, the State having already sacrificed in vain, as we know, hundreds of millions to encourage German colonisation of the Polish parts of the country. It gives a possibly even more peculiar impression when one of the younger pupils of the school, the deserving Heinrich Herkner, who is undoubtedly friendly to the workers' cause, attempts in his book *Die Arbeiterfrage* (The Labour Problem) to win sympathy among the working classes for Germany's well-known external power politics, and positively complains that this policy has up to now met with opposition originating in what he himself calls a deep-rooted ethical viewpoint of the German working class, which says that it is necessary to fight every sort of exploitation and suppression, whether directed against a class, a party, a sex, or a race.

To me it is clear, however, that the German labour party in this respect not only represents the ethical standpoint, as also naïvely admitted by Herkner, but also the clearer vision of the future. Or must we really think of the future as a continuous war of attrition on the part of one race, nationality, language group, or religious faith—and why not one social class also—against the others? If such be the case, it is certain that there is nothing better to be done than promptly to set all books on both classical and other systematic economics back on the shelf or else on the fire; for they are not intended for such a concept of society, they have no learning to give to it. But if, as I hope and believe, one day we recognise that our goal here on earth is to extend the greatest possible happiness to all, of whatever class of society, race, sex, language, or faith they may be—then the pleasant discovery will be made that the economic side of this problem has already been solved in its essentials, and that the solution only awaits practical application. The science of economics, even in the backward state in which, through unfavourable circumstances, it finds itself at present, is possessed in spite of everything of resources capable of making the average material conditions of human happiness incomparably better than they are at present.

THE INFLUENCE OF THE RATE OF INTEREST ON COMMODITY PRICES[1]

THERE is no need to waste words proving how important it is that the exchange value of money or, what is the same thing seen from the opposite angle, the general level of commodity prices, remains as stable and constant as possible. Money is the standard of all values, the basis of all property transactions, and daily becomes more and more so. All commodities are exchanged for money, and, moreover, we produce only in order to exchange, and to exchange for money. What then can be more important than that what constitutes the standard of everything else, should itself retain a constant magnitude? It is true that it is not altogether easy to decide what ought to be meant by a constant money value or a constant average price of commodities—the commonly employed index-number method leaves a good deal to be desired in various respects, as is well known —yet the main difficulty is not there, but as I shall demonstrate presently, in a totally different sphere.

In passing, an opinion may here be mentioned which is rather common but which on closer examination is seen to lack all foundation. Many people imagine that it would be possible to attain still better results if the value of money were, or could be, made not constant but successively variable downwards, so that commodity prices would thus be rising continuously. They consider that the rise in commodity prices would be a continual incentive to industrial enterprise and thus have a fruitful and stimulating effect on the economic life of the community as a whole. It is not difficult, however, to realise that this is a pure illusion. What one person gains by rising prices another unfortunately loses; but it is a general psychological rule that an unexpected gain, other things being equal, can never compare in importance with an equally large unexpected loss. If, on the other hand, the rise in prices took place with such regularity that it could be foreseen and calculated in advance, why, then it

[1] 'Penningeräntans inflytande på varuprisen,' *Nationalekonomiska föreningens förhandlingar under förra halvåret 1898*, Stockholm, 1899, pp. 47–70. Lecture to the Economic Association in Stockholm, April 14, 1898.

would of course be taken into account in all transactions; nothing would be either gained or lost, and we should only find ourselves, after somewhat more trouble, in the same position as if average commodity prices were absolutely constant. Were it therefore in our power to arrange these circumstances as we please, it is fairly certain that all interests would be best served if the standard of value were kept as scrupulously constant as the standards of weights and measures.

And why should this not be in our power? It is true that we can do nothing about the *relative* exchange value of commodities themselves; each time there is a change in conditions of production, it must, at least under a system of free competition, lead to a shift in the relative value of commodities; every effort to regulate this artificially must, in so far as the principles of free exchange are true, necessarily entail a decrease in the sum-total of utility available to the community. But *money prices* and their average level we are complete masters over, since these are ultimately dependent on the choice, which lies with us, of a standard of price. It can also be maintained that the obstacles to a solution of the problem are to be found not so much in the practical as in the theoretical field, and agreement about a constant standard of commodity prices would probably have been reached long ago if there had existed a completely clear theory as to what factors cause the changes actually observed in their general level.

There was a time when economists thought they had largely mastered this question. That was in the golden age of economics, at the beginning of our century, when so many problems, previously obscure and unsolvable, became, as it were, transparent under Ricardo's penetrating eyes. Reading Ricardo's works on money, in particular the little pamphlet *The High Price of Bullion* and its sequel *Reply to Mr. Bosanquet*—which are, incidentally, even by admission of his opponents, probably the finest and most penetrating studies that economic literature can boast in this sphere—we find a perfectly clear and exhaustive, logically coherent treatment of the subject which does not seem to leave room for doubt or dissenting opinion. Essentially this exposition is based on the so-called quantity theory: the relationship between the available, or at least the circulating, amount of money on the one hand, and the amount of commodities to be bought and sold on the other, constitutes for Ricardo and his supporters the decisive factor which determines the level of commodity prices. I for my part am convinced that this theory is fundamentally sound and correct, but as so often with Ricardo the theory was given too one-sided a character; it was too narrow, it was not immediately applicable to concrete reality. It is true that during his lifetime Ricardo succeeded in repelling victoriously all attacks, but after his death there arose on the opposite side a formidable champion against whom the Ricardians now in their turn could not pit anybody quite equal in stature. This was Thomas Tooke, who, with Newmark, was the author of the voluminous work *History of Prices*. Equipped with an infinite amount of practical experience and unhampered by any very great theoretical ballast, Tooke set out to fight the Ricardian theories and to prove that their conclusions in many cases did not tally with reality. It was not true, for instance, that a heavy issue of notes caused a rise in commodity prices, but rather did the issue of notes follow as the necessary corollary of a rise in prices that had already taken place, or as Tooke expressed it: 'That the prices of commodities do not depend . . . upon the amount of the whole of the circulating medium; but that, on the contrary, the amount of the circulating medium is the consequence of prices.' This thesis may be true, in any case it contains a good deal of truth; but unfortunately it does not, as is easily discovered, replace the thesis which it sets out to refute; it tells us, and largely correctly, what the determination of prices does *not* depend on, but unhappily leaves us ignorant as to what it actually does depend on. Tooke's criticism, however justified it may be, is in fact purely negative, and this weakness has not been remedied by any of his successors —in England John Stuart Mill, in Germany Adolf Wagner (who, however, has later changed his point of view somewhat), Erwin Nasse, etc. Nevertheless, the view prevailed, supported, as it seemed, by irrefutable experience. But the vacuum that was formed when the quantity theory was superseded, has in actual fact never been filled. It can be maintained without exaggeration that most modern economists, with the exception of the small group, mainly bimetallists, who in spite of everything still adhere to the quantity theory, lack any real, logically worked out theory of the value of money and its causes, a circumstance which has not of course had a particularly beneficial effect on the modern discussion of these questions.

The most prevalent doctrine nowadays seems to be that the level of commodity prices, and as a consequence thereof the exchange value of money, is determined by causes which have nothing whatever to do with changes in the amount of money available, namely by production and transport conditions for the commodities themselves. It should be noticed that this does not mean changes in the production costs of commodities *in relation* to the production costs

69

of money, i.e. gold at present: a level of prices determined by an increase or a decrease in the amount of commodities available, while the amount of money available remains practically the same would, in fact, simply mean a reversion to the old quantity theory. What is maintained is that commodity prices are determined, quite independently of money, by circumstances which only concern themselves. The matter is conceived roughly thus: by technical progress, etc., the production of first one then another group of commodities is simplified, which thereby fall in price, and when the price reduction has in due course affected the whole series of groups of commodities, the general level of prices will thereby have become a new and lower one, and the exchange value of money will thus have increased proportionately. This explanation is particularly popular during periods which, like the last few decades, show a fall in commodity prices. When prices are rising it is less useful; resort is then preferably made to 'bad harvests,' 'speculation,' etc.

This argument is heard not only from practical men, but just as much from theoreticians, although, it is true, mostly from theoreticians of a school that would prefer to throw all theory overboard. In the second supplementary volume of Conrad's *Handwörterbuch der Staatswissenschaften*, published last year, there is an essay by the well-known Professor W. Lexis at Göttingen, who gives an account of the latest stages in the production of precious metals. He points to the fact that since 1888, in less than ten years, the annual production of gold has been nearly doubled; the supply of gold in the world has probably also increased far more during this period than the population or the production of commodities, yet the general level of commodity prices, at least in the great ports of Hamburg and London, has not risen since 1888, but on the contrary has fallen. It is obvious then, says Lexis, that the determination of prices can have nothing to do with the quantity of money, but depends solely on the conditions of production and transport of the commodities themselves: commodities are produced more cheaply and transported more cheaply, therefore they become cheaper. Nothing could appear simpler, and yet, in spite of this ostensibly convincing argument and in spite of the authority of a Lexis, this opinion must on closer examination be rejected as logically untenable and erroneous. It is contrary to logic, because a price is in all circumstances a relationship between two objects, commodity and money, and how could a relationship between A and B possibly be dependent only on a change taking place in A, but quite independent of changes occurring simultaneously in B? And it is not difficult to demonstrate that it is also factually incorrect. Let us start with the cost of transport. If a commodity is transported more cheaply, it must also be sold more cheaply, it is maintained. Yes, certainly, but where? At its destination of course, in the importing country, where the price was kept up before by the high cost of freight; but what happens in the place of production, in the exporting country, where the high cost of freight has so far made sale abroad difficult? Obviously there the price of the commodity will not fall but rise as a consequence of the increase in demand from abroad. For instance, a commodity is produced in this country at a price of 100 crowns and the cost of transport also amounts to 100 crowns; consequently the minimum price of the commodity abroad is 200 crowns. Then the cost of freight drops to 50 crowns. Probably the price will then drop abroad as well; but it is equally certain that it will rise at home; it would be simplest to suppose that the reduction in freight costs is halved, the price abroad becoming 175 crowns and at home 125 crowns, the difference, 50 crowns, thus corresponding to the new and lower cost of freight. In short, cheaper freights *level out* the differences in commodity prices between the exporting and the importing countries, but do not necessarily in themselves have any influence on the average level of prices. Indeed, there is even one factor which, at least from the point of view of the quantity theory, makes one expect an improvement in means of transport to bring about a rise rather than a fall in commodity prices. As we all know, precious metals and particularly gold are produced practically exclusively in the most remote parts of the civilised world, in the interior of South Africa, in the extreme north-west of North America, etc. The expensiveness of gold in relation to commodities depends largely on the difficulty of bringing to these remote parts the food and other commodities that the gold-miner needs in order to exist. An improvement in transport conditions would thus on the whole lead to cheaper gold, i.e. more expensive commodities. If five sacks of corn are sent from inhabited regions to Klondyke, the freight charge might perhaps absorb four sacks, and only the fifth—to all intents and purposes—arrives at its destination to be exchanged for gold. The consequence of this is that a lump of gold, which in Klondyke is exchanged for one sack of corn, will buy five sacks in the rest of the world—all this is of course only roughly applicable to reality. If transport conditions to Klondyke are improved so that the same quantity of commodities can be sent there with the loss of only three sacks, two sacks or even one sack, the price of corn will fall, that is true—in Klondyke, but for the same reason it will rise

71

in all the rest of the world, which is exactly opposite to Lexis's conclusion.

The case for maintaining that commodity prices are determined by the cost of their production is no stronger. This proposition is certainly quite correct, broadly speaking at least, with respect to the relative values of commodities; but it no longer makes sense when it is extended to the actual prices of commodities, expressed in terms of money. The exception, of course, is in those cases where the relative cost of producing commodities on the one hand and of money on the other has changed; a circumstance which will no doubt influence commodity prices sooner or later, but generally only after some time. It must not be forgotten that the increase in the supply of one commodity, which causes a fall in its price, at the same time means an increase in the demand for other commodities and thus ought in turn to cause a rise in their prices. If farmers obtain a better harvest than usual, they increase their demand for other commodities, and the prices of these rise as the price of corn falls. If, then, a commodity can be produced at less 'cost,' i.e. with less productive power or, as we shall express it for the sake of simplicity, with less work than before, under a system of free competition this will entail, it is true, a fall in the price of this commodity in *relation* to other commodities; but this fall in price need by no means take the form of an equally large fall in the money price of this commodity; it may well happen that the result is partly attained by a rise in the prices of other commodities. Usually this rise is probably barely perceptible; but on the other hand it extends to many groups of commodities, so that the average price level may possibly remain quite unchanged or even rise; and of course the same thing applies to every subsequent improvement in the production of other groups of commodities.

Looked at from another angle—for we are here concerned with an idea so deeply rooted that one can hardly be too explicit in disputing it—the proposition that the price of a commodity is determined by the amount of work (or other productive power) which is put into its production, rests in fact on the tacit assumption that wages remain stationary; for otherwise, e.g., if wages increase to the same extent as the necessary amount of work decreases, there has been no change in the cost of production in money terms. If the conditions of production of one group of commodities alone have been made easier, one is indeed justified in assuming that this will not result in any perceptible change in average wages as a whole, although no doubt in this case too it would be more correct to say that an increase in wages (at all events in real wages) must take place everywhere, be it ever so small. If on the other hand technical progress has made it possible for all or most commodities to be produced with less work than before, i.e. in greater quantities with the same amount of work, it would obviously be absurd to assume wages to have remained unchanged in the meantime. On the contrary, under such circumstances real wages *must* rise, because broadly speaking the fruits of production constitute labour's own reward. It is true that this *can* happen in such a way that nominal wages (money wages) remain stationary, while commodities drop in price, but it can also happen in such a way that commodity prices remain the same or even rise, and nominal wages increase at the same pace or even faster than real wages. It simply cannot be established *a priori* whether one or the other will occur in reality.

In short, the determination of prices cannot possibly depend on the production market alone or the commodity market alone; it must be conditioned in some way or other by the relationship between the commodity market on the one hand and the money market on the other. No matter how this relationship may be understood in reality. If the money market is sufficiently elastic or well supplied, prices can rise, however much the production of commodities may have improved; if conditions are tight in the money market, it is certain that prices will fall, even if there has been no increase whatsoever in the production of commodities.

It is not possible, therefore, to throw the old quantity theory overboard without further ado; with all its weaknesses it is still the only theory that rests on a sound, logical basis. What is in fact required is an attempt to develop its fundamental idea, which in itself is correct, so that it conforms completely with reality. That a theory is found to conflict with experience is not enough to make us stop occupying ourselves with it; it may be enough for the practical man, but the theoretician has to investigate why and to what extent the theory thus found to be incorrect conflicts with logic and common sense. Only this will put him in a position to replace the rejected theory with a new one which is more rational and so in better accordance with experience.

If, then, we test the assumptions on which the quantity theory rests, we easily find that this doctrine would be quite true, assuming a state of affairs where everybody buys and sells for cash and with money of their *own*, that is to say, neither commodity credits nor money loans exist. Under such circumstances, everybody, particularly every businessman, would be obliged to keep large or small *holdings of cash,* partly in order to defray his immediate expenses, to the extent that these are not covered by simultaneous receipts of money, partly as a reserve against unforeseen needs. The sum-total of all these cash holdings constitutes the amount of money in existence or in circulation. The size of the cash holdings depends, of course, on various circumstances, particularly on the nature of the business itself; there are businesses with a large turnover that, nevertheless, demand little cash, because expenses and income roughly correspond; if on the other hand expenses and income accumulate at different times, a business with a comparatively small turnover may need a large amount of cash all the same. It is further and not least dependent on the personal disposition of the owner; an anxiously cautious person may keep so much cash that it is never once during his whole lifetime in danger of being exhausted; a more sanguine person is often satisfied with a minimum of cash, but thus exposes himself to the danger of frequently being unable to effect, for lack of cash, an otherwise desirable purchase at the right time, or of having to hasten a sale unduly for the same reason. But allowing for all this, it is still obvious that, everything else being equal, the size of the cash holdings must be in exact proportion to the prices of commodities; when prices rise the same turnover of commodities must necessarily require the keeping of more cash, and consequently the keeping of less cash when prices fall. If then, to borrow the philosopher Hume's well-known example, everybody woke up one morning with cash holdings of twice the sum of marks, francs or pounds, all prices would soon be doubled; not that everybody would immediately start offering twice the price for their necessities, but in one way or another they would look for some use for their surplus of cash. Even if, under such circumstances, they did not actually increase their consumption, they would still be inclined to effect earlier those purchases which they would otherwise have left till later, and at the same time they would be less anxious to sell their own goods. In short: the demand for all commodities increases, while the supply becomes less pronounced than before, and this must result in an increase in prices, which cannot cease until cash holdings have, as a result of the higher prices, again attained a normal relation to turnover. If, on the other hand, all cash holdings were for some reason cut by half, the result would be exactly the opposite with respect to commodity prices. It is true that the turnover might possibly continue for some time without a change in prices, a greater velocity of circulation of money replacing what was lacking in quantity; but soon the constraint and inconvenience of insufficient cash holdings would make themselves felt; everybody would try to increase their cash holdings and under the conditions laid down above this could only be done by decreasing their demand or increasing their supply of goods, until in time another equilibrium was attained, not by an actual increase in cash, but by a fall in prices to a level compatible with the reduced cash holdings. Thus, under these conditions the quantity theory is perfectly true and correct; but it need hardly be pointed out how little they conform to reality, at any rate with present-day developments in the monetary system. We had assumed that all purchases were effected by cash and by people's own money—yet, in reality, at least in the business world proper, all purchases are made against credit for a longer or shorter period, and every businessman, however solvent, repeatedly has occasion to seek monetary credit for his business. As a consequence of this the keeping of actual individual holdings of cash has virtually ceased in the commercially more advanced countries. Nowadays a businessman's 'cash balance' is only a legal conception: it means his *right* to draw at his bank at any time say 500 crowns on his current account, and, after giving notice, a few thousand more on his deposit account; also bills of exchange and other securities, i.e. claims of various kinds which can be discounted or offered as a pledge and so easily converted into money. But these cash holdings which therefore need no longer be kept by individuals, are not in consequence accumulated by the banks. Only a minor part of the sums for which a bank is at any time responsible actually needs to be kept in the form of ready cash, because the withdrawal of one customer always corresponds more or less to the deposit of another. In so far as a bank's customers transact business with each other, it is in fact not necessary to keep any cash at all on their behalf, but their respective balances can simply be regulated by debiting and crediting to their bank accounts. If we imagine this system developed everywhere to such perfection as it can be said to have attained already in the big banking centres, by means of cheques and a clearing system, and even somewhat further, then all purchases, and in fact all business transactions, could be effected without material coinage simply by means of entries in the books of the banks. Although this is a purely imaginary state of affairs, it is, nevertheless, worth examining a little closer. In reality every existing country's monetary system is a mixture, in different proportions, of these two extremes of pure cash economy (Barwirtschaft) and pure credit economy. If we then investigate the manner in which prices would be determined under one or the other of these two assumptions and if we succeed in finding a law common to both of them, we shall also be able to maintain that this law must apply to concrete reality in all its varying manifestations. Consequently, we shall try to answer the undeniably very interesting question: what factors would determine the value of money and the level of commodity prices, assuming a pure cheque system? Here the quantity theory seems, at least on the surface of it, to have lost every inch of ground, because when (possibly with the exception of coinage for the purpose of change) neither coins nor notes are used in the conduct of business, there is no need for any metallic cash holding, at any rate not for the requirements of internal commerce. However much 'money' is demanded in the banks, they can pay it out without danger of insolvency, since they do nothing about it, but enter a few figures in their books to represent a loan granted or a deposit withdrawn; the cheques and orders drawn against these must necessarily come back into the banks within a few days, and are credited to the depositors as a deposit paid in or a debt paid off. Supply and demand of money have in short now become one and the same thing.[1]

As a matter of fact, the problem presented here lies, with varying degrees of consciousness, at the bottom of all modern discussion of monetary problems. During the discussions before the British Gold and Silver Commission of the years 1887–8, instructive in so many respects, when virtually everybody that Britain can claim of eminence, theoretical or practical, in the sphere of money was heard as a 'witness,' the same question constantly recurs: how could a greater or smaller amount of metal coinage or notes in the banks' safes, or among the public, possibly determine the level of commodity prices, when actually far the greater proportion of all transfers of commodities take place without the help of either, simply by means of credit operations? How, particularly with the aid of the quantity theory, could the low prices already prevalent be explained, when actually all banks were full to overflowing with gold, and interest on money was lower than ever before? The Commission did not, however, receive a satisfactory answer to these questions; some of its witnesses, for instance the bank manager, H. H. Gibbs, well known as a bimetallist, entangle themselves in a veritable net of contradictory ideas, when they give as reasons for

[1] It is presumably superfluous to add that what has just been said applies only to all banks taken together, considered as a unit, not to any one particular bank. Indeed, fundamentally, as we shall soon see, it does not even apply to the banks of one particular country.

the surplus of money the business slump and the low prices of commodities, but, nevertheless, wish to maintain that the latter are a consequence of a supposed lack of gold. Roughly at the same time as these discussions took place there appeared in *Conrads Jahrbücher* (1888) a couple of essays, which attracted a great deal of attention, by the late Professor Erwin Nasse in Bonn, on the causes of the falling commodity prices, and in these the same idea is taken up. Nasse points out how absurd it is, with the means of credit at their present stage of development, to think that the amount of precious metal available in a country could possibly be directly decisive in the formation of prices. In this connection he brings up the question whether and by what means any limits at all are set to an increase in prices taking place with the aid of credit; because at first it might seem as if under these circumstances the formation of prices was left completely 'hanging in mid air.' His own answer is that ultimately the stock of precious metals is the decisive factor after all, in an indirect way, through the foreign balance of payments. The country that led the way in such an 'unsound development of prices' would soon see its trade balance towards other countries deteriorate, gold would flow out of the country, and it would become the task of bank management to exert pressure on domestic commodity prices by raising the rate of discount and thus change the direction of the flow of gold.

It is, however, easy to see that this so-called explanation is quite inadequate. Fundamentally it says nothing but what was known before, namely that the level of prices in one particular country cannot develop independently of prices in other countries, but is ultimately determined by world prices. Obviously, however, this only pushes the difficulties into the background, it does not solve them, because one immediately asks oneself the further question: if the prices of one particular country depend on world prices, on what do world prices themselves depend? And if a temporary increase in prices can take place in one particular country with the aid of credit, why should it not be possible for a similar process to take place simultaneously in several countries? But if that is the case, then there is generally speaking no disturbance in the trade balance, no necessity for the transfer of gold from one country to another, and consequently if the latter factor is the decisive one, as Nasse maintains, prices would still seem to be hanging in mid air.

Logically speaking it does not seem possible to give any other answer to our question than the following: assuming a pure credit economy, the exchange value of money and the level of commodity prices must depend on the price at which 'money' (i.e. in this case credit) itself can be obtained, in other words on *the rate of interest on money*. A low rate of interest must lead to rising prices, a high rate of interest to falling prices. And this is in full agreement with the basic principles of the quantity theory, because a surplus of material money would manifest itself, among other ways, in a lower interest on money. Indeed, the surplus of money could to a large extent only spread among the general public and influence prices by means of the lower rate of interest on loans. It seems, then, as if we had here found a simple principle which ought to be more or less equally valid in all types of monetary system. But, unfortunately, we are once more faced with the same regrettable circumstance: a lack of correspondence between theory and reality. If we compare the diagram given on p. 87 of wholesale prices in Hamburg and England since the middle of this century, on the one hand, and the rate of interest in the central banks and on the open market in Berlin and London on the other, it must be admitted that if it is possible to discover any connection between them at all, it is that a high rate of interest is associated with high commodity prices and a low rate of interest with low commodity prices, rather than the other way around. Faithful to the principle we established earlier, however, we are not going to let ourselves be put out by this circumstance but, for the time being, we shall test the theory itself on grounds of logic.

We shall assume, then, still supposing the existence of a completely flexible and elastic money system, that, *all other things being equal*, the banks lower their rate of interest from, let us say, 4 to 3 per cent. What will be the consequence? A businessman has sold his commodity to a customer against a bill of exchange drawn for three months; he is, however, not enough of a capitalist to be able to advance the value of the commodity itself and therefore turns to a bank to have the bill of exchange discounted. At a rate of discount of 4 per cent he will suffer a deduction of 1 per cent for the three months; if then the bill of exchange is for 100 crowns, he will get 99 crowns for it. Assuming that the bill of exchange is properly cashed, he has consequently in reality sold his commodity at a *cash* price of 99 crowns. If, however, the discount has been lowered to 3 per cent, he will get 99·25 crowns for his bill, i.e. the cash price of the commodity will have risen, if only by $\frac{1}{4}$ per cent. In reality it is improbable that the whole advantage of the credit relief would accrue to the seller; because of competition he would probably have to cede to his customer a larger or smaller part of it by granting him a somewhat lower credit price, i.e. in reality a smaller addition of interest to the cash price. If instead the buyer buys with cash, but with borrowed money, he can, if conditions of credit are improved, obviously pay the seller a somewhat higher price without loss to himself, and will probably be forced by competition between buyers to do so to a greater or lesser extent. It is to be noticed here that the magnitude of the possible rise in prices becomes greater in proportion to the length of time that the credit is utilised. If it is a question only of three-months' credit, the rise in prices will, as I have just indicated, be at the most $\frac{1}{4}$ per cent; if, on the other hand, credit is used for a whole year, the rise in prices can, as is easily perceived, rise to fully 1 per cent, and for two years to nearly 2 per cent, and so on. The rise in prices becomes most pronounced in cases where capital is committed for an infinite period, as in building activity. Take, for instance, a house which brings in 4,000 crowns net in rents. At a rate of interest of 4 per cent the capital value of the house is then 100,000 crowns, and if the current state of the labour market permits as good a house to be built for this sum, building activity is just profitable at the rate of interest in question. If, on the other hand, the rate of interest falls to 3 per cent, the capital value of the house will rise to 133,000 crowns and if similar houses can still be built for 100,000 crowns, building activity then becomes an extremely profitable business. Through competition in the building business, wages, the value of land and the price of building materials will therefore rise—in extreme cases this increase in prices might amount to as much as 33 per cent—and, indirectly, the prices of all commodities that are consumed by workers, landowners and producers of materials will rise to some extent, through the increase in their demand. The most important thing, however, is that this rise in prices, be it large or small, cannot cease at this first stage, but must constantly be repeated as long as the low rate of interest continues. Once a general increase in prices has taken place, an economic equilibrium will soon be established again on the basis of this higher level of prices, and banks will now be able to return to their original rate of interest without thereby causing prices to return to their previous level. This interesting circumstance has already been pointed out by Ricardo from the point of view of the quantity theory: an increase in the amount of money must at first lower the rate of interest at the same time as raising the prices of commodities, but whereas the increase in prices would be permanent, the decrease in the rate of interest would only be temporary, because as soon as prices had adapted themselves to the increase in the amount of money, the surplus of money would no longer exist, and, therefore, neither would the reason for keeping the rate of interest down. Assuming that the banks, nevertheless, maintain the low rate of interest, the consequence of this must be a series of new increases in prices of the same magnitude as the first one. This would appear in a particularly drastic manner, if we were to assume, for the moment, that all production was as favoured by the decrease in the rate of interest as, for instance, building activity. We should then, from the very beginning, witness a very marked increase in all wages and other incomes, and, consequently, in the prices of all commodities and, *among other things, also in rents*. We could assume that by the following October 1st rents, too, will have risen by 33 per cent because of the increased demand for housing—there would be no overproduction in building activity as, according to our assumption, all fields of activity would be equally profitable—our house would thus now bring in 5,333 crowns net, its capital value, even at a rate of interest of 4 per cent, would be 133,000 crowns, and if the banks then returned to this rate of interest, building activity (as with all other activity) could continue, in spite of the higher cost of labour, without loss, although without profit, too. If, on the other hand, banks kept to a rate of interest of 3 per cent, everything would be repeated all over again: the value of real estate, wages, prices of commodities and rents would rise the next year as well, in extreme cases by 33 per cent. There would then be a general increase in prices of up to 33 per cent a year: in less than three years all prices would have been doubled, in six years they would be four times as high, in nine years eight times and in thirty years—a thousand times as high. A tram journey or a 10-öre cigar would cost 100 crowns apiece—all as a consequence of the banks keeping their rate of interest at 3 instead of at 4 per cent for three decades.

This example, of course, is partly a humorous exaggeration, because the supposition was that all production be similar to building activity, i.e. that the mobile capital invested in it be committed for all time; whereas in fact in most fields of production capital is only tied for a short period, for instance, a few years. But even with this reservation there remains a very large increase in prices, which will eventually exceed all bounds, as a consequence of even the most insignificant decrease in the rate of interest, if only this is allowed to work for a sufficiently long time. An *increase* in the rate of interest, however insignificant, ought, of course, similarly to entail an unlimited depression of all prices.

How is it then that in reality no trace has been found of this strange phenomenon? The explanation is extremely simple. We assumed that the banks would lower the rate of interest, *other things being equal*; but this is plainly an assumption at variance with reality: 'other things being equal,' banks do not lower their rate of interest—why should they? Instead, they keep it unchanged until they are forced either to raise or to lower it by *changed* circumstances. Once in a while the reason may be exclusively an increase or a decrease in the actual stock of coinage, resulting, for instance, from changing conditions in the production and consumption of gold, but in most cases changes in the rate of interest are probably caused by an increase or a decrease in the demand for loans, which in their turn are caused by an increase or a decrease in the real or natural rate of interest on capital, and then, as will be shown presently, the result will be quite different, or apparently so, at any rate.

Let us return to the example just used. Because of some circumstance or other—a decrease in the supply of labour with ensuing higher (real) wages, greater demands for rents on the part of landowners, or less suitable land for house-building, etc.—the profitability of new houses has fallen, so that one which is built for 100,000 crowns can no longer be expected to bring in more than 3,000 crowns net. If, then, the banks still kept their interest at 4 per cent, all building activity would be brought to a standstill. In order to be able to grant any building loans, banks would have to reduce their rate of interest to 3 per cent and at this rate of interest house-building would only just be profitable, but in this situation there would be no reason for the demand for labour, building materials, etc., to increase, and so none for prices to increase either. If, however, the banks had still kept the rate of interest at 4 per cent, building activity would probably have got going in the end just the same, but only because workers and sellers of materials would have reduced their demands rather than go unemployed or find no market for their products. Thus on the face of it we here get exactly the opposite effect, unchanged prices in spite of a lowered rate of interest and falling prices when the rate of interest remains unchanged. In reality the principle is exactly the same, however, because although the rate of interest has nominally fallen, it has, in actual fact, remained unchanged *in relation to* the natural rate of interest on capital; and, in the same way, when it remained unchanged nominally, it had in reality risen, namely in relation to the same natural rate of interest, i.e. to the real return on capital in production.

In all probability this simple circumstance contains the key to the riddle. The expressions high or low rate of interest are after all only relative conceptions: a rate of interest is never either low or high in itself, but only in relation to what one can or thinks one can earn with the money at one's disposal by using capital in production. And this latter factor, the natural rate of interest on capital, is constantly subject to changes resulting from circumstances which are partly beyond all human control: a rise or a fall in wages because of a decrease or an increase in the supply of labour, or because of changes in the amount of liquid capital from which the demand for labour primarily emanates; a rise or a fall in the rent of land for the same reasons; finally, the yield from production itself, which can increase or decrease as a result of technical or physical conditions. If then we regard these latter changes as original, as *primum movens*, which is undoubtedly the only right and sensible thing to do, while the changes in the rate of interest on mo ey, on the other hand, are regarded as conditioned thereby, the contradiction with experience to which we have just drawn attention is instantly resolved, and the most important objections which have always been advanced against the quantity theory and theories connected therewith are happily and satisfactorily overcome. For if the natural rate of interest on capital rises, this leads, it is true, to a corresponding rise in the rate of interest on money; but in the meantime, before the rate of interest on money has quite reached the level of the rate of interest on capital, the low level of the rate of interest on money in relation to the natural rate of interest on capital must, in accordance with our earlier analysis, cause a progressive increase in all commodity prices, which is therefore taking place at the same time as the rate of interest on money, in absolute terms, is rising. If, on the other hand, the rate of interest on capital falls, the rate of interest on money will also move downwards; but here, too, the cause must precede its effect, i.e. for a longer or shorter period there will be a combination (higher rate of interest on money than on capital) whereby prices are constantly forced downwards, at the same time as the rate of interest on money is falling nominally.

We consequently arrive at the following general principle:

'At any moment and in any economic situation there is always a certain rate of interest, at which the exchange value of money and the general level of commodity prices have no tendency to change. This can be called *the normal rate of interest*; its level is determined by the current natural rate of interest, the real return on capital in production, and must rise or fall with this.'

'If the rate of interest on money deviates *downwards*, be it ever so little, from this normal level prices will, as long as the deviation lasts, rise continuously; if it deviates *upwards*, they will fall indefinitely in the same way.'

For a more detailed explanation and exposition of this thesis I must refer to my work, *Interest and Prices*,[1] which is to appear shortly, where it has been dealt with exhaustively. I should like, however, to draw attention to yet another circumstance which seems to support it. Not only are the most important objections to the conceptions of the classical monetary theory removed in this way, but it is here also that we find for the first time the only completely satisfactory explanation of the above-mentioned circumstance, usually regarded almost as an axiom in economics, namely, that the level of the rate of interest on money is not in the last instance determined by a shortage or a surplus of money, but by a shortage or a surplus of real capital. The proposition is undoubtedly correct, but practically the only proof of it that has so far been put forward consists of a sort of catch-phrase. It is said that what is lent in reality is not money but real capital; money is only an instrument, a way of lending capital, and so on. But this is not strictly true; what is lent *is* money and nothing else; liquid real capital, in the form of goods, is bought and sold with the money, but is not lent. Negotiation concerning the level of interest on loans is conducted with the owners of the money, not with the owners of the real capital. But the relation of cause and effect immediately becomes clear, as soon as it can be assumed that a lasting difference between the natural rate of interest on capital and the rate of interest on money would at once, according to whether it is itself positive or negative, lead to a rise or a fall in all commodity prices. If a single country is involved, a continuous rise in prices must finally result in an outflow of the banks' reserves, while a continuous reduction of prices, on the other hand, must lead to their saturation with foreign money. In these ways the banks are either forced to raise, or led to lower, their rates of interest. Indeed, in countries where business in general still makes use of metal currency to a large extent, this consequence follows even more immediately, the change in prices also leading to a change in the metal currency requirements of commerce and thereby directly influencing the stock of metal in the banks. But at the same time it must be kept in mind that if something causes an increase or decrease in the level of the natural rate of interest on capital in several or all countries simultaneously, so that prices in different countries move in the same direction, with the means of

[1] *Geldzins und Güterpreise*, Jena, Gustav Fischer, 1898.

credit as developed as they are at present, the impact on the stock of metal need not take place so soon; a difference in either direction between the natural rate of interest on capital on the one hand, and the rate of interest on money on the other, can persist for a long period, with the result that prices throughout this period continue to move upwards or downwards.

It is somewhat astonishing that such a simple—I should like to say self-evident—proposition, even if it has been alluded to here and there in economic literature, has never as far as I know been used as the foundation of a properly worked-out theory of price formation. The explanation undoubtedly lies in the mighty unsatisfactory state the theory of capital and interest generally found themselves in until a few years ago. Older economists, too, knew very well that money and real capital are not the same thing, and interest on money and interest on capital thus two different concepts, and they do not neglect to impress this distinction upon their pupils in general terms; but when it comes to its application, these two concepts are almost without exception 'mixed up in the most inextricable confusion' as Mill expresses it in the introduction to the chapter 'On the Rate of Interest', where unfortunately he himself, in spite of his efforts, has done nothing but help to perpetuate and increase this confusion. Even Stanley Jevons, in his older works on money, was a captive of the same confused ideas; but in the *Theory of Political Economy*, written towards the end of his life, he gives for the first time an outline, even if only in rudimentary form, of a fully realistic theory of capital, which was later fully developed in Böhm-Bawerk's famous *Positive Theory of Capital*. Thanks to these works it is now possible to observe quite clearly, be it only under certain simplifying conditions, the phenomena of capital and interest on capital, as they would appear if liquid capital, production's means of support, was in reality lent in kind without the intervention of money; and only then is it possible to distinguish what modifications are in reality caused by the introduction of money. In the former case, i.e. if capital was lent in kind, there would undoubtedly develop, through the supply of and demand for the available capital, a certain rate of interest on the lending market, which would be the natural rate of interest on capital in the strictest sense. If the actual rate of interest on money corresponds with this figure, the intervention of money will cause no change in the economic equilibrium; money transactions are then only the particular form taken by what, theoretically speaking, could just as well have been effected without the intervention of money. In short, there is no cause for a change in the price level. If, on the other hand, the rate of interest on money deviates from the ideal standard just mentioned, economic equilibrium, and with it the equilibrium of prices, is already *ipso facto* disturbed, and the further course of events will be the one described above.

What has been said, however, offers only indirect empirical proof of our thesis. In order that a theory, even if plausible in itself, is to be more than a hypothesis, direct, positive support for it in experience is required. Unfortunately, in the present case it is extremely difficult, indeed at the moment almost impossible, to produce such support. The reason is obvious. It is a question of showing a connection between three different elements: changes in prices, the level of the rate of interest on money and finally the magnitude of the natural rate of interest on capital. Of these three the first two are just known to economic statistics; but about the third nothing is really known at all. Its general changes over the years can, of course, be inferred from precisely the simultaneous fluctuations in the rate of interest on money; but in that case it is to be noticed that the average *similarity* between these two rates of interest is taken for granted, whereas for us the task is to demonstrate the *difference* between them at any particular moment.

In spite of this obvious difficulty, a direct confirmation of the truth of our proposition or at least of its general principles can, I believe, be gained from the history of commodity prices and the rate of interest upon loans, in so far as this is known. In the *Journal of the Statistical Society*, 1865, Jevons has given a survey[1] of prices for forty groups of commodities in England since the end of the last century. The results he obtains are that from the beginning of the seventeen-nineties an enormous rise took place, which culminated during the years 1810–15 when prices, in terms of gold, had risen by 80 per cent, but in terms of the then somewhat inferior paper money by 90 per cent. Later a still stronger downward price movement followed, so that by the middle of this century prices had fallen to less than half of the prices in 1810, even if these are reckoned in gold. Jevons says he is unable to give the reason for these violent price fluctuations, which, by the way, were probably largely a specifically English phenomenon without any complete equivalent in other countries. He supposes that the reduction of prices during the latter of the two periods mentioned was connected with the expansion of the production of goods which resulted from technical progress; but he admits himself that this argument is

[1] Also published in the work *Investigations in Currency and Finance*.

double-edged, because even during the former period production was by no means at a standstill, quite the contrary, in fact, for that was when the foundations of England's industrial development were being energetically laid. According to our theory, however, the matter seems simple enough to explain. The long wars unquestionably entailed a tremendous sacrifice of liquid capital just at the time when this was being made use of by production to an ever larger extent. The natural rate of interest on capital must consequently have been very high throughout this period; as far as the rate of interest on money is concerned, since 1797, as is well known, there had been in force the so-called bank restriction, i.e. the Bank of England was released from its obligation to redeem its notes with gold and also issued notes of smaller denominations than usual. It thus no longer needed to place any restrictions on its grants of credit, and it did in fact adhere to the principle that money be lent, against sufficient security, to an unlimited extent at the then legal rate of 5 per cent. If then, as there is every reason to believe, the natural rate of interest on capital was actually higher than this, there existed exactly that circumstance which ought to force prices up. After the conclusion of peace there ensued in England a very heavy accumulation of capital, the consequences of which were only partially relieved by foreign lending and, towards the middle of the century, by the building of railways in England. Interest on capital must have been comparatively low during this period; the rate of interest on money also fell, it is true, but the bank rate remained at 5 per cent right up to 1824 and thereafter at 4 per cent until 1836. Such a combination should according to our fundamental principles have brought about a sudden drop in prices and in actual fact the fall in prices was largely completed as early as 1832.

From the middle of the century we possess far more complete and reliable information about prices in England especially through Sauerbeck's price surveys, covering forty-five staple products, and in Hamburg through the price statistics begun by Soetbeer, continued later by Heintz and finally by Conrad, covering no less than 114 articles. As the diagram shows, prices in both places present a fundamental conformity: between 1850 and 1873 a predominating increase in prices appears, although with serious interruptions because of crises. From 1873 up to the present day, on the other hand, an almost uninterrupted fall in prices occurs, so that in so far as bonded store prices in Hamburg and London are any guide, prices now are considerably lower than in the middle of this century.

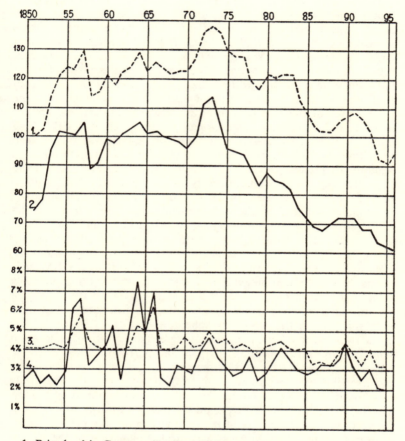

1. Price level in Germany (Soetbeer, Heintz and Conrad; 1847—50 = 100).
2. Price level in England (Sauerbeck; 1867—77 = 100).
3. Rate of interest in Berlin (Reichsbank).
4. Rate of interest in London (Bank of England).

EDITOR'S NOTE.—The original diagram used by Wicksell also included curves showing the rates of interest on the open market in Berlin and London. These have been omitted here in order to simplify the diagram.

87

The explanation of this price movement would seem in the main to be perfectly analogous with the one just given. The period from 1850 to 1873 was not, it is true, like the Napoleonic era, a time of uninterrupted warfare, but, nevertheless, it embraced among others the Crimean War, the Italian War, the very long and devastating North American Civil War, the wars between Prussia and Denmark, Prussia and Austria and finally between Prussia and France. At the same time there falls within this period the enormous industrial expansion which shows itself, for instance, in the completion of the greater part of the European railway network. The natural rate of interest on capital must consequently have been unusually high during this period; the rate of interest on money was indeed also very high throughout, with violent oscillations, as is shown by the diagram of interest rates. Nevertheless, it would seem possible to conclude that it was comparatively low in relation to the natural rate of interest on capital, for the following two reasons, quite apart from many others. The rate of interest in the so-called open market is for several reasons normally somewhat lower than the official bank discount, but during the period in question we find that the rate of interest in the open market almost constantly reaches, indeed, even exceeds the magnitude of the rate of interest in the banks. It seems then as if it had pulled the bank rate upwards with it, probably after first having been forced up itself by a high natural rate of interest on capital. The other circumstance, intimately connected with this, lies in the monetary sphere; the stock of money in the world was greatly increased at this time, partly through the great gold finds in California and Australia, and partly because the United States and, towards the end of the period, France, changed over to inconvertible paper money, and this circumstance has naturally also contributed to preventing a rise in the rate of interest on money. During the last years of the period we even find rather low rates of interest, which, as the rate of interest on capital was probably very high just at that time, gives us a natural explanation of the violent increase in prices which then took place.

Since the beginning of the eighteen-seventies, Western Europe and the United States have both been able to enjoy uninterrupted peace; the accumulation of capital has continued in practically all classes of society and on a scale undreamt of hitherto, and although the development of industry has by no means stood still, it has usually proved quite difficult to find a sufficiently profitable use in production for the accumulating capital. The rate of interest on capital has therefore almost certainly been unusually low, particularly if, as is proper, only liquid capital is considered. It is true that, at the same time, the rate of interest on money has fallen, but, as a mere glance at the diagram would seem to show, probably not to quite the same extent as the fall in the natural rate of interest. Here, too, changes in the monetary sphere, e.g. the slight decrease in gold production until 1888, the withdrawal in France and the United States of circulating paper money, and finally the discontinuation of free silver minting, have undoubtedly contributed to keeping the rate of interest on money higher than it would otherwise have been, and they have thus certainly been one, but by no means the only or even the most important, of the causes of what has happened. As far as the relation between bank rate and the rate of interest in the open market is concerned, the latter has constantly been lower throughout this period, which from an *a priori* point of view must be the case, if both are influenced by a falling natural rate of interest on capital.

Of course I do not by any means consider myself to have offered complete and satisfactory empirical proof of the truth of my proposition. On the contrary, it seems to me extremely probable that a closer examination, in this as in so many similar cases, would show that in order to be brought into full accordance with reality the hypothesis may need modification and completion in some respect or other. If however, as I believe, it proves to be essentially true, its importance, not only for the theory of the monetary system, but in the practical sphere as well, need hardly be emphasised. In the last chapter of my book I have given some hints about the practical side of the matter as well. May I be permitted to confine myself here to the purely theoretical aspect, which, as I pointed out in my introduction, is in fact the most important one for the solution of the present problem. Once a clear insight into the causes of the changes in the value of money and of the present instability thereof has been gained, the men concerned with the practical aspect will surely show themselves equal to the task of availing themselves of this insight to create a completely stable money value to the advantage of world commerce. Once the causes of the evil have been found, the therapy and, above all, the prevention of the disease will prove a comparatively simple matter.

II

THEORY OF PRODUCTION AND DISTRIBUTION

MARGINAL PRODUCTIVITY AS THE BASIS OF DISTRIBUTION IN ECONOMICS[1]

THE theory that marginal productivity, the yield from the 'last' production element, regulates the distribution of products under free competition is attracting an increasing amount of attention in theoretical economics of the present day. This is only natural, since this theory is very closely connected to the modern theory of value, although it is actually much older—it was first put forward by Malthus and von Thünen. We might even say that these two theories are based on the same fundamental idea, the conception of economic magnitudes as essentially changeable, variable quantities. Just as the concept of marginal utility has become the dominant principle in the theory of exchange, after overcoming considerable opposition, its elder brother, marginal productivity, should soon begin to play the same part in production theory.

However, in the form in which it has hitherto been presented, the theory suffers from a certain incompleteness; it contains not a few dubious points which seem to have escaped the majority of its adherents, but which must necessarily be remedied or removed if the theory is to fulfill all the requirements of logical clarity and consistency. I intend subsequently to indicate some of these points, and, where possible, to clear them up. I have been partly forestalled by Ph. H. Wicksteed, the well-known and perspicacious author of *The Alphabet of Economic Science*. The work of his to which I am referring here is *The Coordination of the Laws of Distribution* (London: Macmillan and Co., 1894), which economists have either neglected entirely or, strangely enough, completely misunderstood.

I

PRODUCTION WITHOUT CAPITAL

The problem of economic distribution, considered as a concrete

[1] 'Om gränsproduktiviteten såsom grundval för den nationalekonomiska fördelningen,' *Ekonomisk Tidskrift*, 1900, pp. 305-37.

reality, is extremely complicated, and even if we regard the problem abstractly, confining productive factors to the three well-known main types—land, labour and capital—there are still considerable difficulties in a simultaneous consideration of all three. We will therefore dissect the problem, so to speak, by excluding capital for the time being and confining our attention to the two so-called original elements of production, labour and land, where we take land in its usual sense as the aggregate of natural forces in their original form, with the exception of those operating in the human body.

We will thus be considering production without capital; but it is not necessary for us to regard this conception so strictly that its material aspects, so to speak, disappear when a concrete presentation is attempted; it will suffice if we allow capital to play such an insignificant part in production that its share in the product may be disregarded without appreciable error. We have an example of these conditions if we suppose that production is more or less as in primitive agriculture, beginning and ending during the course of a year, during which time the few simple tools and other equipment used are both made and completely expended. If we also suppose that finished products are not ready until the end of the year, it is difficult to see how any interest on capital could arise under such circumstances, since it does not matter at all then to the producer if he pays his workers in advance at the beginning of the year, or in instalments during the year, or at the end of the year. The first method might even be preferable for him, since he would then avoid having to store the products. However, we will not bother about this, but assume for the sake of simplicity that all wages are paid at the end of the production year, and that out of the wages they then receive the workers maintain themselves for the whole of the following production year. All contracts between workers and landowners, or between these two and a third party as entrepreneur, are thus based on a division of the product at the end of the current production year. What are the principles for this division?

If we first take *the landowners as entrepreneurs*, then, under free competition, the distribution will logically follow the law of wages of Malthus and von Thünen[1]: the increase in the product due to the worker last employed determines both his wage and that of the other workers, assuming that all the workers are equally strong and skilful. For as long as a worker is content with a smaller wage than

[1] Not to be confused with the latter's hypothesis about so-called natural wages, which is often mentioned, though it is at bottom incorrect.

that which corresponds to the increase in the total product which he brings about if employed, it must be advantageous for the landowner to increase his labour force by one, and competition between the employers then raises the level of wages. On the other hand, as soon as an employed worker demands a wage higher than his additional product, that is, than that part of the total product which would disappear if he were dismissed, it is more advantageous for the landowner to decrease his labour force, and competition between the workers leads to a decline in wages everywhere. The remainder of the product, whether it is thought of as rent or as rent and entrepreneurial profit combined, goes to the landowner; or, in modern terminology, wages are determined by the marginal productivity of labour, and the landowner-employer is the residual claimant.

As far as the preceding reasoning has taken us, this remarkable law may be regarded theoretically as infallible. The extent to which it corresponds with reality can only be decided, of course, by investigation of particular cases and, apart from the effect of capital, which we are at present disregarding, it depends primarily on the extent to which our basic assumption, free competition, is realised.[1] In spite of the simplicity of von Thünen's formulation of the law, it actually says as much as the whole of Ricardo's theory of rent. The latter is customarily divided into two parts, one dealing with the successive extension of agriculture to land where the conditions are less and less favourable, the other with the more intensive working of land already in use, so that more labour is employed directly or indirectly on the same acreage. Which of the two occurs, however, may be regarded as important only to the entrepreneur. He will choose the technically most advantageous methods, of course, but the result in either case will be essentially the same: every additional worker, although employed in the most effective manner, produces a smaller additional product than the one before him. Nor does it make any difference that, in his theory of rent, Ricardo considers a gradual application of increasing amounts of *capital* to the land; for closer examination reveals that Ricardo regards capital in this connection merely as representing or embodying an increasing

[1] Experience seems to indicate that the sphere of validity of the law is not small, even when competition is not completely free. There is nothing more common than that employers reply to an increase of wages forced upon them by immediately or gradually dismissing some of their workers because it is not profitable to employ the whole labour force. If the workers do not then support their unemployed comrades out of the trade-union funds, as they have often done in the British unions, the competition of the dismissed labourers in obtaining work must lead to a fall in wages.

95

amount of *labour* employed on the same acreage. The proper role of capital in production, to advance both rent and wages, often for a period of several years, does not appear in the usual theory of rent—and as a matter of fact, this has led to many hasty or incorrect conclusions about rent, especially on the part of English economists.

We could equally well have considered *the workers themselves as the entrepreneurs*, however. The lack of capital which actually prevents them from playing such a part is of no concern to us here, since we have assumed that all workers are provided with the means of subsistence for the whole of the current production period. They are therefore at liberty to take up agriculture or some other form of production, either individually or in groups, by hiring the necessary land from its owners. The process by which economic equilibrium is ultimately established in this case is completely analogous to—or rather the converse of—that just described. The more land a given group of workers has, the greater the product. The product does not increase in proportion to the acreage in use, however, but more slowly, so that each additional acre cultivated by the unchanged labour force yields a smaller additional product. Therefore, from the economic point of view, the workers will extend their demand for land just as long as the additional product from the last acre covers the rent they pay for it. For the sake of simplicity we make the additional assumption here that all land is equally good, though this is not of fundamental importance. If all the land is not taken into cultivation at once, or if, conversely, not all the groups of workers can satisfy their demand for land, then it is easy to see that competition in the former case between landowners and in the latter between workers would lead to an increase or decrease in rent respectively, until complete equilibrium is restored. In other words, rent is here determined by the marginal productivity of land, and wages conversely by the surplus product divided among all the workers in the group—the worker here becoming the residual claimant.

An interesting question now arises to which attention may be turned: will the distribution of the product between landowners and workers be the same for both of our assumptions? Or, to put it another way: if the entrepreneurs are actually, or conceptually a third class of persons, who hire all the labour and land and pay for both in accordance with the law of marginal productivity, will the total of rent and wages exhaust the whole of the product, so that nothing is left over for the entrepreneur as such?

This may seem self-evident, and I myself have always regarded it so, though I have not achieved a satisfactory analysis of the matter. We have assumed that both workers and landowners are free to employ their labour or their land on their own account, or to hire it out to others, whichever they prefer. It might be supposed that if the share of labour in the product is different in the two cases, the difference should soon be cancelled out by competition and similarly in the case of land. In the same way it seems obvious that entrepreneurial profits as such must always tend to zero. For the work and thought which the entrepreneur devotes to the management of production, he should, of course, receive wages like any other worker. If he also uses property (land or capital, though we are not yet taking the latter into consideration), he will of course receive a corresponding share of the product (rent or interest), like any other property owner. But if he were able to obtain a share of the product merely in his capacity of entrepreneur, it seems likely that the whole world would rush to obtain income so easily acquired.

We will see that this reasoning is valid, however, only if a certain condition is fulfilled which has generally been overlooked. To illustrate this, let us consider the production of, say, an agricultural enterprise where 100 workers are employed on land which we take to be divided into 100 units, say acres. We call the annual product P, and we will examine the increase in this quantity if the volume of production is successively increased by the addition first of one more worker and then of one more acre of land. The first of these additional products is the marginal productivity of labour, since we may regard the additional product due to the work of the 101st worker on the given acreage as roughly the same as that contributed by the 100th worker—the product which would be lost if one of the 100 workers were dismissed or left. We denote this quantity by w, since, according to our assumptions, it determines the magnitude of wages. If the amount of land in use is now increased by one acre of equally good land, so that the 101 workers are now employed on 101 acres, it is clear that this also increases the product by an amount which coincides with what we have called the marginal productivity of land; for just as in the case of labour, or with even better reason perhaps, we may regard the additional yield which results when the area worked by 101 workers is increased from 100 to 101 acres as practically the same as the additional yield which would result if the area worked by 100 workers had increased from 99 to 100 acres. As we are supposing that it is the yield of this last acre which determines the rent, that is, which constitutes the rent for one acre of the land, we will denote it by r. The expression for the total increase in the product is thus $w + r$. On the other hand, the total production has been uniformly expanded, with respect to both the acreage and the number of workers, and if we assume that it is carried on in essentially the same manner as previously, the total product should finally have increased by exactly 1/100th, and we should have

$$w + r = \frac{P}{100},$$

or
$$100w + 100r = P.$$

In other words, the wages of 100 workers and the rent for 100 acres are together equal to the whole of the original total product.

This proof may seem generally valid and even self-evident, but actually it is neither. On the contrary, it is not difficult to see that it depends entirely on the assumption that when the volume of production increases uniformly, the product only increases in the same proportion as each of the productive factors, that is to say, that the *scale* of production is immaterial for the result, so that *production on a small scale and production on a large scale yield the same relative return*.[1] This assumption is far from obvious or generally valid; on the contrary, it may be questioned whether it is ever strictly fulfilled, since the advantage of combining and dividing work must always appear to some extent when production is on a larger scale.

On the other hand, this underlying assumption is theoretically a necessary condition for the attainment of economic equilibrium. For, if large scale production is more advantageous than small scale, larger scale operations should unremittingly displace those on a

---

[1] The matter is quite simple from the mathematical viewpoint. If we consider the product P as a function of the number of workers, a, and the number of acres of land, b, the marginal productivities are the partial differential coefficients of P with respect to a and b, so that we have

$$a\frac{\delta P}{\delta a} + b\frac{\delta P}{\delta b} = P.$$

The general solution of this equation is

$$P = a \cdot f\left(\frac{b}{a}\right),$$

where $f(\ )$ is an arbitrary function. In other words, P must be a *homogeneous* and *linear* function of a and b. Among the infinite number of functions with these properties we may select: $P = a^\alpha b^\beta$, where α and β are two constant fractions whose sum is 1. If a and b are changed to $m \cdot a$ and $m \cdot b$ respectively, P becomes $m \cdot P$: that is, production on a large scale and on a small scale yield the same relative return.

smaller scale, only to be displayed in turn by still larger, until the branch of production in question comes under a single giant monopoly, whereupon free competition ceases. In reality, this is not exactly what happens: it may be that for various reasons, and particularly because of the local character of enterprises and their markets, a small enterprise in some out-of-the-way place may coexist with larger ones for some time. This is not to say, however, that the larger firm does not enjoy advantages, because of its better organisation and division of labour, which the smaller one lacks, and it may be able to earn a true entrepreneurial profit in addition to wages and rent (as well as interest). The larger firm cannot be deprived of this profit, since any attempt at active competition on the part of the small firm outside its own territory would be fruitless; and if, by a great economic effort, the smaller firm were to establish itself on the same footing as the larger firm, this would only lead to the ruin of both, since the market is not big enough for two large firms in the same industry. Thus, the larger firm possesses an actual monopoly—which may have the same significance as a legal monopoly—simply because it was first in the field. We should not forget that the modern development of communications necessarily implies an increase in the advantages of large-scale operations, and therefore tends to hasten their ascendancy. The branch of production which has offered, and is still offering, most resistance to this change is agriculture; but there are some indications that future developments in this industry may also be in the direction of large-scale operation. But although more or less monopolistic enterprises are constantly gaining ground, there are still fields where free competition prevails, or almost so, since production on a small or large scale give approximately the same returns. Our theory is completely applicable to such fields: true entrepreneur's profit theoretically does not exist; in production without capital, wages and rent would share the whole product, and the amounts they received would be determined by the marginal productivity of labour and land respectively, whether it is the workers or the landowners or third parties which act as entrepreneurs. And, so long as such a field exists, the marginal productivity will set the standard of wages and rent for the whole field of production, although, where workers or landowners are themselves the entrepreneurs, wages and rent can of course only conceptually be distinguished from entrepreneur's profit where the latter does occur.

As far as I know, the views set out here were first put forward by Wicksteed in the work mentioned above. But Wicksteed presents them in a different context, since the main purpose of his book is to defend the theory of marginal productivity against earlier ideas on the problem of distribution. He mentions the important condition referred to here more or less in passing, as something self-evident. I myself read Wicksteed's book when it was first published without noticing this detail, and without finding anything new in general. It was not until later, when my own speculations had led me to the same result, that I found on closer examination that Wicksteed had forestalled me. The fact that his work has received such scant attention is most probably due to the abundant use of mathematical symbols and a certain lack of lucidity. *Walras* appears to be the only one to have paid any attention to it in an appendix to the third edition of his *Éléments d'économie politique pure*, where it is mentioned and criticised in detail. Walras contends, and rightly I think, that the fundamental features of Wicksteed's theory are to be found in Walras's own theory of economic production. But he also maintains that his theory is more generally valid than Wicksteed's: Wicksteed is said to have established the law of marginal productivity only for the case where the total product is a *linear and homogeneous* function of the productive factors (as I have just pointed out, this is the mathematical expression of the fact that production yields the same return on a small scale as on a large), whereas Walras considers that he himself has proved the proposition 'dans sa plus grande généralité,' without any restrictions. In this he is mistaken, however. Actually, he makes what he regards as a self-evident assumption, that competition between entrepreneurs makes the entrepreneurial profit tend steadily to zero, unless there is monopoly. But it is not difficult to see that this assumption involves the very condition that we postulated, namely, that the product is independent of the scale of production. If such is not the case, but if instead an enterprise on a larger scale is, say, more profitable than one on a smaller scale, the entrepreneurial profit cannot disappear or even tend to zero; for either the smaller enterprise will simply run at a loss or the larger shows a positive surplus over and above production costs, wages and rent (together with interest). So Wicksteed's treatment of the problem is particularly commendable, and not at all deserving of the scornful dismissal accorded it by Walras.

The Influence of Technical Inventions on Rent and Wages

We are now in a position to take up, at least partly, a question of the greatest practical importance, that of the influence of certain technical advances—mechanical inventions, for instance—on the shares of the different production factors in the total product, with special reference to wages. We cannot answer this question fully, of course, before we have discussed the role of capital in production. Apart from their property of being or representing capital, however, which we will come to later, machines also modify to some extent the ratio in which labour and land may replace one another in production, thereby changing their relative marginal productivities, and consequently, by our theory, their shares of the product. It is this aspect which we will now consider, avoiding for the time being the further complications which enter into an already involved problem when the third production factor is taken into account.

The most obvious thing about machines is that they 'save labour,' that is, they allow us to produce the same amount with less labour, or a larger amount with the *same* labour. On the other hand, it might be thought that this greater productivity of labour should lead to, or at least make possible, higher wages; on the other hand, it is commonly believed that machines render some workers redundant, and the competition of the unemployed forces wages down. It would seem, therefore, that two opposing tendencies operate simultaneously, and that the introduction of machines either benefits the workers or injures them, according to which tendency is dominant. As is well known, opinions on this point have varied a great deal in the course of time. Formerly, when the old mercantilism held sway, no one doubted that labour-saving machines or methods took the bread out of the mouths of the workers, and not only they, but also the authorities, often stubbornly opposed the introduction of new machinery into industry. The victory of the physiocratic school led to a reversal of opinion in this respect, since, according to its doctrine, goods are always ultimately exchanged for other goods, giving rise to a demand for these other goods. An increased productivity of labour should therefore bring about an increased demand for other articles previously consumed on a small scale or not at all, and hence to an increased demand for labour for their production. Machines could at most cause temporary unemployment and redundancy for certain groups of workers, but in the long run their effect must be beneficial, leading to increased opportunities for work and an increase, not a decrease, in wages. This optimistic view in its turn suffered a setback when *Ricardo* introduced into the third edition of his *Principles* a chapter 'On Machinery,' and showed in a seemingly irrefutable manner that other labour-saving methods might occasionally be advantageous for the employer even when it did not give an increase in the product, but a *decrease* instead, if the entrepreneur's *net profit* increased at the same time. The workers could not, in such a case, be compensated by an increased demand for other commodities.

The question has remained in this somewhat unsatisfactory state since then, but I believe the theory of marginal productivity will enable us to put it on a firmer basis, and to replace the vague, and in places even incorrect, reasoning by something better. Actually, the expression 'productivity of labour' has no comprehensible meaning when it is applied to production as a whole, since this is always the *combined* result of labour and natural resources. It is therefore the common productivity of labour and land which is increased by the machine; it is not possible to determine how much of the increase is to be attributed to the different factors of production—indeed, the question is meaningless. The productivities of labour and land acquire independent meaning only at the margin of production, in that it is there that they are, or may be thought of as, economically interchangeable. But an increase in the total product arising from technical innovations in production need not imply an increase in the marginal productivities of all production factors—and certainly not a uniform increase; it may even happen that the marginal productivity decreases for one factor, while increasing all the more for another. Either the marginal productivity of labour may increase at the expense of that of land, and therefore wages at the expense of rent, or conversely rent may increase at the expense of wages. Examples of the former kind could be expected where an invention has the effect of increasing natural resources, as when previously neglected sources of natural power—coal, waterfalls, etc.—are brought to use, previously useless land made productive, with or without preparatory treatment, the practice of fallowing replaced by crop rotation, and so on. In such cases, it is possible, or at least conceivable, that rents will decline both absolutely and relatively, so that the whole benefit of the increase in production—or perhaps even more—accrues to the workers. (It may be objected here that changes which conflict with the interests of the landowners could never come about, but we will shortly see that this objection cannot be maintained.) The opposite effect might be feared if an invention has the immediate result of rendering labour superfluous without bringing new natural resources into operation, as in the case of new agricultural machinery for sowing, harvesting and threshing, which replaces human labour with the labour of draught animals on a large scale. Of course, even here an increase of the product is not impossible (we shall see later that, *theoretically*, there must always be such an increase), for, if the same product can be achieved with fewer workers, the remaining workers should be able to produce something, so that the final result is a greater total product; but it seems to be beyond doubt that this result is nevertheless compatible with a decrease, and even a considerable decrease, in the *marginal* productivity of labour.

It may be objected here that the landowners would not be willing, or even able, to consume their increased incomes from rents directly, in kind; they would rather direct their consumption to luxury goods, and thereby increase their demand for human labour, so that wages would again rise. But it is not difficult to see that this tendency is of only secondary importance. It may modify the preceding result to some extent, but it can hardly reverse it. As a matter of fact, the problem could easily be formulated in such a way that this objection would be quite inapplicable: for instance, we might suppose that a society existed which was restricted by natural conditions to producing one, or just a few, staple articles, and which must acquire all other commodities by trade with other places or countries at exchange values determined in the world market, where they have no say in the matter. Another possibility is that the landowners might actually consume their net product in kind, using it to rear hounds, horses for hunting and racing, etc. In neither case would there be any question of compensation for the workers in the form of a further demand for labour.

On the other hand, it appears on closer examination—and this seems to me to be of particular interest—that Ricardo's objection is theoretically untenable. It is inconceivable that the size or value of the gross product could decrease under free competition, if we assume for the sake of simplicity that exchange values are fixed, as in the first of the examples just given. This might even be said to be self-evident, since anyone who found himself in a position to increase production with the existing means of production would be able, as an entrepreneur, to reap a profit. As I will show, Ricardo has failed to draw the ultimate conclusions from his own assumptions. It is true that Ricardo sets out from the standpoint of capital and its division into circulating capital—or the wage fund—and fixed capital. Nevertheless, his reasoning may be applied under our simplifying assumption of production without capital, and it is open to the same objections in both cases.

Let us assume that the introduction of certain labour-saving machines, e.g. the mowing machine and the horse-harrow, have made

103

dairy farming and fodder crops more profitable for every farmer than the growing of grain, in such a way that although the exchange value of the former products is less, the net yield is greater, because of the labour saved. The immediate consequence of this will be that one or more farmers will change to the more profitable production. If all the others were to follow their example, there would naturally be a fairly considerable decrease in the total product or its value, *but this does not happen.* For, as soon as some workers become redundant because of the initial change and wages therefore fall, the growing of grain crops will become more profitable, and will absorb the unemployed in a more intensive application of labour—something which Ricardo overlooked. It can be proved rigorously that economic equilibrium here requires a division of production between the old and the new methods, such that the net profit of the entrepreneur is the same in both cases, and the total product or its exchange value is the *maximum* physically attainable. So that it does not decrease, but *increases.*[1]

The modifications involved in this reasoning if changes in exchange values are also taken into account do not appear to disturb the main result. We may therefore assume that production is maximised under free competition in any case, although this may very well be accompanied, or even *helped*, by a decrease in the share of the total product going to one production factor—in this case, labour. It is at once

[1] For the sake of conciseness, I will give the proof only in its mathematical form. If x and y are the numbers of workers employed per acre in the first and second types of production, respectively, and the corresponding production functions are $f(x)$ and $\phi(y)$, and if m acres are used in the first type of production and n in the second, we have to find the conditions under which the expression

$$mf(x) + n\phi(y)$$

attains its greatest value, where

$$m + n = B$$

and

$$mx + ny = A,$$

B being the total number of acres and A the total number of workers available in the whole of the industry in question (here agriculture). Differentiation and elimination readily give the conditions

$$f'(x) = \phi'(y)$$

and

$$f(x) - xf'(x) = \phi(y) - y\phi'(y).$$

The former means that the marginal productivity of labour, and therefore wages, are the same in both types of production; the latter that the rent per acre is the same for both types of production.

Hence the partial change-over to the new type of production, which at first sight seemed to entail a decrease in the total product, actually leads to maximisation.

104

evident from this that those who regard free competition as an adequate means for bringing about the greatest possible *satisfaction of needs*, or sum of enjoyments for all the members of the society, are very much mistaken.

It might be supposed that this result would not arise if the workers themselves were entrepreneurs, or, on the other hand, that a change of production which led to a decrease in rents would never be accepted by the landowners as entrepreneurs; but both possibilities can be realised under perfect competition. For the individual entrepreneur who is confronted in the market with a certain definite rent or wage, any technical change which increases the magnitude of his product is in itself always economically advantageous. The fact that the contrary may be true if all the entrepreneurs adopt the same position does not affect the individual's reaction as a rule, provided that agreements, cartels, and the like, do not impair free competition. It is nevertheless remarkable that, from the technical point of view, production attains its maximum under multilateral free competition—at least so long as our assumption that the product is independent of the scale of production is fulfilled. Co-operation between workers to raise their wages, or between landowner-employers to lower them and thereby raise their rents, would both contribute to a *diminution* of the result of production, and only under real social collectivism would the maximum technically or physically attainable product again be reached.

What has been said here in no way implies that in the great majority of cases inventions and technical progress may not be beneficial in both directions, that is to say, in increasing the marginal productivities of both labour and land and their shares of the product. As a matter of fact, according to the ordinary rules of probability, such benefits are extremely likely as soon as the increase in total productivity is sufficiently widespread. If the tremendous upward surge in all branches of production during the last two hundred years has none the less brought about a relatively insignificant, and sometimes doubtful, improvement in the workers' situation, while rents have increased many times over, as much as a thousand times or more in some places, the main cause of this is to be sought in the disproportionate increase in one of the production factors, labour, owing to the great increase in population. This increase would have progressively lowered the marginal productivity of labour, and with it wages, if other conditions had remained unchanged; or—what amounts to the same thing, though to a superficial observer it tends to fog the issue—where technical progress is continually being made, the rise in population hinders the otherwise inevitable increase in wages which follows therefrom. Unfortunately, not even collectivism is of any assistance against this self-created handicap—not in the long run, at any rate.

If we are to summarise this long inquiry into a single conclusion, we have to regard the total product as dependent on co-operation between two factors, labour and land, neither of which can be dispensed with entirely, although either of them may be so in part. If they both increase simultaneously at the same rate, the product also increases in at least the same proportion, but usually faster because of the division of labour which becomes possible. If only one of them increases, it leads in general to a less than proportionate increase of the product, and therefore to a decrease in the marginal productivity of the factor in question. Technical inventions always increase the product, so that the same amount of labour and land produce more; marginal productivity likewise increases, usually for both factors, but sometimes—and perhaps not so seldom—for one only, the other's marginal productivity and share of the product either remaining stationary or diminishing.

It is scarcely possible to give a simple and intelligible criterion which will indicate whether the one possibility or the other will occur. But, in accordance with what we have just established in our criticism of Ricardo's reasoning, it does seem possible to assert that as soon as some change of production leads employers to reduce the number of workers without a rise in wages having compelled them to do so, this is a sign that the marginal productivity of labour has fallen, and a decrease in wages will follow. On the other hand, a technical advance which is favourable to labour must from the very beginning give rise to an increased demand for labour and increased wages. But what we have said here applies in the main to the interplay of wages and rent; the appearance of capital in the field of production leads, as we shall see, to not unimportant modifications of our conclusions.

II

CAPITALISTIC PRODUCTION

Our most obvious course is to apply the proposition we developed in the preceding section—that the share of each production factor in the product is determined by that factor's marginal productivity—to the more or less well-defined economic concept called *capital*.

As a matter of fact, this is what von Thünen attempted to do. In the same way as the additional product of the last worker regulates wages, so the rate of interest on all capital, according to von Thünen, is determined by the yield of the last portion of capital brought into use. This may seem obvious, for so long as an entrepreneur obtains a larger return on the capital he uses in his production than the interest which he needs to pay for capital he borrows, or which he himself can obtain on capital he lends, he will clearly be inclined to increase his use of capital. Conversely, if the interest on borrowed capital is higher than the yield on the last portion of the capital used in his production, he will restrict his use of capital, as much as possible, to the most necessary purposes or to the most profitable branches of production.

However, a closer examination of the problem shows that the analogy between interest on the one hand and wages and rent on the other is not complete. As regards labour and land, the law of marginal productivity applies to the whole economy just as well as it does to every private undertaking; as long as there exists in any region a moderately good worker or acre of land which, though employable, is incapable of increasing the total product by an amount corresponding to the prevailing wages or rent, these latter must, theoretically, fall. (It is another matter that a limit may exist below which wages either cannot fall for physical reasons or must not fall for social ones.) But in the case of capital, as it is usually conceived, this proposition applies only to each private entrepreneur, wages and rent being regarded as given quantities, determined by the market. If we consider an increase (or possibly a decrease) of the whole of the social capital, it is not at all true that the increase (or decrease) of the whole national product which follows will provide a norm for the level of interest. For, in the first place, the new capital competes with the old, and thereby contributes mainly to an increase in wages and rents, perhaps without any marked effect on the technical aspects of production. The rate of interest does therefore fall, of course, but it is certainly not necessary that it should fall to zero or anything approaching zero, even if the additional product associated with the new capital is almost zero. For the actual rise of wages and rents may absorb the surplus of circulating capital so that the capital just fulfils production needs, in spite of the fact that production really has hardly increased at all.

This peculiar circumstance was pointed out by me several years ago in an article in *Conrads Jahrbücher*, and subsequently in my book *Value, Capital and Rent*, but at that time I was not clear why there was a defect in the analogy between interest and wages and rent. The explanation is quite simple, however, and is bound up with the fact that, whereas labour and land are measured in the *appropriate technical units*, e.g. working days or working months, acre years, and so on, capital is usually reckoned in terms of its *exchange value* either in money or in an average product, that is, in a unit *extraneous* to itself. From the practical point of view there are very good reasons for this practice, of course, but it is a serious theoretical anomaly, as Wicksteed has also pointed out. The contribution to production made by a piece of technical capital, e.g. a steam engine, is not determined by how much it costs, but by the horse-power it develops, as well as by the excess or scarcity of such machines. So, if capital were also measured in technical units, in this respect the defect would be removed and the analogy completed; but productive capital would then fall into as many categories as there are types of tools, machines, raw materials, and so on, and a unified treatment of the role of capital in production would be impossible. There is nevertheless a way out of this dilemma, if we consider the common, or at least similar, origin of the various capital goods. Capital is itself always a product, of course, the fruit of the union of labour and land. All capital goods, however different they may seem, can always finally be resolved into a certain amount of labour and a certain amount of land, and all that distinguishes this labour and land from those considered previously is that they belong to *earlier years*, whereas we have been considering only current labour and land which is directly applied to the production of consumption goods. But this difference is sufficient to justify the establishment of a special production category alongside labour and land, to be called capital. During the period when labour and land are being stored up, they are able to assume forms which are impossible for them in their crude state, and they enhance the effectiveness for a great many productive purposes—as Böhm-Bawerk in particular among modern authors has shown in such a masterly fashion. In the main, the following presentation of the theory is in complete agreement with Böhm-Bawerk's ideas on capital; though I think it is possible to formulate it in a manner more simple, more consistent, and more practically useful than that which is to be found in his famous work, *Positive Theory of Capital*, and which I myself have always followed hitherto, in the footsteps of the master.

We may thus regard capital as a single coherent mass of stored-up labour and stored-up land, accumulated over the years. The inclusion of land is important. English political economy has always suffered from a failure to recognise that a part of capital is stored-up land; John Stuart Mill even flatly denied it. And yet there is no doubt that this component is as important as the other. Although certain of the more refined tools and machines receive their main value from the human labour incorporated in them, domestic animals and certain raw materials are examples of a type of capital whose main value arises from the land incorporated in them. Indeed, untended forest, the fish in our rivers and lakes, etc., are solely produced by natural forces. But it is clear that the majority of capital goods are a combination of stored-up labour and stored-up land; and although these two components are actually fused, we may separate them conceptually, just as it was possible to separate them in considering labour and land as factors of production. Subsequently we will therefore talk about labour-capital and land-capital as conceptually distinct elements of the whole mass of physical capital.

We now have to consider the stratification of this mass with respect to *time*. Here, too, we will proceed to our goal step by step, and hence we first assume that, besides the current labour and land devoted directly to the present year's production, there is labour and land saved from a single previous year in the form of various capital goods, which we also assume to be completely used up in the current year's production. Naturally, a considerable increase of the total product would be brought about if these capital goods and the whole of the available labour and land were used to produce goods intended for immediate consumption; but it is obvious that in such a case the gain would be quite transitory, being achieved at the expense of the sacrifices of the earlier year, and leaving the production of the following years in the primitive non-capitalistic state. We must therefore suppose that a part of the current year's labour and land is saved as capital for the production of subsequent years and so on. And since we are going to simplify the problem by considering *stationary* conditions, we will assume that the amount of labour and land saved in this way is the same from year to year. When once the production of capital is complete, just as much labour and land will be used for the production of consumer goods each year as was used previously in the case without capital; but since some of these resources have now been saved from earlier years, i.e. are in the form of capital, the final product will generally be considerably larger than previously, and even increasingly larger the larger the proportion of labour and land applied in this stored-up form—to a certain limit, at any rate.

109

How much of the increase in the product is to be ascribed to each of the co-operating production factors cannot be determined in this case either; it must not be supposed that the whole increase is due to capital—for here, too, the shares of the various factors are determined by their marginal productivities.[1] Since we have assumed that the exchange of a certain amount of current labour or land for the same amount of stored-up labour and land increases the product, it follows at once from this that the marginal productivities of stored-up labour and stored-up land are greater than the corresponding current magnitudes—at any rate, up to a certain limit which is not reached in practice. This marginal productivity, and the share of the product determined by it, are primarily compensation for the capital expended in actual production; but also something more. Under stationary conditions, the exchange values of goods and services remain the same from year to year, so that anyone who purchases labour and land in order to transform them into capital for use in the next year's production can always count on receiving more products or exchange value than he gives. This surplus is what is called interest. We thus arrive at the following simple definition:

Capital is stored-up labour and stored-up land; interest is the difference between the marginal productivity of stored-up labour and land and that of current labour and land.

As far as I can see, these few words contain all that can be said in explanation of the phenomenon of interest. Of Böhm-Bawerk's three main grounds why 'present' goods have a higher value than 'future' goods, the first refers to the different relation between needs and their satisfaction now and in the future, and the second to the subjective under-estimation of future needs and over-estimation of future resources. Both these aspects are important, but they really only concern the accumulation of capital and consumption loans, which are economically its *negative* form, since they diminish the supply of capital for productive purposes that would otherwise be available. It seems to me that for a systematic presentation it is better to consider first the effects of a stock of capital, already accumulated, before considering the causes which affect this stock of capital and possibly change its magnitude. We thus come to Böhm-Bawerk's third main ground, the *technical* superiority of commodities or means of production available at an early stage over those which are not available until a later stage. His reasoning in this connection

---

[1] Our basic assumptions—that there is free competition, and that the scale of production does not affect the relative return—have the same significance here as with non-capitalistic production, of course.

is essentially the same as ours here, but a comparison will show that it is considerably more complicated and less easily comprehensible. This seems to be mainly due to the fact that Böhm-Bawerk has not made the simplifying assumption of stationary economic conditions, although his reasoning is not thereby rendered more generally valid. I think he makes the mistake of trying to prove too much when he states that any current means of production, e.g. a working month available now, is in every respect superior to one available in the future. This is not true, of course. There are very many technical instances where current labour and land must be used, and cannot be replaced by stored-up productive power. But this is not the point at issue, which is concerned with the fact that the *marginal* productivity for the stored-up productive power is greater. This is simply due to the over-abundance of current labour and land for the purposes to which they alone are applicable, whereas the stored-up labour and land do not suffice for all the many uses to which they might advantageously be put—a circumstance to be explained by restrictions on the accumulation of capital.

It is clear that, within the limits imposed by the one-year investment of capital that we are considering, the rate of interest as we have defined it must be the same for all enterprises and applications, with the particular implication that the marginal productivity of the stored-up land, and its share of the product, must be in the same proportion to that of current land as the marginal productivity of the stored-up labour is to that of the current labour. Otherwise, it would be profitable to store more labour and less land the next year, or vice versa. It should here be pointed out in passing that the technical renewal of capital from year to year in no way renders it impossible for the private individual to accumulate and store capital for use in the more distant future. Such an individual need only buy up labour and land in the market in one year, sell them in the next in the form of tools, fat stock, etc., simultaneously buying labour and land to repeat the same operation.

A less simple question is that of the influence of capital on the shares of the product assigned to current labour and land, in other words, on the magnitude of wages and rent. The fact that their marginal productivities are less than those of stored-up labour and land does not mean that the former may not have risen through the use of capital. Indeed, such a rise might be regarded as an obvious consequence of the capitalisation of production: each year's direct production of consumption commodities employs decreasing amounts of current labour and land as the method of production becomes more highly capitalistic, and it might be supposed that the marginal productivities of these production factors would therefore naturally increase. The matter is not so simple as that, however. It is true that a relative decrease in one production factor should lead to an increase in its marginal productivity, *other things being equal*; but the accumulation of capital is usually accompanied by inventions and technical progress, so that it is quite conceivable, despite the increased use of capital and the rise in production, that the marginal productivity and share of the product of either current labour or current land, or both, will decrease rather than increase. It is not until production at a particular technical level is saturated with capital that we can count of an increase in wages or rents, usually both, while interest decreases. Expressing this in our terminology, we might say that the marginal productivity of current labour and land increases, while that of stored-up labour and land decreases, so that the difference between them is gradually reduced and may finally disappear altogether, interest consequently falling to zero; the capitalist's share of the product then merely corresponds to the stored-up labour and land, that is, to the capital itself.

Before such a situation had time to arise, however, what would actually happen is that the one-year investment of capital would be replaced by something more permanent. We will therefore inquire into the conditions for this change; but it will be sufficient if we consider the storing of labour and land for not more than *two years*, i.e. investment for either one or two years. Our findings for this case may easily be extended to production processes and investment periods of any duration. Here, too, we will disregard the transition period during which capital is initially accumulated and distributed over the whole of the production period, and just consider the situation when complete economic equilibrium again has been established. Each year's production now involves, besides current labour and land, certain amounts of these factors which have been accumulated and capitalised during the two preceding years. If stationary conditions are to prevail, *two* fractions of both current labour and land, corresponding precisely with the amounts just mentioned, must be withdrawn from the direct production of consumption goods in the current year. One fraction of each is set aside for use in the following year's production, and the other for that of the year after. But this does not conclude the list of capital groups, since there are also categories of labour and land which were accumulated during the preceding year, and which are intended for use in the following year's production; they may be regarded as a kind of goods in transit during the year we are considering.[1] In a similar manner, if capital is stored for up to three years, the labour-capital in existence at any instant is divided not just into 3 distinct groups, but into 6 = 3 + 2 + 1, and analogously for investment of longer duration, so that the number of capital groups may be thought of as increasing in both height and breadth, or quadratically, with respect to the number of different capital ages. This applies to land-capital as well, of course, and, as we shall presently see, it is a circumstance of considerable importance.[2]

[1] Actually, the various annual groups of capital are not always strictly separate, but are often combined in the same capital good. We will return to this matter later.

[2] It may be easier to visualise all this by considering the following graphical presentation, intended to represent production for 1900. We suppose that the current year's original supply of labour and land is represented by two rectangles, and in the case of one-year capital investment the left hand one of these represents the fraction of the productive power which is used directly during the year, the right hand one the fraction which is stored from the preceding year and used during the current year, and the equal rectangle above this the fraction of the current year's labour and land which is carried over for direct use the next year.

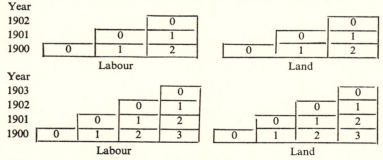

The following figures, which illustrate the present amounts of current and stored-up labour and land corresponding to investment for either one or two years, or for one, two or three years, respectively, should be self-explanatory.

The figures 1, 2, 3 signify that the capital in question is 1, 2, or 3 years old, i.e. originated in 1899, 98 or 97; 0 denotes current labour or land, which is used either directly in the current year's production or is being stored as capital for production in subsequent years. The year given to the left indicates that the productive power on the same horizontal line is used during that year for the production of consumption goods.

If we return to the one-year and two-year investments, it is clear that even the labour and land which is stored-up for two years will yield according to its marginal productivity. If we consider how extremely primitive the implements, domestic animals, etc., would be which were due to investments of only one year, and what an immense improvement in the technique of production would result from the adoption of two-year investment in many fields, it is easy to see that the marginal productivity of two-year capital may, within quite wide limits, be considerably higher than that of one-year capital, and higher still than that of current labour and land. But that does not mean that two-year investment would be profitable in every such case. For that to be so, the three quantities mentioned must stand in a certain definite relation to one another, corresponding to that involved in the calculation of compound interest. In other words, if the marginal productivity of one-year capital—land and labour stored-up for one year—stands in the proportion $1 \cdot 05 : 1$ to that of current labour and land, so that one-year capital yields 5 per cent interest, the marginal productivity of the two-year capital must be at least $1 \cdot 05$ times that of the one-year capital, and therefore $1 \cdot 05^2$ times that of current labour and land, so that the yield of the two-year capital must be at least $10\frac{1}{4}$ per cent for the two years. This is obvious, for otherwise everyone who wished to save capital for two years or more would prefer to divide up a two-year investment into two successive one-year investments.

It might be asked whether the two-year interest might not be permanently higher with respect to the one-year interest than the above compound relationship, since such a higher ratio cannot be levelled out so easily, owing to the fact that those who wish to regain their capital at the end of one year have no alternative but one-year investment. In an advanced economic system, however, credit makes an appearance here as a powerful levelling factor. As long as the size of the total social capital remains unchanged from year to year (and, of course, still more if it is continually increasing), it is of no importance to the individual capitalists how long the term of investment is. On our assumptions, therefore, to those who wish to recall some or all of their capital and consume it, there would correspond others wishing to build up new capital to the same amount. The transfer of capital from the former to the latter, and of its equivalent in consumption goods in the opposite direction, could then be accomplished by a single credit operation, without it being necessary to liberate any real capital in the technical sense. In actual fact, rates of interest for long and short loans do tend to equality; the difference which actually exists is probably best regarded as an increased risk premium for long-term loans. It is not difficult to see that if this levelling process has taken place, the total profit on capital each year, that is, the surplus marginal productivity of all the groups of capital employed during the year, is equal to *one year's interest* on the exchange value of the total capital, since each group of capital is regarded as representing the labour and land incorporated in it, *together with the accrued interest.*

Capital will therefore be divided between one-year and two-year investments (for the time being we will disregard possible investments over longer periods), in a certain proportion such that the above relation between the marginal productivities is always satisfied. It might be supposed that if capital increases, i.e. if there is an increase in the amount of labour or land or both which is stored-up from year to year, the new capital, and therefore the whole capital, would be distributed in the same proportion as the old capital was between the two investment periods. However, this will not be so in general. In accordance with what we have said before, such an increase must lead to a decrease in the marginal productivity of stored-up resources and a simultaneous increase in the marginal productivity of current resources. Provided the decrease does not affect two-year capital to an exceptional extent, it is evident that the balance between the two fractions of capital will be tilted toward the longer investment term. The interest on both the one-year and two-year capital falls, but the latter is now much more than double the former, perhaps two or three times as large, as may easily be seen from a numerical example. In other words, two-year investment of capital becomes relatively more profitable than before, and will be extended to new fields, whereas one-year investment will increase but little, or may even decrease. This has an important consequence as regards current labour and land. Increased investment in itself tends to diminish the amount of current labour and land available for direct production of consumption goods, and therefore tends to raise their marginal productivities. But if a relatively larger proportion of this investment is devoted to two-year capital, and is thus divided into two groups, each of which is used only every other year, it is obvious that the amount of stored-up labour and land put to use every year decreases, relatively at least. At the same time, the amount of current labour and land which has to be stored each year to replace that which has been used up also decreases, and more of these productive factors are therefore available for the direct production of consumption goods for the current year, with a consequent reduction in

115

the marginal productivity of current labour and land. This property of capital, that it grows, as it were, more in height than in breadth, therefore provides a counterbalance to the tendency of an increase of capital to raise wages and rents.

Other things being equal, however, the latter tendency can never be quite halted; the increased capitalisation does lead to a definite increase in wages and rents, although not to the same extent as we might at first suppose. But the situation is quite different if some technical invention makes long-term investment more profitable (in the absolute sense) than previously, and there is no accompanying increase in the total capital. The consequence of this must necessarily be that capital diminishes 'in breadth': a greater amount of current labour and land is therefore available for direct production of consumption goods each year, and their marginal productivities and product shares may diminish, although this is not a necessary consequence because the invention increases the total product.[1] The capitalist-saver is thus fundamentally a friend of the worker, but the technical inventor is quite often his enemy. The great industrial inventions which have from time to time revolutionised production have, as has been possible to observe, initially brought many workmen to beggary, while capitalists' profits soared. It is quite unnecessary to explain this away by 'economic friction' and the like, because it is in complete conformity with rational theory. But it is really not just capital that is to blame. As a matter of fact, if the accumulation of capital were to continue, the damage would be repaired: interest rates would fall, and wages would rise—at any rate, unless the workers themselves counteract this tendency by a large increase in their numbers.

The groundwork of our theory of capital is now completed. The complications involved in passing from abstract theory to the concrete phenomena of society are not matters of principle, and, especially in a mathematical treatment, present few difficulties. The most important of them are due to the fact that, on the one hand, labour and land *from several years* are incorporated in the same capital good; while, on the other hand, capital goods are not entirely used up in one year's (direct) production, as we have hitherto

---

[1] It is thus undoubtedly true that the 'transformation of circulating capital into fixed capital,' i.e. the change-over from short-term to long-term investment, may often injure the workers; but Ricardo was mistaken when he supposed that this was a consequence of a simultaneous decrease in the total gross product. This idea is theoretically untenable, as is quite easily proved. Under perfect competition, the gross product always tends to the maximum physically possible with the existing means of production.

116

assumed, but often give many years of service, so that the productive power embodied in them may be expended over a succession of years. In general, it is impossible to say how much, and which part, of it is used each year. But here too the law of marginal productivity must nevertheless be fulfilled in equilibrium. Otherwise, it would be profitable to apply more—or less—productive power at some point of production either in such a way that the amount of production factors applied at some other point simultaneously decreased —or increased—or, alternatively, to raise—or lower—the value of the capital good. For instance, suppose a machine takes four years to complete, and is afterwards used for ten years before it is scrapped. And suppose that if one more day's labour had been used in the first year of the machine's production, its value would have increased by, say, three days of current labour during the last year of its use, i.e. the first working day would have yielded about 8 per cent per annum, since $(1 \cdot 08)^{13} = 3$ approximately. This rate of interest must coincide with the prevailing rate in the society, because if it were higher it would be profitable in the future to apply more labour to the kind of machine in question, and if it were lower it would usually be profitable to use similar machines of slightly lower quality and shorter life, requiring less labour and land for their production.

It is, of course, another matter that some investments, e.g. in houses, roads, certain soil-improvements, etc., attain such an age that the theoretical adjustment of the capital goods with regard to quality and quantity cannot be realised in practice. Unless we wish to extend our observations to periods of time in which centuries are small episodes, we must rest content with the statement that there is a continual *tendency*, perhaps very incompletely realised, towards adjustments of the kind indicated above. This reservation applies especially to periods of intense industrial development, where economic equilibrium is usually conspicuous by its absence.

It would be very interesting to apply our theory to many of the controversial questions about capital. For example: whether improvements in land should be reckoned as land or as capital; whether dwelling-houses and other very durable consumption goods are capital in the technical-social sense, or only from the point of view of the private economy; whether the means of subsistence of the worker should be reckoned as capital, and, in this connection, whether the source of wages is capital or the products which are completed year after year; and to what extent the so-called wage fund (or rather, wage-and-rent fund) theory is tenable.

But such a discussion here would involve far too great a digression —and, as a matter of fact, would show that the whole controversy often hinges merely on an unclear formulation of the point at issue—so I will merely say a little in conclusion about the *accumulation of capital*. In our society, the accumulation of capital is mainly in the hands of private enterprise, although the state does sometimes accumulate capital. From the theoretical point of view, the individual should always carry his accumulation (or consumption) of capital just so far that the marginal utility of capital goods is the same in the present as in the future. If by sacrificing 1 crown this year he can expect to obtain 2 crowns in ten years' time, it is a question of whether 2 crowns then has larger or smaller subjective value for him than 1 crown now. The answer naturally depends on many circumstances: among other things, on the amount the person in question may wish to save during the next few years. In particular, it is important to notice that the rate of interest has a double effect here: a high rate increases the yield of present saving, and consequently its future marginal utility, but at the same time it promises a more ample satisfaction of future needs if saving continues at the given rate, and in this way *lowers* the marginal utility of future goods for the individual. It may even happen that the second tendency overcomes the first, so that for some individuals a low rate of interest may be better encouragement for saving than a high one. Individual accumulation of capital is thus a rather complicated phenomenon. But if we look at a society as a whole with an almost stationary economy, we see that complete economic equilibrium can never occur, and the accumulation of capital can therefore never cease until the rate of interest falls to zero, which implies that the annual product has reached the maximum physically possible. For as long as stored-up labour and land provide even the smallest excess of marginal productivity over that of current labour and land, a sacrifice on the part of the average individual now—if it is not altogether too large—must give a larger compensation in the future.

The fact that this ideal future state, so long looked forward to by economists, is slow to arrive depends presumably on *two* circumstances. One we have just pointed out: that the accumulation of capital is largely in the hands of individual members of the society. As Böhm-Bawerk has observed, the individual is very much inclined to under-estimate future needs and to over-estimate future resources, mainly perhaps on account of the uncertainty of the future. He does not know for certain whether he himself, or those whose welfare is his interest, will actually gain anything by his sacrifices; and even if the accumulation of capital always leads to an increase of production as a whole, he has no assurance that an enterprise in which he invests his savings will be among the successful ones. In both these respects, the collective system appears to be superior to private enterprise, offering better guarantees for more vigorous accumulation of capital.

But an even more important factor is involved: the tendency of present-day economies to differ so widely from the stationary type. Technical progress and increase of population both lead to an increase in the rate of interest, as we have already seen—the former as a rule, the latter without exception. In spite of the continual accumulation of capital, capital never succeeds in satisfying a productive process which is incessantly increasing in scale. This takes a particularly extreme form in colonial countries where development is very rapid: the interest rate there often reaches fabulous heights.

But it is obvious that these are exceptional circumstances, which must sooner or later, presumably during this century, give way to a much slower development—quantitatively at least—and possibly even to completely stationary conditions. Interest will then fall, and will account for quite a small fraction of the total product, both relatively and absolutely. That does not mean that the role of capital in production is then finished, of course; on the contrary, in such circumstances, it has reached its climax, but capital then gives its services for little or no remuneration, like land when it is to be had in abundance. The mature-capitalist system resembles in one respect the otherwise so entirely dissimilar primitive, non-capitalistic system of production, in that labour and land share the whole product between them, or practically so.

This situation is not particularly desirable, however. The gulf between the classes with property and without it must become practically impassable when land, capitalised at a very low rate of interest, attains almost infinitely great exchange value. Even now the greater part of what is commonly called capital and interest is really land and rent, and the so-called annual savings of the nations consist to a large extent of increases in the capital value of land. There is also the profit from the many different sorts of *monopoly*, which, as we have already seen, are often merely founded on an initial advantage in timing which competition does not succeed in levelling out.

It is, then, far from being the case that a decrease in the rate of interest would bring about the solution of the social problem, as has sometimes been suggested. That would remove only one of labour's

119

rivals—and perhaps not the most important—for the fruits of the social product; whereas it would strengthen the title to income which is the most disputable from the ethical point of view—that which is based entirely on the private ownership of natural resources, or the almost comparable possession of monopoly rights.

ON THE PROBLEM OF
DISTRIBUTION[1]

IN an article in this journal in 1900, and subsequently in my published lectures, I endeavoured to elaborate the theory of marginal productivity as the norm for economic distribution; in other words, the proposition that the respective shares of the productive factors in the product are determined under free competition by the change in the product which would result from a slight increase or decrease in the factor concerned, if the other factors remained unchanged. This theory, which is clearly somewhat analogous to the theory of marginal utility, is without doubt destined to play a considerable part in theoretical economics. Von Thünen's proposition that it is the additional product of the last worker which determines wages, and the yield of the last unit of capital invested which regulates interest, and ultimately even Ricardo's theory of rent, with the generalisations of it introduced by Schäffle, Mangoldt, and others, are really only applications of this law. In fact, we may say on the whole that all attempts at a rational solution of the distribution problem are in the last analysis based on reasoning which, if pursued to its logical conclusion, would lead to the formulation of a marginal productivity principle of distribution.

There is, however, an *error* in the presentations mentioned above, and I would like to take this opportunity of correcting it, especially as the theory gains thereby in general validity and completeness. In agreement with the English economist Wicksteed, I have stated that the proposition in question is only true under one important restrictive condition, namely, in branches of production which obey the law of 'constant returns,' as Marshall calls it, that is, where small and large scale production give the same relative returns. If we attempt to apply it to cases where production on a larger scale leads to a more than proportional increase in the product ('increasing returns'), an obvious contradiction arises, since the wages, rents and interest determined in this way would come to more than the total

---

[1] 'Till fördelningsproblemet,' *Ekonomisk Tidskrift*, 1902, pp. 424–33.

product. This is connected with the fact that in such circumstances a real and lasting equilibrium is theoretically impossible, because the firms which operate on a larger scale must gradually drive the smaller ones out of the market, to be themselves engulfed by yet larger concerns, until in the end the whole of the industry in question comes under the control of one more or less giant enterprise possessing an actual, if not legal, monopoly.

My opinion was confirmed by the fact that I had already arrived at the same result independently of Wicksteed. Moreover, the criticism of Wicksteed which Walras put forward in the third edition of his *Éléments d'économie politique pure*, after consulting the Italian economist Enrico Barone, seemed to me *a priori* incorrect, since Walras assumes it to be a self-evident fact that the cost price and the sales price of the goods must be the same under free competition; in other words, he assumes that the enterprises' real profits are reduced to zero by general competition between entrepreneurs, so that for the work and risks they have undertaken they receive only a reasonable remuneration, calculated in the customary way, which is regarded as included in the costs of production—but nothing in excess of this. It seemed to me that this involved the assumption that both large and small scale production must give the same return since if large and small enterprises operate side by side in the same branch, and the former are more profitable, then one of the two following alternatives must occur: either the smaller firms run at a loss, which they cannot continue to do indefinitely, or else the larger ones reap an extra profit after all costs have been paid at the same rates as by the smaller, who cannot eliminate this extra profit by competition.

I have found on further reflection, however, that on this point I did Walras—or rather his collaborator, Barone—an *injustice*, and that the law of marginal productivity actually has a far greater field of application theoretically than either Wicksteed or I had hitherto imagined.

As I now see it, not all the possibilities are exhausted by the categories 'increasing,' constant, and diminishing returns.'[1] On the

---

[1] What is usually called (by Marshall, among others) 'diminishing returns' in agriculture, for instance, does not actually constitute another category separate from the other two. It is of course true that increased applications of labour and capital to *the same acreage* will not in general give a proportionate increase in the product, but the same thing applies to an equal or even greater extent to all other production, as soon as one of the necessary elements of production—e.g. the raw material—cannot be expanded at the same rate as the others. The expressions

contrary, when a productive enterprise expands, in the general case, it passes through more than one of these phases: for example, the product may initially increase faster than the scale of production, but subsequently more slowly. There is no doubt that such cases often occur in reality. Sometimes, the very nature of the operations involved implies, of necessity, a restriction of the scale of production: thus in building a house, a ship, a locomotive, and so on, a certain limited labour force together with the appropriate capital is definitely the most advantageous economically. A builder who has four medium-sized houses to build will presumably do better to employ twenty-five men, say, on each house, than to let one hundred men work on each house in succession. But even in the proper manufacturing industries, it must often happen that the technical gain resulting from the division and concentration of labour is ultimately outweighed by the increased costs for the longer transport of raw materials and the extension of the sales area.

Thus in all such cases it is not only a certain proportion between the productive factors which is most advantageous technically, but also a certain form of operation, or scale of production. We now come to the remarkable circumstance, which Barone had pointed out but which I had overlooked, that although remuneration of the productive factors in accordance with the law of marginal productivity is impossible while production has not achieved its most advantageous scale, it is nevertheless quite possible once production has reached this limit, its maximum value, which it must also be regarded as tending towards under free competition.

This circumstance is clearly connected with the fact that the enterprise passes from increasing to diminishing returns at this maximum and may therefore be regarded momentarily as being subject to *constant* returns.

Since this connection is undeniably of great importance and interest, I will endeavour to illuminate it further without the use of Walras' and Barone's mathematical symbols, or at least without resorting to others than those found in elementary mathematics.

The matter is quite simple when only a single production element is considered—a case which, admittedly, is rare in practice. If, for instance, production is such that only 'free' natural resources are

'increasing' or 'constant' returns presuppose that all the production elements may be increased as desired. But if, as has sometimes been maintained, agriculture on a *small* scale were always to give a higher yield than on a large scale, agriculture would *then*, but only then, provide a direct contrast to those industries where the yield increases, even relatively, almost continuously with the scale of production.

employed, and if technical equipment is so little and the time of its application so short that interest on capital may be neglected, *labour* will be the only production factor involved economically. If we now suppose that the labour force and the division of labour are successively increased, we may assume that the product first increases, even relatively, so that every worker on an average produces more than formerly. But this cannot continue indefinitely: there must be a limit. But where is the limit? Clearly at that point where a new worker is able to increase the product or the value of the product by precisely that amount which the other workers produce *on an average*. If his additional product continues to be larger than this average, then the average itself is increased by the addition of his labour, and the most advantageous scale of production has not yet been reached; if, on the other hand, his additional product is smaller than the average, the average is decreased by the addition of his labour, and the most advantageous scale of production has already been exceeded, so that it would be more profitable to let this worker and others after him form a new working group. Here then the marginal productivity, the additional product of the last worker, coincides directly with the average productivity of labour. It follows at once that if the former determines wages, the total of wages will be exactly equivalent to the value of the product, so that there will be no surplus for the entrepreneur *as such* (i.e. apart from the above-mentioned remuneration for his work and risks), though on the other hand he will not suffer any loss.

Perhaps this will be easier to understand if we consider an arbi-trarily chosen numerical example, set out in tabular form, where for

No. of workers in the group	Value of the whole product of labour	Value of the last worker's additional pro-duct	Average value of product per worker
1	2·00	—	2·00
2	5·00	3·00	2·50
3	9·00	4·00	3·00
4	14·00	5·00	3·50
5	20·00	6·00	4·00
6	27·00	7·00	4·50
7	35·00	8·00	5·00
8	42·00	7·00	5·25
9	48·00	6·00	5·33
10	53·50	5·50	5·35
11	58·75	5·25	5·34
12	63·75	5·00	5·31

simplicity we allow the magnitude of products to be represented by their money values.

The table should be self-explanatory. The third column gives the increase in the product due to each new worker, so that each figure there is equal to the difference between the corresponding figure and the one above it in the second column. It will be seen that the increase in the value of the product rises for each of the first seven workers. But the increase due to the eighth worker is only the same as that for the sixth, that for the ninth the same as that for the fifth, tenth increase still less, and so on. Regardless of this, the *average* product increases all the time until the tenth worker, and it is not until the eleventh that the average product begins to decrease. The most advantageous arrangement of production in this case is therefore with ten or eleven workers in each group, and because of the competition between the entrepreneurs, it will be the 'last,' i.e. approximately the eleventh, worker's additional product which determines the wages of all the workers, whereby the value of the whole product covers wages exactly. As already pointed out, this assumes that the most advantageous scale of production is actually realised. If the entrepreneurs halted for some reason at groups of seven or eight workers, wages paid in accordance with the marginal productivity would swallow up considerably more than the whole value of the product. (On the other hand, if the size of the working groups exceeded the most technically advantageous arrangement— which could only occur by mutual agreement—this would be the most advantageous for the entrepreneurs, since they would acquire a surplus, profits of enterprise, if the workers were paid according to the marginal productivity, which is as a matter of fact the highest wages they could obtain under free competition among themselves.)

If we now consider the general case where several factors of production—labour, land and capital in their various forms—are involved at the same time, the situation appears at first sight to be much more complex, but, actually, it is possible to reduce it to the one we have just been considering. Let us suppose for the moment that the *proportion* in which the various productive factors contribute to the total product is given in advance as the only possible one—for instance, because of the technical nature of the process in question— so that for each employed worker μ acres of average quality land and ν units of capital are required. In such a case we could regard the combination 1 worker $+ \mu$ acres of land $+ \nu$ units of capital as a new production factor, a new productive unit, and everything which was said previously about labour as the single production

125

factor may now be applied to this new unit. When production is on the most advantageous scale, the marginal productivity, i.e. the additional product of the last unit of the new production factor (always 1 worker $+ \mu$ acres of land $+ \nu$ units of capital), will coincide with the average productivity of such a complex unit, and if competition between the entrepreneurs implies that the remuneration for each such unit is determined by its marginal productivity, the total remuneration will correspond exactly to the total product. All that remains is to determine the share of each component production factor in the complex unit. Now since, in reality, the proportion between the factors is not determined in advance, for they may replace one another in most cases, it is not difficult to see that this distribution will also necessarily be determined according to the marginal productivity of each and every separate factor. These marginal productivities consequently become the final principle of distribution, since we assumed that each complex unit is extremely small in comparison to the scale of the whole enterprise, and thus its marginal productivity is equal to the sum of the separate factors.

The same result may be reached by a somewhat different way, very similar to the proof given by Barone. For the sake of simplicity, we will assume that only *two* production factors are involved, e.g. labour and land. If, first of all, their productive shares, i.e. wages and rent, are given as to size, it would be the task of each entrepreneur to arrange the production factors used in his processes in such a way that he obtains as large a profit as possible; in other words, to ensure that each unit of the product is manufactured at the smallest possible cost. If the wage is w, the rent per acre r, and if he employs a workers and b acres of land in the same productive group,[1] the total cost of the goods manufactured by the group is clearly $aw + br$, and if we divide this expression by the quantity manufactured, which we denote by Q, we obtain the average cost per unit of the product, k,

$$k = \frac{aw + br}{Q}$$

The entrepreneur will endeavour to make k as *small* as possible. This problem can only be solved, in reality, if the manner in which Q depends on a and b is known, but we can easily establish two formal conditions for a correct solution which will suffice for our purposes. If we suppose that the number of workers increases by

[1] Translator's Note: In the original b was used instead of w, and h instead of b —otherwise they are the same in both the original and the translation.

one man, while the acreage employed remains unchanged, the total production costs will increase by the amount of a single wage, while the product will increase by an amount which we call the marginal productivity of labour, denoted here by q_a. In other words, if the quantity a changes to $a + 1$, the numerator of the above fraction increases by the quantity w, and the denominator by q_a, which is in general itself a variable quantity, dependent on a and b. Whether the whole fraction, which is equal to the average cost k, thereby increases or decreases clearly depends on whether w/q_a is greater or smaller than k. As long as it is smaller, k cannot have reached its minimum value, and a necessary condition for this is therefore that (approximately)

$$\frac{w}{q_a} = k$$

In a similar manner, if we suppose that the acres of land employed with an unchanged labour force increases by 1 acre, we arrive at a second necessary condition for a minimum of k:

$$\frac{r}{q_b} = k$$

where q_b denotes the marginal productivity of the land.

These two equations provide us with an answer to our question. For on substituting $w = kq_a$ and $r = kq_b$ in the expression for k, and cancelling k we obtain

$$Q = aq_a + bq_b.$$

In other words, when production is arranged in the most advantageous manner possible, the whole product is equal to the sum of the marginal productivity of labour multiplied by the number of workers and the marginal productivity of land multiplied by the number of acres, which is exactly analogous to what we found before when we were considering only one production factor.

In the special case considered by Wicksteed and me, where production on a large scale and production on a small scale give the same return, it is easy to see that the above equation is *identically* satisfied, i.e. it is valid for all possible values of a and b. In the general case, it is only valid as a *maximum condition*. It is satisfied for those values of a and b which correspond to the most advantageous production arrangement, but not otherwise.

We have been assuming that wages and rents are given fixed

quantities. If we dispense with this assumption, and assume instead that they are gradually raised by competition between the entrepreneurs to achieve the best possible results, the entrepreneurs must react to each change in wages and rents by an adjustment of the productive groups. As long as q_a and q_b remain larger than w and r respectively, $k < 1$, and the numerator of the fraction is therefore less than the denominator, which means to say that the entrepreneur's own costs are less than the value of the product, so that a true entrepreneurial profit occurs. This profit is the same for each productive group, so there is nothing to prevent it from being reduced to a very small amount by competition between the entrepreneurs. The condition for it to be zero is that $k = 1$, which implies that $w = q_a$ and $r = q_b$, so that with full economic equilibrium the shares of each productive factor in the product are equal to their marginal productivities.

It has been objected against reasoning of this sort that it is not always possible to regard the product as a 'mathematical,' continuous function of the productive factors. One example given in support of this is that of a clothing factory employing one hundred machinists at one hundred sewing machines; the dismissal of one machinist would mean that one machine would stand idle, and the breakdown of one machine would mean that one machinist would be without work. It is therefore impossible to consider the marginal productivity of labour as something separate from that of the machine or capital, and consequently impossible to decide what labour's and capital's shares of the product are by this method.

But it is only necessary to modify the above example slightly, and in a way which is fully in accordance with reality, to fit it in with the requirements of the theory. The factory in question is probably engaged in more than one sort of manufacture, so that in addition to the sewing of straightforward work where each machinist is continually using a machine, there is probably also finer work which requires much hand-sewing, where one machine is sufficient for two operators, let us say. So, if the number of machinists diminishes slightly, all the machines can still be kept in full use by a slight adjustment of production involving an increase of the plain sewing and a decrease of the finer work. Adjustment in the opposite direction could accommodate a slight surplus of machinists. The change in the total product which would follow an increase or decrease in one factor would be quite distinct from that resulting from a change in the other factor. It is also quite easy to see, especially with the assistance of a numerical example, that the additional product which results from successively increasing first one and then the other production factor is the same as that arising from equal simultaneous increases of both factors together in complete accordance with the theory, and as we assumed earlier.

Seen in this light there does not as a rule seem to be anything to prevent an exact treatment of economic phenomena. But it is important to remember that such a treatment can only establish certain *tendencies* which may in actual fact be counteracted or even cancelled by other forces, among which 'the force of inertia' and the strength of tradition and habit may be counted among the foremost.

Although Wicksteed's reservation as regards the applicability of the law of marginal productivity cannot be admitted from the strictly theoretical viewpoint, it nevertheless does not seem to be without significance in practice. For if the most advantageous productive group is small, this is practically the same as if the branch of production in question follows the law of *constant* returns. It is then always possible to obtain the same relative return in large-scale industry as in small-scale industry by dividing manufacture among smaller units, by dividing up large areas of land, etc. If, on the other hand, the opposite situation prevails, and large-scale production is more advantageous, it is true that, taken abstractly, a certain scale of production may still be the most advantageous technically, but if this scale of production is near to or higher than the consuming capacity of the society, equilibrium cannot occur until production is actually monopolised. But once the most advantageous scale of production is so large that there is only room in a country or a district for a few firms in the industry, then it is no longer possible to assume that these firms compete actively with one another, because it is so easy for them to combine and achieve a monopolist position to their mutual advantage.

Another circumstance having a similar effect is the geographical distribution of production and consumption—hitherto neglected to an undue extent by economists. Two producers of similar goods located in different places can seldom compete with one another effectively except where their natural sales areas overlap. Each of them has a definite advantage over his competitor in the region closest to him, and up to a certain limit he is free to exploit this advantage. Consequently, the prices of goods within these immediately adjacent areas will be higher than in the common sales area where there is full competition—perhaps absolutely higher, but certainly relatively (with respect to costs). Since no producer is inclined to carry on even a part of his production at a loss, his costs, wages, rents, etc., will be adapted to the least profitable part of his production, and a surplus will then appear for the more profitable part, which may reasonably be called true entrepreneurial profit or interest on an actual monopoly.

As far as I can see, therefore, the reflections on this topic in the works referred to are not affected in any essential way by the above modification of the underlying theory.

THE 'CRITICAL POINT' IN THE LAW OF DECREASING AGRICULTURAL PRODUCTIVITY[1]

THE doctrine of relatively diminishing returns from agriculture when labour or capital intensity is increased, has never enjoyed any remarkable popularity among the general public, just like the Malthusian population theory, of which it is really only another expression. Economists—who are no less sensitive to the sweetness of popularity than other people—have therefore endeavoured as a rule to soften the unfavourable impression of these theories of theirs. They prefer to speak about the decreasing returns from land 'after a certain limit,' leaving it an open question as to whether this limit has already been exceeded or whether it perhaps still lies ahead of us, whether it is a question of a movable or a fixed limit, and so on. They often present Malthus's theory of population trends in a similar manner, as if it merely referred to certain vague conditions in a more or less distant future, whereas it actually serves to explain why poverty, want and misery have been the lot of the broad mass of the population, always and everywhere, at all times and in all countries.

This sensitivity is but little appreciated by most of their readers, however, who with some justification conclude, on the contrary, that the economists do not really understand the things they write about, and that in general their warnings need not be taken seriously.

I was led to these reflections by an article in the June number of this journal,[2] where the author did his best in thirty-three pages to refute or cast doubts upon the whole of the law of decreasing agricultural productivity.

His main argument, which he uses almost unceasingly throughout the whole of his long article, is that a law about agricultural returns under varying conditions must be of a technical or scientific kind;

---

[1] 'Den "kritiska punkten" i lagen för jordbrukets avtagande avkastning,' *Ekonomisk Tidskrift*, 1916, pp. 285–92.

[2] 'Om gränsen för jordbrukets intensifiering' (On the Limit for the Intensification of Agriculture) by C. Rohtlieb.

131

and since the classical economists who first formulated the law certainly had a very imperfect conception of the physical and chemical forces regulating the magnitude of the final product, he thinks that we should not be surprised if they were mistaken. And this would be the case here, too, because it is sometimes actually possible to increase the product in far greater proportion than that by which the capital or labour involved has increased—for instance, by applying chalk, potash, phosphates, etc., to land where these substances are at a minimum, or, by draining waterlogged land, and so on.

We have here a confusion of ideas which can most easily be seen if we reflect that the increases of production mentioned might just as easily have occurred *without* any increase of either labour or capital, merely by a more suitable arrangement of the labour and capital already available, in so far as these could be liberated and transformed. It is then clear that Rohtlieb is not talking about the same thing as the protagonists of the law of agricultural productivity. These latter assume that the technical leader of agricultural production, if not at the peak of contemporary knowledge, has at least reached *a certain average level of agricultural skill and experience*, and endeavours to find out to what extent the result of his operations would increase or decrease, if different amounts of the general agricultural production factors were placed at his disposal.

It is clear that, with this assumption, the product must be a mathematical function of the quantities of labour, land and capital used: if we denote these quantities by a, b and c respectively—the second expressed in units of land-area of a certain quality, the latter for the sake of simplicity in money—and the average product per annum by p, we may write

$$p = f(a, b, c).$$

Unfortunately we know little about the detailed properties of this function. The agricultural research stations are responsible for providing us with the necessary data, but they have not done so.

One important property of the function in question *is* known, however, or rather is self-evident: it must be *homogeneous and of the first degree*. In other words, if we substitute for a, b and c the quantities $2a$, $2b$, and $2c$, for example, we have

$$f(2a, 2b, 2c) = 2p,$$

and the same thing applies, of course, if instead of the number 2 we have any number m, be it whole or fractional.

132

This equation merely expresses the well-known fact that two agricultural enterprises producing the same sort of products (a little more will be said about this shortly), one on a small scale and the other on a larger, will give essentially the same returns. This is, moreover, implicitly recognised by Rohtlieb, when he says on p. 194 that 'production is increased by every simultaneous addition of these three factors'—I assume that the increase referred to is uniform, as nothing is said to the contrary.[1]

It is clear that if a uniform increase of all three production factors leads to a proportionate increase in the product, an increase of only one or two of them cannot lead to the same increase in the product.[2]

This in itself proves the law of agricultural productivity. Consequently, no deeper knowledge of the details of agricultural technique is required for this purpose (which does not mean to say that such knowledge would not be of great advantage even to economists). The fact on which it is based is not immediately technical but economic—i.e. quite simply the existence of a *rent* on land or of a *price* for its ownership. If it were possible to increase the return from a constant area of land proportionally by increasing the capital and labour, i.e. if the equation

$$f(2a, b, 2c) = 2p$$

were valid, then it must follow that

$$f(a, \tfrac{1}{2}b, c) = p = f(a, b, c)$$

In other words, the farmer could produce with the capital and labour at his disposal just as much on *half* the land as on the whole of it. Is it conceivable then that he would be willing to pay out a considerable amount for the tenancy of the remaining land—or, if he wishes to own it, a high purchase price for its possession—when, according to our assumption, it would be of no use to him?

[1] It is true that he adds some reflections that there must be a 'certain proportion' between these factors, and so on, but this is based on another confusion, which I shall point out later on.

[2] One simple form of the function in question which would fulfil the conditions mentioned—with a suitable choice of units—is

$$a^{\alpha} . b^{\beta} . c^{\gamma} = p,$$

where α, β, γ are three fractions whose sum is *unity*. An increase of 10 per cent in labour a would then increase p by about 10 . α per cent, and an increase of 10 per cent in capital c would increase p by 10 . γ per cent, the two increases together giving 10 $(\alpha + \gamma)$ per cent. Not until the area of land, b, also increases by 10 per cent does the product increase by 10 $(\alpha + \beta + \gamma)$ per cent = 10 per cent.

133

As previously mentioned, this assumes that the farmer in question possesses at least an average technical ability. If discoveries and inventions were to *raise* this technical standard to any considerable extent, the product would of course be much greater as regards quantity or quality. But that does not mean that the law of agricultural productivity would cease to be valid, or even that it would be 'suspended,' as Rohtlieb expresses it. We should simply have to deal with a *new* function, for example,

$$\phi(a, b, c) = 2p \text{ (or } 3p, 4p, \text{ etc.)},$$

but this function is also homogeneous and of the first degree, so that an increase in only one or two of the production factors would still only lead to a proportionately smaller increase in the product.[1]

In several places Rohtlieb is guilty of another confusion—an extremely common one, unfortunately—between relative yield and profitability in agriculture. For example, when he says on p. 194 that a certain proportion between labour, land and capital is preferable to any other, this statement is completely meaningless unless one sets out with a definite *price* for each of these factors. Otherwise, how could it be anything but advantageous for the landowner to have at his disposal unlimited amounts of labour and capital in the case where he did not need to pay anything for them? This brings us to agricultural *profitability*, however, which is quite another matter. The relative yield is the product divided by the amount of labour (if for the sake of simplicity we confine ourselves to this factor only) and is not directly concerned with the price of labour. Profitability, on the other hand, is the *difference* between the value of the product and the sum of wages, and is therefore completely dependent on the level of wages. Similarly, when we read on p. 128 'that at the present stage of agriculture there is no fixed and insurmountable limit to yields,' this may possibly apply to profitability, which in turn may increase further if wages fall or, what is basically the same, if the price of agricultural products rises, and which, moreover, usually increases with every technical advance. But if the statement is intended to mean that the critical point at which the law of

[1] It is not entirely inconceivable that a series of technical advances might lead to such a sudden increase in the area of land worth cultivating that the law of agricultural productivity would cease to be valid for a time, whereupon rent would also disappear at the same time. There does not appear to be any historical example of this, although the fall in European rents which resulted from North American grain competition in the 1870's and 1880's—i.e. due ultimately to the opening up of the prairies for commerce—did point in this direction to some extent.

agricultural returns begins to be valid has not yet been reached in Sweden, it is quite absurd, for this point was certainly passed some hundreds or even thousands of years ago. Some years back, in criticising Waterstradt in *Thünen-Archiv* (which Rohtlieb does not seem to have noticed), I endeavoured to show that this so-called critical point must have been passed—at least as far as *private* agriculture is concerned—as soon as the spontaneous products of the soil—timber in the natural forest, wild grassland, etc.—had achieved economic value. For, compared with these products, which are obtained practically *without* the employment of labour or capital, all products that are won *with* the assistance of labour and capital must indicate relatively decreasing returns.

It must be admitted, however, that this viewpoint is too one-sided. If instead of private agriculture we consider the agricultural production of a whole country, and try to apply the above equation, which may be written in the form

$$F(A, B, C) = P,$$

where the capital letters refer to the total labour engaged in agriculture in the whole country, the total area of land, etc., and the *whole* of the national gross product of agriculture. It is perhaps no longer true that this function is homogeneous and of the first degree, since the combination and division of labour in a large country (or in a large continuous area of land) can profitably be carried farther than in a small country. In this case a proportionate increase of the product is possible even if one of the factors (land) remains constant. When a colony is first begun, it may happen that the mutual help which colonists can give one another in the building of roads, the arrangement of markets, the organisation of trade and credit, and so on, may for a time make every new immigrant welcome, even if the earlier settlers' free right of disposition over the land are curtailed thereby.

Lastly, it must also be admitted that the formula 'decreasing returns' leaves much unsaid. So long as agriculture provides a good living, one should of course be happy that as many people as possible may find a livelihood on the surface of the earth, even if a thinning-out of the population would increase the yield per unit of labour employed. But whatever we may think in this respect, it is important that we do not deceive ourselves with false reasoning or sophistry.

The statistical material which Rohtlieb puts forward to show that our agriculture may be further intensified before the law of decreasing returns comes into operation seems to me to be devoid of real significance. The fact that our small farms yield a gross product per hectare of considerably greater value than that of the large farms would be proof of something if it were a question of the *same type of product*—but it is not. It is reasonable to suppose that an analysis of the production of the larger farms would show that the yields per hectare for certain of their crops, e.g. sugar-beet, or mangolds, are considerably higher in value than the average for the other crops— though it does not follow that the crops giving the more valuable yield could advantageously be extended to the whole area under cultivation. It may be that a market gardener produces on one hectare a harvest equal in value to that which an ordinary farmer produces on ten hectares. But it cannot be concluded from this that the whole of the country's land should be cultivated as one great garden, as we cannot live on cauliflower or asparagus alone, and it would probably be impossible to produce the large quantities of manure necessary for garden cultivation. Nor does the increase in the 'amount of turnover' per hectare for small farms in recent years prove anything, since the price increases for agricultural products exert influences in two different directions: they increase the money value of a harvest which does not itself change, and they make profitable an increased intensity of cultivation which would not have been profitable before.

Finally Rohtlieb tries a little *social economic* reasoning. He asks whether a more intensive agriculture should not be regarded as desirable for the country as a whole, although it might be unprofitable from the viewpoint of the private economy, and whether it should not therefore be encouraged by appropriate means, even if the general public were obliged to recompense owners whose rents consequently fell, in whole or part, below zero. He suggests that 'it is precisely this problem that lies behind the controversy about the justification of protective tariffs, though other problems are also involved' (p. 200).

He seems to forget—or at any rate he does not examine the point further—that if the capital and labour allocated to agriculture must be taken from *industry*, the gain for the 'national income' might be very doubtful. It may, however, be admitted that if we bring the problem to a head and regard it exclusively from a rather narrow national point of view, then such an antagonism between private and national interests could be imagined. Suppose, for instance, that the price of *timber* products of all kinds became so high, and the price of agricultural products so low because of competition from foreign grain and other foodstuffs, that the best course for the landowners was to stop growing crops and to *devote all Swedish land to forest*. This is not altogether inconceivable, and since forestry even, together with associated manufactures, certainly could not employ more than a fraction of the labour and capital which is now employed directly or indirectly in Swedish agriculture,[1] it is clear that such a revolutionary change would necessitate the emigration of some Swedish labour and capital. From a national point of view, in the narrow sense, this would presumably be regarded as a serious loss; but from the point of view of the *world economy*, it would be a definite gain, since from this viewpoint it is naturally most advantageous if those parts of the world best suited to forestry are used for forestry, and if agriculture is carried on where conditions are most fitting, even if the former regions become more sparsely and the latter more densely populated than now.

But this situation is not likely to arise in the near future, and so long as the transfer is confined within the boundaries of this country it may be regarded as a gain *even* from the purely national viewpoint. The obstacles raised by legislation, be it through making afforestation more difficult or through encouraging agriculture artificially by means of tariffs, seem to be deleterious, and should thus be abandoned—only at the same time it would be necessary to ensure that the unearned wealth which might then fall to the fortunate owners of forest and of the arable land on which agriculture would subsequently be concentrated would be put to more generally beneficial use.

Perhaps sufficient has been said. Nothing can be more desirable than that these vital questions should be subjected to thorough scrutiny. But it seems to me that Rohtlieb has presented the results of his reasoning and of his evidently wide studies of the literature in too undigested a form. In particular, he should learn to distinguish between the technical and the economic aspects and, within the latter, between agricultural profitability—which is a matter for the private economist and of only limited interest for the political economist—and relative returns—which are entirely a matter of political economy, or rather, of population.

[1] Rohtlieb charges me (p. 201 n.) with having overlooked the fact that the labour (and capital) used in agriculture does not only include that which is employed directly on the land in question. From my review in the 1903 issue of this journal of the book by Pohle, which he himself quotes in this connection he, would have discovered that I am not altogether unacquainted with this circumstance; but we need not go into the question whether my reasoning in the passage to which he refers would have been altered in any essential way by the inclusion of this point.

III

ON THE WORK OF HIS CONTEMPORARIES

VILFREDO PARETO'S
COURS D'ÉCONOMIE POLITIQUE[1]

IT was never an easy task to write a good textbook of political economy, and today it has become more difficult than ever. The scope of this subject has expanded a great deal in recent decades, on the one hand because of important researches in the historical and statistical fields, and on the other through no less important and penetrating achievements in the field of pure theory. It is certainly not given to everyone to master both these fields at the same time, or even to have the art of presenting their principal results concisely and lucidly. I do not think it could be maintained that Pareto has successfully overcome all the difficulties involved, but this work of his is nevertheless a valuable addition to the none too abundant modern textbooks. It is full of interesting comparisons and acute remarks, and the writer everywhere strikes his reader as a sincere man of research and a person of understanding. I wish to emphasise this expressly to begin with, since in the following I will be obliged for lack of space to confine myself to those points where my opinion differs from that of Pareto.

If I am not mistaken, Pareto was originally an engineer and mathematician, and in economics he is an outstanding practitioner of the mathematical method developed by Cournot, Walras and Jevons. The present volume contains several mathematical formulations and proofs of propositions considered, but the mathematics is relegated to the notes, so that the text may quite well be read without any knowledge of mathematics. In general theoretical considerations he follows Walras closely—too closely, really, since some of the less successful ideas of the classical Walrasian work are taken over either directly or insufficiently improved, as I will endeavour to show.

In an introduction to the theoretical part of the book, the modern theory of subjective utility is first developed, a concept for which

[1] Two reviews in *Zeitschrift für Volkswirtschaft, Sozialpolitik und Verwaltung*, 1897, pp. 159–66, and 1899, pp. 95–100, of Vilfredo Pareto, *Cours d' économie politique*, professé à l'université de Lausanne. Lausanne: F. Rouge; Tome I, 1896, pp. viii, 430, and Tome II, 1897, pp. 426.

Pareto wishes to introduce the term *ophélimité* (from ὠφέλιμος, useful). He calls marginal utility *l'ophélimité élémentaire*—why not rather 'finale' or 'marginale,' since it refers to the *last* element? Like Edgeworth, Pareto stresses that the marginal utility does not in general depend only on the amount of the commodity in question, but to a greater or less extent on the available amounts of all the other commodities as well. If we regard the total utility of the combined stocks of commodities held as a function of all these stocks, the marginal utility of each commodity is the increment of this function relating to the acquisition of one unit of the commodity, or, to express it mathematically, the partial derivative of this function with respect to the quantity of the commodity in question.

According to Pareto, however, such a total utility function *will not always exist*; it does not exist in those cases where the utility depends not only on the quantities of commodities available, but also on the different *combinations* which may be practicable (p. 10, the footnote). This distinction seems to me superfluous, because it must obviously always be assumed that each subject chooses from the possible combinations of commodities that which is best suited to his requirements, and that he knows how to modify his initial consumption plans appropriately if a greater or smaller amount of the commodity in question is at his disposal during the particular consumption period. If this assumption is not made, it is not possible to speak of the marginal utility as a function of the commodity quantities held.

The most important criticism I have to make of Pareto in this field concerns his treatment of the question of mutual gain in free exchange—or, what amounts to the same thing, the economic significance of free competition. Only six years ago Marshall uttered a warning against regarding the gain of utility arising from free competition as a maximum *in the absolute sense*, as it is, strictly speaking, only the greatest possible gain achievable *at the prevailing prices*, i.e. at the equilibrium prices.[1]

The fact of the matter is simply this. The market prices under free competition are approximately the prices at which the supply and demand for the respective commodities balance one another, so that every trading subject is able to satisfy his desire to buy and sell. This cannot be the case for any other combination of prices: if the

---

[1] *Principles*, 2nd edition, pp. 506 ff. Böhm-Bawerk, in his well-known essay 'Grundzüge der Theorie des wirtschaftlichen Güterwertes' (Basic Principles of the Theory of Economic Value), *Conrads Jahrbücher*, Bd. XIII, 1886, in criticism of Schäffle, has also demonstrated the invalidity of this widespread notion.

supply of one commodity exceeds the demand, the demand must exceed the supply for the others. Consequently, even among those whom a price change has favoured, not everyone, perhaps nobody, will be able to satisfy all his inclinations to trade. But this does not mean to say that they may not have concluded more advantageous transactions than they could have done at the equilibrium prices of free competition.

It is not even possible to maintain that the *combined gain* of all the subjects involved is in the economic sense greatest under free competition. In fact it is possible to prove that this is the case only when certain definite conditions are fulfilled; otherwise it is possible to put forward a combination of prices for which the combined economic gain is greater than that attainable under free competition.[1]

Pareto appears to have quite overlooked this important fact, however. Throughout his book he reasons as if the gain from exchange were an absolute maximum under free competition, and that, moreover, it is so for each trading subject (which actually

---

[1] For each trading subject, the quantity of a commodity A received in exchange may be denoted by x, and the quantity of a commodity B given in the exchange by $y = px$, the prices being those obtaining under free competition. If ϕ is the total utility function for the subject in question, the change in this function corresponding to a *small* change in the price p, is given very nearly by the expression

$$\frac{\partial \phi}{\partial x} \Delta x - \frac{\partial \phi}{\partial y} (p\Delta x + x\Delta p)$$

But since $\dfrac{\partial \phi}{\partial x} = \dfrac{p\partial \phi}{\partial y}$, in accordance with the fundamental law of free exchange, this expression may be simplified to

$$-\frac{\partial \phi}{\partial y} . x . \Delta p$$

If the corresponding expressions for all the trading subjects are added (the x's being alternately positive and negative), we obtain

$$- \Sigma\left(\frac{\partial \phi}{\partial y} . x\right)\Delta p.$$

This expression is in general non-zero, and may therefore be made > 0 as a rule, since the sign of Δp may be changed as we wish. An exceptional case occurs when the marginal utility of the commodities is the same for everyone concerned (e.g. if they all own the same amount), whereupon the above expression becomes

$$- \frac{\partial \phi}{\partial y} . \Sigma x . \Delta p$$

which is identically zero, because $\Sigma x = 0$. The proof may easily be extended to any number of commodities.

143

involves a mathematical absurdity, since it is not possible to determine a series of magnitudes so that *several* variables depending on them *simultaneously* attain their maximum). In his treatment of production, distribution, the accumulation of capital, and even in his formulation of monetary theory, this erroneous conception recurs time and again, rendering his conclusions invalid. However, he is not as biased as some of the *harmony economists* in their easy optimism that the prevailing distribution of wealth is manifestly an infallibly holy outcome of free competition. But as soon as this distribution is accepted as a fact, Pareto says that free competition must provide everyone with the greatest satisfaction of needs (possible in the circumstances), since labour, land and capital are then applied to those uses which give the highest possible yield.

This argument seems attractive, but it is far from adequate. What can be proved is simply that under free competition the worker receives the greatest possible wage *compatible with the current state of rents and interest* (just as the landowners and capitalists obtain the greatest possible yield compatible with the current wage situation). But this does not in any way signify that the workers, for instance, could not by economic collaboration improve their position within limits, at the expense of rents and interest.

In this latter case, and similarly in the contrary case when the capitalists combine against the workers, it is admittedly a question of advantage to one side associated with a more or less definite disadvantage to the other. But there are cases where, without detriment to the interests of anyone concerned, the total gain of utility may be greater—occasionally considerably so—than that actually obtained under free competition such as that at present existing in the private sector. As Marshall, among others, has so beautifully shown,[1] this applies to all enterprises for which the 'law of increasing returns' is valid, for instance, to all enterprises such as transport companies, theatres, publishers of books and newspapers, which always, or nearly always, have certain 'general costs,' in consequence of which the costs fall proportionally as business increases. It is likely that Pareto would have been encouraged to revise his views very considerably if he had paid attention to the appropriate passages in Marshall, whom he has quoted himself as a matter of fact.

The theories of production and of capital are developed by Pareto in the same way as by Walras, except that he emphasises more strongly than his predecessor the capital aspect even of consumable

[1] *Principles*, 2nd edition, Bk. V, Chs. XII and XIII. Cf. also my *Finanstheoretische Untersuchungen* (Investigations in Public Finance) pp. 125–38.

commodities, which certainly makes the Walrasian definition of capital, 'commodities which serve production *more than once*,' all the more peculiar.

Nevertheless I have to repeat against Pareto the main substance of the objections I raised in my *Value, Capital and Rent* against Walras's method of procedure.

The exchange value of 'productive services,' i.e. labour and the utilisation of land and capital, is equal to the combined value of the consumption goods produced with their help, assuming that the entrepreneurial profits, over and above wages (including the salaries of the leaders of the enterprise), monopoly income, etc., are reduced to zero by the competition of the various entrepreneurs. The magnitude of the remuneration of each productive factor, like the exchange value of each consumption good, is therefore determined by supply and demand in the same way as in the simple exchange of commodities. The entrepreneur figures in the 'market for productive services' as a buyer, in the 'commodity market' as a seller, whereas the worker, the landowner and the capitalist are sellers in the former and buyers in the latter. Indeed, if these three categories are regarded in the most *general* sense, there is no other class of consumers.

So far, so good—the comprehensiveness of Walras's scheme cannot be denied—but it is here that the difficulties begin. Pareto says that the balance of production may be taken over any period, e.g. one calendar year, provided the period is the same for all branches of production. But it is obvious that we can scarcely expect any production to extend over this period. When finished consumption goods emerge from the production process at the end of the year, they will have started the year partly as raw material or even as half-finished goods; if there were only productive services to begin with, the year would generally end with only half-finished goods, or with only preliminary work concluded, which could not be sold on the 'product market.' Pareto believes that he can avoid this difficulty by explaining that 'raw materials may be treated as productive services in this respect.' Very true! But these productive services were applied not in the year in question but in a previous year (or else the goods in question are not sold until some later period); it is consequently impossible to enter them on the accounts for the current year. To grasp the implications of this oversight, we have only to consider that technical capital is also 'in this respect' equivalent to productive services, in the last analysis to the services of labour and land. If we followed Pareto's bookkeeping practices, we would arrive at the strange conclusion that

145

technical capital does not yield interest in the true sense, and that the product should be divided between the workers and the landowners.

E. Barone has recently shown in a really brilliant manner how Walras's theory of production may be completed, so that all theoretical blemishes are removed.[1] This is accomplished simply by adding another relation to the 'logical relations' formulated by Walras for the quantities concerned; that is to say, by relating them to the *length of the production period* or the investment period, thus bringing into the foreground this exceedingly fruitful idea, which was indicated by Jevons, but first exploited to the full by Böhm-Bawerk. Unfortunately this reasoning is quite alien to Pareto, apart from some apparently fortuitous suggestions on p. 40. After this introduction the rest of the book is taken up with an exhaustive discussion of the different types of capital. The first chapter, headed 'Les capitaux personels,' deals at length with the *question of population*.

Pareto is in the wider sense of the word a Malthusian; he shows conclusively that the present rate of increase of the population of Europe is quite exceptional, and that it must slow down considerably in the probably not too distant future. In the circumstances, his numerous jibes at Malthus rather surprise me, especially as they are most often directed against the legendary Malthus rather than the real Malthus. 'Malthus's errors' are due to the fact that, from the admitted indispensability of a not too rapid increase in the population for the welfare of a people, he drew 'the false conclusion that all other factors exert no influence' (?). He thus invalidates his own objections to socialism, says Pareto, for if the contribution of governments to the suffering of a people is so insignificant, it would be just as well to try a socialist system as any other.

Pareto here overlooks the fact that for Malthus the system of government, for all its real or alleged defects, is still of importance, since it originates and, so to speak, adapts itself under the pressure of the law of population. His main objection to communism or, as he expressed it, to 'systems of equality,' was that if parents ceased to be responsible for their children, the necessary restriction of the population could either not be accomplished or could only be realised by the imposition of repressive measures. Whether he was right in this we will not consider; but he was not guilty of the formal errors which Pareto attributes to him.

Regarding the well-known 'series,' Pareto states that Malthus said

[1] 'Studi sulle distribuzione,' *Giornale degli Economisti*, February, March 1896.

'the means of livelihood increase in an arithmetical progression'—which is 'definitely incorrect.' But such a silly statement has been uttered only by the legendary Malthus; what Malthus really said was quite different—that the means of livelihood in countries with an old-established culture does not increase in even this modest proportion, which would imply that subsistence in all twenty-five years (that is, the period in which the population could double under favourable circumstances) would increase by the same absolute amount as it constituted at the beginning of the century (as Malthus wrote). This has been completely confirmed up to now. Pareto stresses, however, that the population of England has almost two times doubled during the last century, but the wealth of the English people per individual has nevertheless increased during that time. In the first place we may remark that the period for this doubling is much longer than that assumed by Malthus—almost twice as long; and, moreover, it is well known that England obtains most of her foodstuffs from her colonies, so that she is in this respect something like an industrial town in a broad agricultural region. According to Pareto, Malthus was not less mistaken with regard to France, as he expressed in his political economy the fear that the unrestricted division of estates in France would lead to overpopulation and impoverishment of the country, 'if these consequences were not mitigated by great caution in conjugal life.' Malthus's error here is presumably that he could not predict with certainty this latter result (mitigation by caution)—which is surely excusable, especially as the connection which some recent writers have drawn between the sub-division of estates in France and the fall in the birth-rate there is still an open question, and is left as such by Pareto some pages farther on.

The chapter on circulating capital is prefaced with a lengthy section on money. It is difficult to see why Pareto should place monetary theory at the beginning, as it usually comes at the end, but it is to some extent due to his fundamental attitude to money, with which I am afraid I find myself unable to agree. He stresses (p. 181 and in several other places) that 'it cannot be repeated too often that money is properly only one kind of capital amongst many others used in production and exchange.' For my part, I would like to emphasise just the opposite. In my opinion it cannot be repeated too often that money is not just one kind of capital among many others, but something *sui generis*. The other forms of capital serve production and consumption by their *substance*, money only by the *meaning* people assign to it. There is thus never enough of the other forms of capital (up to a limit, at least); whether or not the world's stocks of money are larger or smaller is a matter of complete indifference, however. It is only the *function* of money that is of importance economically; but this function can be fulfilled just as well by half the amount of money as by twice as much. How could an economist fail to perceive such a palpable difference?

In accordance with this view of his Pareto (unlike Walras here) rejects all attempts to set up an invariable measure of value. He considers that all such attempts only infringe the law of a maximum of *ophélimité*; 'for if money becomes dearer because it is of greater service and not merely for some artificial reasons, then this is an expression of the condition for maximising utility, as in the case of all other goods' (p. 262). This entire reasoning is thus based on the much-mentioned theory of maximum gain under free exchange, whose invalidity I have already established. But what is 'artificial' and what 'natural' in such cases? The whole monetary system is ultimately artificial through and through. If a farmer borrows a certain amount of gold in order to improve his land or to buy out his co-heir, and in return undertakes to pay back an equal sum of gold after some years together with interest accruing thereon, also in gold, although his yield is corn and other farm products—has he not engaged in a thoroughly artificial business transaction? And when, as a consequence of gold becoming dearer, all commodity prices fall, so that he is obliged to redeem his capital debt with perhaps twice as much of his products as he would have needed to pay at the original prices, will he find any comfort in the thought that gold has only become dearer because each coin now 'renders greater service'?

Pareto shows himself yet more severe against inconvertible paper money, which he refers to throughout as 'false coinage'—which is rather exaggerated, since such money used as legal tender is not usually issued as anything other than what it really is. According to him, devaluation of paper currency delivers an unearned profit not only to all debtors but also, and more particularly, to all entrepreneurs, because, as experience shows, wages lag behind at the original low level for a long time—'at least some years'—in accordance with the law of inertia, despite the increase in the prices of all commodities.

But both these consequences are just as likely to occur if 'genuine' money suffered a depreciation of value—the famous 'maximum d'ophélimité' could do nothing about it. Moreover, although it is a fact that the workers have several times suffered from the issue of paper money, it is questionable whether the real reason for this is the one given here. It should be borne in mind that the issue of such money is usually accompanied by a *diminution in real capital*, because the Government by this measure takes over a considerable part of the country's circulating capital for non-productive purposes. Real wages must therefore fall, and the result would be more or less the same if the Government had, for instance, secured the necessary revenue by means of an internal loan, except that money wages would probably also decrease in that case. If, on the other hand, the issue of excess paper money occurred as a consequence of bank loans to private entrepreneurs on too easy interest conditions, it seems probable that the rise in prices would be in the main a *consequence* of the increase in money wages, so that the latter would occur first.

The rapid rise in wages in Germany and elsewhere after the Franco-Prussian war, when the world's supply of money increased by a considerable amount, illustrates that the effect of the law of inertia which is supposed to operate in the realm of wages is rather exaggerated. According to Pareto, the workers too are often interested in an increase in the quantity of money; but is this solely due to their ignorance, as he maintains?

Pareto is of the opinion that even during a crisis the issue of credit money does more harm than good, for in delaying the unavoidable price crash it prevents the crisis 'from liquidating' (whatever that may mean), lengthens it, and increases its intensity.

The history of monetary crises in England, where the temporary repeal of Peel's Bank Act has always proved to be the appropriate means of allaying the worst of the panic, does not appear to confirm this view.

Obscurities, and even contradictions, also occur in this section. The purchasing power of money is defined as the increment of welfare (*de bien-être*) that an individual can obtain if a very small additional amount (one unit) of gold is placed at his disposal. The purchasing power of money is thus *different* for different persons, and even for the same person in different wealth situations, and, as Pareto explicitly states, may rise or fall when *prices remain unchanged*, if the general level of the social welfare changes.

This is not the sense in which the term 'purchasing power of money' is customarily used, nor is it the sense in which Pareto himself later uses it. It is undoubtedly not easy to define this concept, but any acceptable definition must be such that the purchasing power of money remains unchanged when prices do not change.

Pareto objects to the customary methods of calculating the so-

149

called index numbers, that 'they pay no attention to the most important of all goods—labour—which, if taken into account, would alter all the results' (p. 281). The footnote on the same page leads us to conclude that he means by this *personal services* such as those provided by doctors and lawyers which do of course figure in our consumption in the wider meaning of the word, just as much as do commodities. There is nothing to object to in his comment; but for the sake of completeness house rents, etc., should also be included. Labour *as such* is a production factor, not a product. If we are to decide whether money has become dearer or cheaper relative to things consumed, the level of wages has as little to do with the index numbers as has the rate of interest or the rent of land.

The other two sections of this chapter, which deal with 'Savings and their Yield' (*l'épargne et son loyer*) and 'The Banks,' and the last chapter on 'Fixed Capital' (*les capitaux fonciers*) leave less scope for comment. Though there is a strange-sounding statement that 'since the payment of rent for goods cannot occur unless they are someone's property,' 'the socialists are right when they assert that in a state where capital is owned in common, interest on capital cannot exist. None the less the question of what would replace it, fascinating though it may be, has no place in the discussion of interest,' and so on (p. 315).

This is not at all in conformity with what Pareto maintains everywhere else—that the transition to a socialist state would *not* bring about any essential change in the organisation of production, the allocation of capital, and so on. If this were so, then everything would be practically as before with regard to the rate of interest, except that it would be paid to the state instead of to private persons.

In considering banking, Pareto once more stresses the distinction between a system with 'genuine' money (i.e. metal currency or convertible banknotes) and one with paper money. In the first case, a diminution of savings would compel the banks to raise their discount rate *immediately*, whereas in the latter case this consequence would make its appearance slowly and hesitantly, probably after formidable crises, such as have occurred 'in recent years in Italy and the United States' (p. 387).

There is a difference, as everyone will admit, but the word 'immediately' must be taken *cum grano salis*. In recent years, when the principal banks of Europe were overstocked with gold several times over, and the permissible limit for note issues usually far from attained, it is difficult to see how a small decrease in savings could *compel* the banks to raise their rate of interest. The real difference between metal and paper currency is in the last analysis that the former enjoys general (international) credit, whereas the latter enjoys only local credit. The banks of a particular country, if they must redeem their notes, are forced to adapt their interest policy to their stock of currency metal, exchange rates, and so on. But if the banks of all countries have the same interest policy, for whatever reason it may be so, are they not in complete control of this policy? And even with a system of 'genuine' money, are there not wide limits within which they may effect at will a raising or lowering of all prices, before the exhaustion of their bullion reserves compels them to alter their rate of interest? These are questions regularly evaded in the discussion of monetary matters, though it is obvious that they are among the most important.

It is just because I have so high an opinion of Pareto's works and of the school to which he belongs that I have permitted myself this detailed criticism of his views. It must be admitted in all fairness that some of the questions dealt with belong to difficult realms of political economy, where no one—and certainly not myself—could describe his own ideas as definitely correct. But in other cases it seems to me that Pareto could easily have avoided the errors I have mentioned by a more careful consideration of the matter, or by more thorough perusal of the relevant modern literature. The value of the book is in any case considerable, but it would thereby have been greatly enhanced.

I look forward with the greatest interest to the second volume of this work, which is to deal with economic organisation, distribution and consumption.

II

Lack of time has hitherto prevented me from complementing my review of the first part of Pareto's work, previously published in this journal, with a similar one for the second part, which had already appeared at that time. This is in fact no easy task. The book is too important, and coloured by too warm a conviction to be disposed of superficially as mere hack work. Nevertheless it seems to me that it unfortunately contains not a few inadequate, and even dubious, passages, which should be pointed out in the interest of the author himself and of his readers. Because of shortage of space, I must again confine myself to points on which my views diverge from those of Pareto. The excellent qualities of the book, its abundance of matter, the concise, often original, and in general sufficiently clear presentation, the intimate union of empirical and rational methods on the classical pattern, speak for themselves, and seem already to have attained full recognition.

The most damaging fault, one which in my opinion distorts the whole of Pareto's reasoning, is that already mentioned in my review of the first volume, namely, Pareto's erroneous conception of the economic significance of free competition. He takes as established —and considers that he himself has proved it strictly mathematically —that free competition implies the greatest possible total of satisfaction or *ophélimité* conformable with the actual distribution of property, not only to the society as a whole, but to each class of it, and even to each member of each class. As previously shown in some detail, this is entirely incorrect. It is only in special cases, e.g. when all the subjects in an economy are in precisely the same economic situation, possessing the same amounts of capital and land, and so on, that free competition has this property, and then only for the system as a whole. It is obviously inconceivable that every individual should attain a maximum of satisfaction.

It is interesting to observe how Pareto reacts when this unfortunate idiosyncrasy comes up against facts. For instance, he admits (pp. 137 ff.) that trade unions are able to exert an important influence on the welfare of their members and of the working class as a whole. But according to him this can only happen either if they help to overcome economic friction for the workers—enabling them to exploit a favourable economic situation, for instance—or if they encourage a higher standard of life—by inducing their members to decrease their numbers by emigration or a lowered birth-rate—or if they lighten the pressure of taxation for the workers by organising their political activity. Otherwise, which means principally with regard to the important problem of the distribution of commodities, there is in his opinion with one exception to be touched upon shortly, 'no further room' for associations of workers (p. 135) in the economic equilibrium system, the conditions of which are sufficiently determined by the principle of free competition. I think this contention is altogether incorrect. A correct theory would show that, just as the economic collaboration of employers can force down wages to the bare living minimum, the collaboration of workers can bring about a raising of wages, which has no other theoretical limit than the direction of the entire yield of land and capital into wages. That the further consequences of such action could be rather to the disadvantage of the workers need not be considered in this connection.

However, with regard to the so-called 'coefficients of production' —the amount of capital and labour necessary for the production of

152

unit quantity of a commodity—Pareto has rightly shown (pp. 84 ff.) that free competition on the whole will lead to the same result as, for instance, the economic activity of a socialist state which endeavours directly and consciously to attain the social maximum of commodities from the means available. Thus, he remarks, if the present total product were *distributed* appropriately, there would be no fundamental difference with regard to the ultimate goal between the present society and a socialist one. Unfortunately he subsequently forgets all too frequently the important word *if* in this statement, or he confuses this statement (cf. p. 101, § 735) with the erroneous one mentioned above, that the relatively best possible distribution of commodities would be ensured by the system of free competition. Moreover, he makes the tacit assumption in his proof that, in the first place, current production always knows beforehand exactly how it is to adapt itself to the needs of the society, so that there is no 'anarchic' squandering of productive forces, and further, that the entrepreneurs are always in a position to produce on the scale most favourable economically—altogether propositions that the socialists, as we know, in general most animatedly contest.

In a rather inconsistent fashion, Pareto then (p. 100) stresses that the workers are able to modify the distribution of commodities to their own advantage, because they can effect unilateral changes in the above-mentioned coefficients of production, e.g. by refusing to work with certain machines. But such behaviour on their part would inevitably involve a 'destruction of wealth,' and in Pareto's opinion would inflict a loss on the other members of the society greater than the possible gain to the workers. The former remark is probably correct, but not the latter; for if profit and loss are conceived of in the subjective sense, as they are by Pareto in the lines that follow, they are not simply proportional to the quantities of commodities gained or lost. It is possible that the entrepreneur loses more money or goods than the workers gain, but the gain of *ophélimité* to the latter is nevertheless greater than the loss to the former.

The passages referred to all occur in the chapter on 'Production.' The doctrinaire overestimation of free competition recurs in the next chapter, which deals with 'Commerce.' Pareto shows with p_{xyc} and p_{xyb} (pp. 222 ff.) that the imposition of an import or export tariff always leads to an increase of the direct and indirect coefficients of production for the country concerned, hence to a net loss of utility. But a closer examination of his reasoning reveals that it depends entirely on the tacit assumption that the measures in question have no effect at all on the coefficients of production and commodity prices in the *other* countries. This assumption cannot be accepted without justification: the opposite contention, with its well-known consequences, is in fact one of the most familiar arguments of the protectionists.

It does not occur to Pareto to ask whether the removal of certain tariffs would not have an unfavourable effect on the internal distribution of commodities, depressing wages in favour of capital profit, for instance, though this is quite conceivable in view of what has been said above.

In short, he has oversimplified the complicated theoretical problems of foreign trade,[1] which of course does not prevent him from being for the most part in the right. His many practical examples are in fact very convincing.

Whether the viewpoint from which he judges commercial speculation is also correct is less certain. It is true that speculation helps to establish a more appropriate economic distribution, but this by no means exhausts its economic significance, and least of all the significance of arbitrage transactions. Recent findings in this field have indicated that these may be regarded as a sort of *insurance* transaction, in which the producers and merchants play the part of buyers of insurance and the speculators that of sellers. It cannot be reasonably maintained that only those who have some rational *prior knowledge* of future prices should speculate, as Pareto suggests. The very reason why transactions about the future such as shipping and fire insurance contracts exist seems as a rule to be bound up with the *impossibility* of such prior knowledge.

Regarding *crises*, which are treated in the fourth chapter of the second book, Pareto puts forward certain ideas which I think may be described as more notable for their originality than for their profundity. Whatever one may think about this difficult matter, it does at least seem certain that crises arise only because of *faulty* judgment of the economic situation. Such errors, made by various persons in various directions, cancel one another in the ordinary way; but they may in special circumstances reinforce one another,

---

[1] Pareto is guilty of yet another oversight in this connection. He mentions (pp. 218 ff.) that a transition to free trade may be accompanied by a *lasting* change (e.g. a decrease) in the general level of commodity prices, and states that the producer will therefore suffer, especially *if he has contracted debts* on which he has to pay interest in the form of a fixed amount of money. Two lines lower down, however, he makes the peculiar statement that this disadvantage to the producers is only transitory, disappearing as soon as economic equilibrium is restored. This can of course not be true, when the producers are burdened with money debts on which interest has to be paid.

causing either too great a tension or slackness in the market. Pareto's explanation bears only a superficial resemblance to this view, for in some vague way he associates a rhythmic movement with both consumption and production, and crises are supposed to arise from mutual reinforcement of these rhythms. He undertakes to show (p. 283 and elsewhere), once again with the help of mathematics, that even with the most simple conceivable assumptions, excluding any faulty judgment of the situation, such a rhythm of alternate expansion and contraction of consumption might very well set in. However, the success of his proof is no more than apparent, owing to some very striking mistakes of mathematics and logic.[1]

[1] It is assumed that a person who daily receives a certain sum of money, r_s, saves part of it, and devotes the rest to the consumption of—for the sake of simplicity—a single type of good (A). The satisfaction pertaining to the savings on the one hand, and to the consumption on the other, depends therefore solely on the amount of money saved daily, r_e, and the amount of goods consumed, r_a, or may be considered as functions (the marginal utilities), ϕ_a and ϕ_e, of each of these quantities. The former satisfaction tends to increase savings, the latter consumption. But, as Pareto correctly points out, even if these two forces are not in equilibrium, the consequent changes in consumption, etc., will not take place *at once*, but only after some delay. In other words, forces of inertia ('the force of habit') come into operation, and analogously to the so-called resistive forces of mechanics, oppose every change in consumption or saving, and are only gradually overcome.

(The idea in question is actually developed by Pareto himself on pp. 9 ff., unfortunately in a rather careless fashion.) These forces, of which nothing more is known, are denoted by f_a and f_e.

By analogy with the principle of virtual work in mechanics, we have

$$(\phi_a - f_a)\delta r_a + (\phi_e - f_e)\delta r_e = 0$$
or
$$\phi_a - f_a = P_a(\phi_e - f_e),$$

where p_a denotes the money price of the good (A), assumed to be constant. We also have the equation

$$r_a \cdot p_a + r_e = r_s.$$

Pareto now puts $r_a = a + x$, where a is an arbitrary constant and x a variable that may be assumed very small when necessary. He then expands the difference $f_a - p_a \cdot f_e$ in powers of x as far as the *second*. He says then that the constant a may be so chosen that the coefficient of first power of x *disappears*, so that the expansion now contains only the second power. However, this is actually *impossible*, as could be seen *a priori*. Each coefficient contains the sum of two quantities (not the difference, which Pareto obtains through an error of calculation), and these two quantities must be negative since they are derivatives of the marginal utility functions.

He further assumes that the resistive forces are proportional to a power of the 'acceleration' (of the consumption and savings respectively), and he states that this power must be an *even* one, 'pour que la résistance au changement de vitesse ait lieu également dans les deux sens.' But the *opposite* is true: since the resistive

155

Pareto's treatment of this subject seems to me to be not entirely satisfactory in other respects as well. According to him, the upward period of a crisis is characterised by increasing consumption and increasing *production* too. I very much doubt whether in the latter case the opposite does not apply, at least as regards consumption goods. Pareto himself says that large amounts of capital are immobilised in such periods. This of course means that a larger proportion of the available workers are engaged in *preparatory work*, which yields nothing for the moment. It is then impossible for the others to produce consumption goods on the usual scale. It seems likely that this is one cause of the rise in prices.

Pareto's concluding remark about the part played by nature in crises in the economy clearly stands or falls with his view on the necessity of the rhythmic movement mentioned previously, for which he has not been able to advance a shadow of a proof.

We finally come to the third book, where the author develops in the first chapter his well-known theory of the *distribution of incomes*, which he himself regards—not entirely without justification—as a notable scientific achievement. He proves that the distribution of incomes in different societies and even in the same society at different times may be expressed, almost without exception, to a sufficient approximation by a single very simple mathematical formula, but with somewhat different values for the constants involved, and by a formula, at that, which differs from the curve of random variations encountered in probability theory. This proof is without doubt a very noteworthy achievement, and one which promises to yield fruitful results on further investigation. This praise cannot be

---

forces oppose both increases and decreases of the rate of consumption or of saving, the mathematical expressions for them must contain *odd* powers. It is simplest if they are taken to be proportional to the *first* power of the acceleration, as in mechanics. If we make this assumption, and if we terminate the expansion in powers of x at the first power, which as already mentioned cannot be zero, we obtain in place of the differential equation given by Pareto (p. 284), which leads to periodic solutions, the following very simple one:

$$\frac{dx}{dt} = 1 - mx,$$

which integrates to

$$x = \frac{1}{m} - ke^{-mt}$$

where 1 and m are given constants and k an integration constant.

Expressing this result in words: the daily consumption approaches a certain most advantageous limit continuously and always *from the same side*—just as simple *a priori* considerations require it to do.

extended to the rest of his reasoning, where he endeavours to apply the proposition and exploit it for his own general liberal standpoint. He deals with the much-discussed question of whether and under what circumstances the inequality in the distribution of incomes becomes smaller or greater in different countries. Pareto remarks, quite correctly, that this expression is rather vague, and should be replaced by something more exactly defined. He cites a passage from Leroy-Beaulieu, according to which the progress of the welfare of the lower classes of the population is at present more rapid than that of the middle and upper classes and in the future will be increasingly so. Leroy-Beaulieu describes this as a 'rapprochement des conditions sociales,' à 'moindre inégalité entre les fortunes.' In supposed conformity with this, Pareto puts forward the definition that the inequality of incomes has diminished if the number of poor decreases with respect to the number of rich, or what amounts to the same thing, with respect to the total population; and in general, if the number of persons with incomes below a certain limit x *decreases*[1] relative to the number with incomes above it (and this for all values of x) (p. 120).

He then undertakes to establish a result which he prints in heavy type (and which completely contradicts the formula for income distribution previously mentioned): *a diminution of the inequality of incomes can only occur if the total of incomes increases faster than the population.*

The steps of the proof are correct, and yet, if I am not greatly mistaken, the whole proposition rests on a *self-delusion.* Closer inspection reveals that Pareto's definition does not at all coincide with what Leroy-Beaulieu intended, nor with what is customarily understood by the equalisation of incomes. Leroy-Beaulieu refers to an improvement of the economic situation of the lower classes during which the position of the upper classes remains relatively unchanged. This is equivalent to an alteration of the social pyramid, in which the apex remains relatively fixed, while the base is pushed upwards, producing a compression or flattening of structure. Pareto's definition implies rather that for every level of incomes, the part of the social pyramid below the limit in question becomes relatively smaller than before, and the part above relatively larger. It can be seen without mathematics that this need not always correspond to a compression of the social pyramid, but may equally well

---

[1] The text has 'augmentent,' not 'diminuent'; but this must be a printing error —despite Pareto's explicit assurance that he means 'this and nothing else.' He himself uses the definition above subsequently.

correspond to an elongation in certain circumstances (i.e. to *increased* inequality of incomes), according to whether the apex or the base remains relatively unchanged. Pareto's general formula gives us no information about this question at all. Thus he has in reality proved *nothing*.

In view of the complexity of this particular subject, I must admit the possibility that I have misunderstood Pareto on some point. But it seems to me that revision of the section concerned is called for even in that case, simply to clarify the matter.

The faults mentioned here—if my criticisms are in fact justified— are the more serious since the more important of them involve erroneous use of the rational or mathematical method, which Pareto is particularly anxious to show his readers is superior to the ordinary procedure. But I think it would be wrong to underrate the virtues of the book merely because of these and similar faults, especially as they are in part due to oversights. Even if it is necessary to read the book with caution, no one will read it without profit. For, whatever defects one may detect in Pareto, one can *never* accuse him of the very worst of all in a writer: *lack of ideas*.

VILFREDO PARETO'S
MANUEL D'ÉCONOMIE POLITIQUE[1]

DURING 1897 and 1899 I discussed at some length in this journal the two parts of Pareto's *Cours d'économie politique* that had then appeared.[2] The present work, which is essentially a translation of that published in Italian in 1906, is not merely a continuation of the *Cours*; it contains a great deal of quite new material, and draws with profit on the author's assiduous work in the field of theoretical political economy. Unfortunately it also contains—though not to the same extent as the *Cours*—many propositions and assertions which seem to me doubtful or even incorrect. I hope to deal with the most important of these in the following pages, though I wish to point out that the questions at issue are *very* complicated, and that I do not put forward my own opinions as in any sense infallible. Pareto once applied to himself the Italian proverb, 'solo chi non fa, non falla'—only he who does nothing is never wrong. He added that 'la critique est aisée, l'art est difficile.' Nevertheless, there can be no doubt that the work of the critic is not always easy, if it is to be useful and to the point.

The book is divided into two parts, of which the first, and more expansive, is intended for readers with little mathematics. An 'appendix' of 133 pages is also included. This is a comprehensive presentation of the theories of consumption and exchange, of production and distribution, which are only briefly referred to in the earlier

---

[1] Review in *Zeitschrift für Volkswirtschaft, Sozialpolitik und Verwaltung*, 1913, pp. 132-51, of Vilfredo Pareto, *Manuel d'économie politique*, Paris: Giard et Brière, 1909, pp. 695.

[2] It appears that these reviews have not come to the notice of Pareto, or he would surely have paid attention in his new publication to at least a few of the many comments I made there. Regarding one of the points taken up by me—his attempt to use the elementary propositions on consumption and saving to build a theory of crises, and even to give it a mathematical formulation—he does now state quite frankly (*Manuel*, p. 216, footnote) that the whole argument was incorrect and based on erroneous considerations. Of course, he may quite well have arrived at this conclusion on his own, by a simple examination of the formulae he used.

sections of the book. The appendix requires the reader to know some mathematics—in fact rather a lot, since the subtle formal language of the calculus of variations is used in one or two places. This part of the work will therefore be a closed book to the majority of readers, though from several points of view it is the most important and interesting. On this account I intend to devote most attention to it here, and will endeavour to present the main ideas and my comments on them in a generally comprehensible form. I admit, however, that it is only after repeated reading that I have been able to grasp the author's meaning, and perhaps not always with complete success then. The paucity of words in his definitions or elucidation of formulae sometimes exceeds the permissible limits. He attributes this to the lack of space, but if he had, say, simply sacrificed the first two chapters of the book and the greater part of the seventh, which are for the most part taken up with sociological considerations with little bearing on the real core of the book, he could have gained some two hundred pages, and would have had more than enough space to lighten the heavier parts—which include *more* than just the 'mathematical' sections.

The first part of the appendix is occupied with the question of whether, and to what extent, it is possible to devise a proper measure of the marginal utility (in Pareto's terminology, *ophélimité élémentaire*) of a commodity, and for the total utility of a commodity or combination of goods. According to Pareto, this is possible only under one of two conditions. Either the marginal utility of a commodity must depend solely on the stock held of *this* commodity, and not on the possession of stocks of other goods; or we must have the special case (in my opinion, scarcely conceivable) where the marginal utility in question depends only on the quantities of goods owned, though the total utility also depends on the *order of their consumption*.

The method of proof is not without interest from the mathematical point of view, although it depends on an *illusion*, as I presently hope to show. Pareto states that he begins from the *indifference curve* introduced by Edgeworth (the combinations of commodity quantities which the consumer regards as equally satisfactory). He makes considerable use of this concept elsewhere in his book, but it is easy to express his argument without using this approach, interesting though it is.

Suppose that a boy has 10 apples and 100 nuts. Let us further assume that in order to obtain 1 more apple he will give *at most* 9 nuts, but that he will ask for at least 11 nuts in exchange for 1 of his apples. *In his present economic position* he therefore values 1 apple and about 10 nuts equally highly. If we assume that the pleasure of eating a nut is the same for each nut of 10, we may assume that he values an apple as highly as exactly 10 nuts; in other words, the ratio of the *marginal utilities* of apples and nuts is 10 : 1 for him at that instant. Experience may show that this ratio changes with his stocks of apples and nuts, in such a way that when the number of apples increases the ratio *decreases* proportionally, and when the number of nuts increases it *increases* proportionally; so that if both stocks increase in the same proportion, the ratio of the marginal utilities remains unchanged.

We may express this mathematically by saying that if x is the number of apples in the boy's possession at this instant and y the number of nuts, and ϕ_x, ϕ_y the marginal utilities of apples and nuts respectively,

$$\phi_x : \phi_y = y : x.$$

It is well known that the law of *exchange* may be theoretically derived entirely on the basis of such a relationship which will in general be different for every individual, though it may be considered to be given approximately by experience. On the other hand, it does *not* suffice for a proper measure—whether absolute or relative—of the magnitude of each *separate* marginal utility, that is to say, for each individual in each economic situation. Nor, therefore, does it suffice for the formulation of a measure of the total utility. It should not be supposed, in the case we are considering, that ϕ_x is proportional to y, and ϕ_y to x. This would mean that the satisfaction of obtaining another apple depended *only* on the stock of nuts, and the satisfaction of another nut only on the stock of apples, whereas it is in fact clear that each satisfaction depends primarily on the size of the stock of the *corresponding* commodity. There are an infinite number of possible expressions for ϕ_x and ϕ_y in terms of *both* x and y—mathematically simultaneous functions of x and y—which fulfil the above relation.[1]

Consequently, according to Pareto, the measure of utility will in general be entirely indeterminate, though it could be expressed in

[1] However, for reasons we will not elaborate here, ϕ_x and ϕ_y always are restricted to expressions which are the partial derivatives with respect to x and y of one and the same function. In the particular case we are considering $\phi_x = y$. $F(x . y)$, $\phi_y = x . F(x . y)$, where F is an arbitrary function of the product $x . y$. In fact, the general expressions ϕ_x and ϕ_y are in customary mathematical notation the partial derivatives with respect to x and y of the function $\phi(x, y)$, which in this case would give expression for the amount of *total* utility of both stocks.

161

terms of a separate index. Utility cannot be directly measured—Pareto denies the possibility of such direct measurement in the elementary part of his book (Ch. IV, §33). In the case where the marginal utility of apples depends only on the stock of apples, and that of nuts only on the stock of nuts—that is to say, when ϕ_x is a function of x only, and ϕ_y of y only—Pareto says that all ambiguity is removed, and it is not difficult to see that then ϕ_x and ϕ_y are given by the expressions

$$\phi_x = \frac{A}{x}, \ \phi_y = \frac{A}{y}$$

where A is a constant factor of proportionality. Summation (integration) then gives an expression for the total utility, $\phi(x, y)$, of apples and nuts, referred to a particular initial situation:

$$\phi(x, y) - \phi(1, 1) = A(\log x + \log y),$$

A being the same constant as above, and the logarithms natural. The factor A (and the initial value $\phi(1, 1)$) is still indeterminate, but under the given assumptions it could be asserted that the total utility of apples and nuts increases *logarithmically* with the stocks of the same (determined for a certain consumption period), that is, that it increases (decreases) in arithmetic progression when the stock of one commodity (or both) increases (decreases) in geometric progression.

This would indeed be a remarkable result: *indirectly*, by the simple comparison of two (simultaneous) marginal utilities, to obtain a measure for each of them and, moreover, for the total utility of the commodities in question! Unfortunately Pareto overlooks the fact that his assumption—that the marginal utility of a particular commodity is dependent only on the stock of that commodity—necessarily implies that the marginal utility may be *directly* measured. It is of course quite *feasible* that the desire for a further apple should depend only on the number of apples already possessed (and similarly for nuts). The *confirmation* of this, however, requires the comparison of the desire for an apple *in each of two different economic situations*, where the number of nuts available for consumption is different and the number of apples the same. If the desire for an apple does not change, the assumption is borne out, and so on.

If the assumption is *not* borne out, it would have been just as easy to establish, for instance, that with a stock of twice as many nuts the acquisition of three-quarters of an apple would give as much satisfaction as the acquisition of one apple in the original situation, and with half the number of nuts, the acquisition of one and a half apples would give as much satisfaction as that of one apple originally. Suppose it is established in this way that the marginal utility of apples (with the stock of them unchanging) varies in proportion to the square root of the number of nuts, and likewise for the marginal utility of nuts with respect to the stock of apples. Then consideration of the original equation (see p. 161 above) yields in the same way two expressions for the marginal utilities

$$\phi_x = A\sqrt{\frac{x}{y}}, \ \phi_y = A\sqrt{\frac{y}{x}}$$

and for the total utility, reckoned from the origin, the function

$$\phi(x, y) = 2A\sqrt{x \cdot y},$$

where ϕ_x and ϕ_y are the partial derivatives of this latter function. It is thus possible to obtain unambiguous measures of the marginal utilities and the total combined utility, even though the former depend on the stocks of *both* commodities, *contrary* to the condition stated by Pareto.[1]

As to Pareto's *second* case, where the total utility depends on the order of consumption, though the marginal utilities depend only on the amounts of the commodities held, it is hardly worth wasting many words, in my opinion. In the first place, the whole supposition seems to me to be implausible, as I have already mentioned. If we suppose that a farmer could be compelled by some governmental decree to use the whole of his stock of ice in winter and the whole of his stock of fuel in summer instead of the other way about, this would obviously have a marked effect not only on the total utility of the two goods, but also on the marginal utility of each of them. Normally a slight addition to his stocks of both would probably be welcome; in the situation we are considering, on the other hand, he would most decidedly decline any increase. But if for the sake of argument we are prepared to accept Pareto's assumption,[2] the objection previously advanced still holds good: the observation that

[1] The difficulty of a proper measurement of utility or marginal utility really lies in the fact that it is necessary to compare two satisfactions which occur in two different situations, and which are therefore separated *in time*. This presupposes a good memory: whether it is on that account to be regarded as 'impossible,' I leave to the psycho-physicists to decide.

[2] In one place, on p. 553, the marginal utility functions P_x, T_t, etc., are also taken to be dependent on the order of consumption. This must be a printing error; otherwise the whole thing is quite incomprehensible to me.

there is such a relation as the one in question obviously involves the comparison of the marginal utilities of one of the commodities in two different situations—where the order of consumption is different. Such a comparison is equivalent to a direct measurement of the marginal utilities, however. To use Pareto's roundabout, indirect method would be to force doors already open.[1]

The next point gives less scope to objections of principle. Pareto develops in an elegant fashion the well-known equations of Walras for exchange under free competition and at the same time endeavours to make the phenomena of supply and demand more comprehensible by a discussion of the higher derivatives of the utility function. That is much to be appreciated, if only it were not made unnecessarily difficult to read by carelessness on the part of the author. For instance, on pp. 876 and 877 there are no less than seven manuscript or printing errors which obscure the meaning to some extent (besides the assignment of two incorrect numbers to equations); and on p. 581 two different symbols ($M_{3 \cdot 1}$ and R_2) are

[1] Pareto states that he was induced to take up this enquiry—to me of little value—by a remark of his countryman, the mathematician Volterra. But I consider that what he refers to is to be regarded in quite a different light.

It is a matter of an ordinary differential equation of the first order, which might be derived approximately from experience by means of appropriate observations, and which after integration gives the system of indifference lines or surfaces (etc.) valid for the individual in question. Volterra points out that when three or more commodities are involved, this differential equation may prove to be unintegrable. Pareto seems to think that this would happen under the above-mentioned highly artificial conditions, where the total utility depends on the order of consumption, whereas the marginal utility or the ratio of the marginal utilities of the commodities in question depends only on the amount consumed. Another, and much simpler, explanation may be given, however: the simultaneous existence of *several* relations between the amounts of commodities consumed.

Our consumption of *provisions* is a good example here. Suppose that a person makes his daily fare of three foods—say bacon, peas and potatoes. Then, neither indifference surfaces nor indifference lines exist for him, not even in the proper sense a *choice* of or preference for a certain combination of these commodities, because, if he is to live and not to starve, he must evidently consume fairly well-determined quantities of all three foods in order to obtain the physiologically necessary amounts of fats, protein and carbohydrates (we will disregard the possibility mentioned recently that these nutrients may be substituted for one another). It is not until a fourth food (e.g. bread) becomes available to him that he has a choice between different combinations of these four commodities, not until there are five commodities, does a system of indifference lines appear (a simple infinity of variations between the commodities), and not until there are six do indifference surfaces appear, and so on. The last two cases are thus the first where a differential equation depending on his individual taste exists, although it is obvious that the differential equation will as a rule be unintegrable without *other* relations to eliminate the necessary number of variables.

used in the same formula for quantities actually identical. Moreover, the theorem on p. 578 (at the end of §49) is *false* as far as I can see: the author has made a mistake in the sign of one of the quantities involved. The error is fortunately of no great consequence, although he does refer to the result on a later occasion.

More important to me is the lack of sufficient emphasis on the fact that economic equilibrium under free competition always constitutes a problem which is partly *indeterminate*—and in the case of only two (trading) subjects exchanging, for the greater part indeterminate. Admittedly the theory provides the necessary number of 'equations' for free competition on the open market, when it is assumed that a definite system of equilibrium prices is in operation from the start. But this assumption is only fulfilled approximately in reality, and is quite inappropriate for individual barter outside the market.[1] Pareto, however, only deals with this case as a preparatory step to the general theory of the market, and he considers it to be of slight practical importance, as Marshall does too. But this seems not to be true: in our day, when a 'price war' is being waged between more or less distinct opposing armies—employers and employees, buying and selling cartels, and so on—it is obvious that we have quite good instances of individual (isolated) exchange. The economic theorist should be on his guard against applying to such phenomena conclusions or 'laws' which have been formulated on the basis of assumptions referring to situations entirely different in their main features.

Regarding *monopolistic* pricing (especially when production is excluded), Pareto is, in my opinion, guilty of a serious error of reasoning. He stresses—and even 'proves' (which is not particularly difficult)—that *two* (or more) monopolists cannot exist side by side in the same commodity branch. This is self-evident if the maximum profit of a monopolist is considered in the absolute sense. But he then states that monopolistic positions in *different* groups of commodities may very well be compatible with each other. Actually, however,

---

[1] In order to obtain the necessary number of equations in this latter case, Pareto assumes—without attempting to justify the assumption—that the two subjects engaged in the exchange must 'move' along certain curves, which are *predetermined* apart from a single parameter. If we consider as such curves two right lines with their common direction undetermined, what this assumption amounts to is simply that the amounts of commodities exchanged must be in the same ratio as the marginal utilities *after* the exchange. This is not generally true for isolated exchange, however, as Edgeworth showed some time ago (*Giornale degli Economisti*, 1891). Cf. Marshall, *Principles*, Appendix 12, and my *Value, Capital and Rent*, pp. 61 ff.

compatibility is as impossible here as in the first case. Pareto's proof depends on the assumption that the price of one of the monopolised commodities is *fixed* for the moment. In other words, he poses the problem of making the profit of each monopolist a maximum, while *assuming* that the other monopolist or monopolists maintain the prices of their goods at the level they have already reached. Such a setting of the problem is not self-contradictory, of course. One could likewise consider, in the case of two or more monopolists in the same branch of commodities, the problem of maximum profit for one of them when the others persist with the *sales levels* they have already reached. As we know, Cournot dealt with the problem of two or more monopolists in this way. However, this assumption is also somewhat arbitrary, though I do not think it is implausible.[1]

Pareto gives a correct enough presentation of the theory of *production* and of exchange under the influence of production, if we accept his general assumptions—which we will consider later. Amongst other things, he quite correctly points out that a proper equilibrium with uniform selling-prices is impossible for productive activity which follows the Marshall 'law of increasing returns'; for instance, when the only costs occurring are certain general ones and, in addition, special costs of unvarying relative size. He treats the problem of dumping admirably from this approach in an earlier part of the book. Nevertheless, it would have been more correct to say that economic equilibrium cannot occur under free competition with such assumptions. For the entrepreneur who *first* extends his production would be able to drive all his competitors from the field, until a single monopoly or monopolistic combination was attained. On the other hand, if it is assumed that the unit cost follows the law of *decreasing* returns—i.e. that it increases relatively as the magnitude of production increases—an assumption often more in accord with reality—each competitor will sooner or later arrive at an optimum

[1] Pareto's treatment of this case is based on the assumption that each of the two monopolists (in the same branch of commodities) regulates his price or his sales in such a way that he will receive a maximum profit, assuming that his competitors continue with the *profit* they already have. If this is so, it is easy to see that the two conditional equations (in Cournot's sense) are temporarily *identical*, and equilibrium (neutral) must therefore occur at *every* price. By itself, this assumption is only one of the many possible, and at that, one of the least plausible. If it is introduced into the other case (monopolists in different commodities), the result obtained directly from Pareto's formula is *quite the same*, since equations (93) on p. 598 must be *completely* differentiated in terms of p_y and p_z. It is rather curious but also instructive that such a practised mathematician as Pareto could have overlooked this.

level of production (as Pareto himself points out in another place). When there are a sufficient number of enterprises to provide active competition, each of them may be considered as a given production unit, and the law of 'constant returns' will then operate for that entire branch of the economy—more or less as in agriculture.[1]

The rest of the apprendix deals mainly with the intricate problem of 'Maximum *d'ophélimité*,' that is, the question of whether, and to what extent, free exchange, production and distribution under omnilateral free competition are able to ensure the greatest possible total utility in the social sense.[2] From what Pareto said on this subject in his *Cours d'économie politique*, I could not then draw any other conclusion than that he associated himself with Walras's viewpoint in this respect. According to Walras, each of the trading subjects will obtain the greatest possible profit compatible with *a uniform system of prices* (and with the original economic position of each of them). This viewpoint is of course quite untenable, as even the simple proposition on monopoly profit shows. Furthermore, it cannot even be stated that the combined profit of both or all the trading subjects is a maximum under such circumstances—although Launhardt wrongly believed that he had proved just this. It can in fact be strictly demonstrated that the proposition is only true under very special conditions, i.e. when all the subjects are initially equal economically; otherwise, it would always be theoretically possible to replace the system of competitive prices by another yielding an increase in the total utility (see the footnote in the first of my reviews mentioned earlier).

However, Pareto has protested in later articles in *Giornale degli economisti* that his viewpoint has been confused with that of Walras. In order to preserve the proposition about the maximum *d'ophélimité* under free competition, he now puts forward a peculiar definition of the concept, to the following effect (*Manuel*, VI, 33, and Appendix, §89): 'We say that the members of a group in a certain position enjoy a maximum *d'ophélimité*, when it is impossible to move even a little from this position in such a way that the utility pertaining to *each* member of the group increases *or decreases*' (the italics are mine—

[1] The well-known law of diminishing returns from *land* has quite a different significance, and should not be confused with the above term, as, unfortunately, it only too often is—even by Marshall on occasion.

[2] In the well-known discussion of the productivity of a national economy in the general assembly of 'Der Verein für Sozialpolitik' (Wien 1909), these questions were touched upon on several occasions, though in such a superficial way that opinions in themselves quite compatible were made to appear irreconcilable opposites.

K. W.). The last addition sounds very peculiar; if the utility cannot *decrease*, it would have been just as reasonable to speak of a *minimum d'ophélimité*.

What is meant, however, is simply that, in the situation referred to, every *infinitely small* change is accompanied by a profit for the one and a loss for the others involved, or if there should happen to be a loss for all, it would be of a higher order of smallness, and therefore, practically speaking, zero. As Pareto himself points out, *finite* deviations from the situation in question may very well lead to a loss of utility for all concerned.

What does the whole of this terminology signify really? That which Pareto gives as a description of the maximum *d'ophélimité* actually constitutes a definition of free competition. When it is possible, by extended trade or by increasing production, to bring about an increase of the utility pertaining to each partaking subject, or of only some of them without loss to the others, it is inconceivable that such changes would *not* be introduced if the economy were free.[1] This does not mean to say that the result of free competition might not be a huge profit for a few, though their attainment of a maximum *d'ophélimité* could not possibly, for the society as a whole, counterbalance the impoverishment or rather lasting pauperism of the greater part of the population. Why, then, use a terminology which stands in direct contradiction to the ordinary usage of language?

Pareto maintains that the utilities of different persons are '*heterogeneous quantities*,' which cannot possibly be compared with one another. '*No bridge*, comme disent les anglais.' But is this correct? Are we human beings so made that we are unable to form some

[1] Pareto includes on pp. 649 ff. a proof of his proposition which he had previously put forward in *Giornale degli Economisti*, 1903, with the assumption that exchange takes place *at constant prices*, and all subjects involved act in accordance with his 'Type I,' i.e. none of them endeavours *consciously* to exert an influence on prices. ('Type II' signifies that one (or more) of the subjects trading withholds available commodities from the market—because of a monopolist position, for instance—in order to obtain for himself better prices and higher profits.) But the proof is just as good, and in fact somewhat simpler, if no assumption is made as to the constancy of prices. It may be based on the fact that the *last* portions of the commodity stocks transferred in exchange must be in the same ratio as the marginal utilities of those engaged in the exchange. The difference between Types I and II proves to be of no importance in *this* connection. It is of course possible, and very frequently happens in fact, that a monopolist sells different parts of his stock at different prices, either to different classes of consumers or (more often) at different times of the consumption year, in order not to be left with an unsaleable remainder of commodities or productive power. According to Pareto's definition, this establishes a maximum *d'ophélimité*, though the consumers may be outrageously exploited!

adequate picture of the joys and cares of our fellows, or to compare in any way the intensities of their feelings with our own? If not, what material basis can there really be for the idea of *justice*, whether in government or in social distribution? Pareto himself admits that in a collective society ('Type III') distribution of the social product must follow certain 'ethical' principles. Whatever we take these principles to be, however, every kind of deliberate distribution must presuppose an *estimation* of the needs and reasonable pleasure of life of one person with respect to another—if it is not to be a question of justice in caricature.

The only thing that is correct and noteworthy in the whole of this reasoning is the fact that the current mode of production, depending on free competition and for the most part dominated by private economic considerations, must from the theoretical point of view result in the greatest possible total of products or exchange value, in the same way as would rational production in some conceivable collective society; that is to say, if we consider just the question of *production*, and disregard both distribution and the pricing of finished goods, as we might well do if, for instance, the prices of commodities within the economy considered were determined in the foreign market.

This proposition is obviously of the greatest significance and importance, and, as far as I can see, it is perfectly correct when formulated with due care.[1] A positive demonstration of it is of little interest here, for that is quite simple, as a matter of fact. It depends in the last analysis on the consideration that, if more products of exchange value could be achieved at any point of the field of production with the labour or other productive power available, the private economic interests would inevitably direct the necessary productive power to that point. But what is of the greatest importance—and what Pareto, with all his learned formulae, has quite forgotten—is to explain the apparent or real contradiction between this proposition and the impressions and opinions of everyday life. No less an economist than Ricardo attempted to show, in the well-known chapter 'On Machinery' added to the third edition of his

---

[1] Under more realistic conditions, where also prices are variable, it is only possible to formulate or demonstrate it *in rough outline*, since it is impossible to make a *direct* comparison of separate commodities or services. E. Barone seems to have overlooked this in his otherwise interesting article in *Giornale degli Economisti*, 1908, 'Il ministro della produzione nello stato collettivista.' He states that under free competition the total income of the society is an exact maximum, although this can be precisely proved only with the above simplifying assumptions. Barone's own mathematical proof of the proposition is therefore in error.

Principles, that the private advantage of a producer might very well be better suited by a *decrease* of his gross product, instead of an increase, and in doing so he appears to have been expressing what experience teaches us. For instance, when the invention of certain agricultural machines put the landowners in a position to replace human labour by draught animals, which consumed a considerable part of each year's harvest; or when they converted arable land to permanent pasture in order to reduce running costs; or when, as has happened in Sweden, arable land and pasture is afforested because of the high price commanded by timber—who would not draw the *prima facie* conclusion that the increased net profit is achieved at the cost of a decrease in the gross return, evidencing an open conflict of private and social economic interests? The new legislation against the sawmill companies in Sweden is actually based on such considerations.

Nevertheless, the proposition mentioned is presumably quite correct: Ricardo did not follow the thread of his reasoning to its end. In a *closed* economy, where there is no transfer of capital or labour to or from other economies, only exchange of commodities with them, the transition to production with smaller gross return can *never* be made *universally*, only partially. The labour or capital freed by such a change would find employment in other (old) productive activity, which would consequently experience an increase of intensity, bringing about a new equilibrium with (total) gross returns in fact *higher*, not lower than previously. On the other hand, if the economy in question is *open*, it may very well happen that the new position of equilibrium is not reached until capital or labour has been transferred abroad, so that the raising of the gross returns occurs only in the world economy, not in the restricted nationalistic sense. But in both cases the change may be accompanied by diminution of wages, and perhaps also by a diminution of capital profits, i.e. to the advantage of the landowners only. Indeed, the case considered does involve such a diminution.

Nevertheless, the maximum attainable product can only be reached in this way. Even a socialist society could not contrive a form of production better or more advantageous in the technical-economic sense, though it would of course ensure that the increase in the product did not fall to the good of a few while the livelihood of the broad mass of the population deteriorated, but instead improved the lot of all.

There is no trace of any such considerations in Pareto.[1] He is

[1] I have given this subject a very thorough treatment in my *Lectures*, I, pp. 133 ff.

content to derive a more or less self-evident proposition by the elegant formulae of the calculus of variations—which is more likely to obscure the matter for the majority of his readers than to illuminate it.[1]

Moreover, Pareto's proof is valid only when it is a question of production *without capital* or employing a technically fixed amount of capital. In other cases, an agreement of the capitalists or entrepreneurs to introduce a production period longer (installation of machinery, etc.) than that which was most advantageous to them under free competition, might very well lead to an increase in the social product (as I have shown in my *Value, Capital and Rent*, pp. 128–30) although a simultaneous reduction of wages would be necessary here too. This means that an economy operating at Type II in Pareto's terminology (see the note on p. 168), instead of Type I, could give rise to an increase of *ophélimité*.[2]

This brings me to the last and most important of my criticisms of Pareto's general theoretical viewpoint. His theory of production, like that of Walras, deals solely with the concept of production *without capital*. The technical aids to production are regarded as inexhaustible funds, so that they could as well be described as some peculiar types of fertile soils. Although Pareto mentions on several occasions a 'transformation dans le temps' as characteristic of capitalist economies, he nowhere draws the necessary conclusion that the time scale of this transformation must have a decisive effect on both the result of production and the proportion of capital devoted to the distribution of the product. Among all the algebraic symbols he uses in his theory of production, there is not one denoting the length of the investment period. Furthermore, the entire mathematical treatment of the problem is formulated as if this time dimension were of no economic importance. The buyers of raw material and of labour are taken to be *simultaneous* consumers of the finished goods which has been produced with the help of these. It is obvious that this is not what happens. In conformity with this

[1] It is not really a question of the proper use of this calculus, since the differential equation which is supposed to give the solution is *identically* fulfilled, according to his assumptions, so that it only remains to find a maximum with respect to the limits of the integral concerned. Even then, in my opinion, the whole of this proposition, 'ce résultat important de la théorie,' could have been demonstrated with somewhat simpler means.

[2] I do not suggest that this is more than an apparent exception from the general rule, because a hidden construction of new capital is in fact *enforced* here, at the workers' expense. But the case is at least worthy of separate consideration. Pareto has of course passed over it unsuspectingly.

obvious deficiency in his presentation, Pareto makes no attempt to put forward a formula for the rate of interest on capital.[1]

This is the only respect in which Pareto differs from the 'École Autrichienne,' or the only one of any significance—since the 'nombreuses raisons' (p. 543, n. 2) which, he maintains, distinguish him from them are not easily perceptible. It would be difficult to contend that the distinction is to his credit, however. I could not stand as champion for every detail of Böhm-Bawerk's edifice of theory; but in order to convince oneself that it represents a definite step forward from the older ideas to which Pareto is still faithful, it is in my opinion only necessary to consider the formula which Walras (in the introduction to the later edition of his *Éléments d'économie politique pure*) put forward as *his* solution of the problem of interest, as against that of Böhm-Bawerk. If conditions are assumed to be *stationary*, Walras's seemingly so meaningful formula reduces itself to the simple relation

$$F(i) = 0$$

where $F(i)$ is the total of new savings as a function of the rate of interest, i. In other words, the equation now says that under such circumstances the incentive to construction of new capital must have disappeared. This is correct, but insufficient, for we also want to know why and how a given total amount of capital warrants a certain definite rate of interest. We can find the answer to that question only by following a particular line of thought: by considering *the effect of time* on production and distribution, by considering the effect of a virtual lengthening of the production process. This is what is really new in the new theory of capital, and an absolutely indispensable element of every rational theory of capital. A few earlier writers—Ricardo, von Thünen, Senior, Jevons and others—had a presentiment of it, or even expressed it clearly to some extent, but first it evolved to a definite systematic form in the hands of Böhm-Bawerk.

---

[1] Probably with the idea of filling in this gap, Enrico Barone, in the article in *Giornale degli Economisti* previously mentioned, has attempted to derive the different rates of interest from the production equation, assuming capital and production factors to be products of the continuous process of production. But he also omits all mention of the length of the investment period for the total capital. His attempt must therefore be rejected as invalid, and it is not difficult to demonstrate this in detail. It is to be regretted that this highly gifted economist, who in his earlier writings gave promising signs of approaching nearer to Böhm-Bawerk's viewpoint, now seems to have fallen back into the old unsatisfactory track, out of blind admiration for Pareto.

I can be briefer with the other, more elementary, parts of the book. There is no doubt that they contain a multitude of fine, perspicacious points, and there is no reader who might not study them with profit. The author's self-criticism could have been a little more rigorous in several places, however. The graphical presentation of exchange phenomena which he prefers (which is closely similar to that of von Auspitz and Lieben) has the advantage over the older method (of Walras) that it gives the supply and demand for *both* the exchanging parties in curves of the *same* general form. But it seems to me rather doubtful whether this advantage is not won at the expense of disadvantages of another kind. However that may be, the author succeeds, in pp. 193–5, in creating such confusion around the simple question of the movement of prices during mutual competition between sellers and buyers that each participant in the market seems to be competing with every other one, which obviously makes no sense.

In the ninth chapter he makes an attack on Ricardo's well-known theory of comparative costs (in international trade)—an attack which I think must be described as utterly unsuccessful. As a matter of fact, this famous theory has fallen into discredit in recent times for no clear reason. Lexis has made it the subject of an adverse criticism which appeared without amendment in all the editions of *Schönbergs Handbuch*, and which has recently been accepted as an authoritative refutation of the Ricardo theory (e.g. in the opinions of several participants at the Antwerp Free Trade Congress); the criticism is, however, actually based on self-contradictory suppositions, and is practically worthless. Pareto has now taken his pitcher to the well. He occupies no less than eight pages with computations (of an elementary type this time) intended to establish that Ricardo's theory applies to a 'possible case,' but definitely not to a 'necessary' one. But his whole argument is based on the neglect of a condition or modification of Ricardo's proposition, which, although indispensable, is almost self-evident. As is known, this says that if there are two craftsmen who both know how to make shoes and hats, but of whom one is more skilful than the other in *both* crafts—his superiority being *greater* in one craft than in the other—the two of them will prosper better if the more skilful (absolutely or relatively) shoemaker restricts himself to making shoes, the more skilful (absolutely or relatively) hatmaker to making hats. But this naturally involves the assumption that the *market* for both hats and shoes is *sufficient*; otherwise, if the demand for hats is too small and the demand for shoes too large, for instance, the hatmaker will be obliged to make shoes *as well*, even though the more skilful shoe-maker continues to ply his trade. The same thing applies to countries engaged in commerce together. Theoretically, only one of them may completely relinquish production of 'commodity A,' while the other always produces at least part of its requirements of 'commodity B.' In practice, however, there is seldom question of the *complete* abandonment of manufacture of any commodity when large groups of commodities are involved, for reasons easy to comprehend. If a country is faced with the alternatives of producing either nothing at all of a certain commodity or the whole of its requirements of that commodity—this is really the tacit assumption in Pareto's computations—the decision would often be contrary to the letter of Ricardo's proposition. But what does this go to prove? Surely no more than that Ricardo did not write tales for children, but addressed himself to men of independent thought! Pareto might have spared himself and his readers the eight pages of his criticism.

As already mentioned, the seventh chapter, on 'Population,' lies somewhat outside the realm of the rest of the book. Pareto unfortunately takes no explicit position with regard to this question, so important for economics. It seems to me, though, that he treats T. R. Malthus with rather more respect than he did in his *Cours*. Perhaps the huge rate of emigration from Italy in the meantime has set him thinking. His fine theory of the conditions for a levelling of incomes —theory of the *proportioning* of incomes is what it should now be called—again appears in the field at the beginning of this chapter without the slightest explanation of his peculiar definition of this concept.[1] Pareto complains that he is misunderstood on this point, despite his precise definition of his meaning. But the criticism—mine, at least[2]—is directed solely against his use of common expressions in a sense quite different from that of customary usage, with the result that he *seems* to have proved something that he has not proved, and which is furthermore not true. This error is the more remarkable in that Pareto cites in this connection P. Leroy-Beaulieu, who has defined the term 'répartition des richesses' in an entirely different manner, a manner which, although a little diffuse, accords with general usage.

---

[1] 'En général, lorsque le nombre des personnes ayant un revenu inférieur à *x* diminue par rapport au nombre des personnes ayant un revenu supérieur à *x*, nous dirons que l'inégalité *de la proportion* des revenus diminue' (p. 390). It is questionable whether this statement (stressed by Pareto) is reconcilable with the rules of logic. What is 'the inequality of *a* proportion'?

[2] See above, pp. 15 ff.

This brings me to the end of what is probably a too detailed criticism. I should be very sorry if it has given the impression that I should not appreciate the merits of Pareto, or wish to designate the whole of his life's work as a 'quantité negligeable.' Any such judgment would certainly be wrong. For my part I have learnt a great deal from his books, and I advise anyone who wishes to make himself familiar with the present position of economic theory not to neglect Pareto's works, especially the *Manuel*. I consider, however, that we must reject the claim which has repeatedly been made by Pareto himself and his Italian admirers, that he has accomplished no less than a revolution in our science. One might rather say with regard to such claims, that most of the truths stated by this gifted economist are not new, or are at most in a new form, while what is really new is, unfortunately, to a great extent, not true.

BÖHM-BAWERK'S THEORY OF CAPITAL[1]

THE theory of interest on capital which Böhm-Bawerk put forward more than twenty years ago has been well to the fore in theoretical economic discussion ever since, and particularly during the last decade. That is sufficient proof of its importance, *even* if smaller or greater parts of it in the end may not be able to withstand scientific criticism. I have faithfully read through what must be the greater part of this critical literature, and my long-standing admiration for Böhm-Bawerk's achievement has not been diminished thereby, although it has led me to take up a more definite position with regard to some of the points at issue. Most of the objections raised against Böhm-Bawerk are, in my opinion, undoubtedly based on misunderstandings and incomplete comprehension of his arguments. But, of course, a writer cannot be said to be entirely blameless if his presentation is not sufficiently lucid and precise to exclude the possibility of misconceptions arising in the mind of a reasonably attentive reader.

The work I mainly intend to deal with here is *Positive Theory of Capital*, the *second* of his more important books.

There have been *relatively* fewer critical objections to his earlier historical work, *Geschichte und Kritik der Kapitalzinstheorien* (History and Criticism of Interest Theories), which was subsequently published in a new and considerably enlarged edition—a huge, almost too comprehensive, volume of seven hundred pages. The appearance of the second work also diminished interest in the first in some ways, for, once in possession of a fully rational theory, it is less important to remind ourselves of all the earlier, more or less unsuccessful attempts; our interest is rather directed towards the origins of the more correct conception that may be detected in earlier writings, side by side with the mistakes.

Nevertheless, even this first work is of considerable value: it might

---

[1] 'Böhm-Bawerk's kapitalteori och kritiken därav,' *Ekonomisk Tidskrift*, 1911, pp. 39–49.

be said that Böhm-Bawerk here shows quite definitely the worthlessness of all those attempts to explain the phenomenon of interest which do not lay sufficient emphasis on the fact that the *time factor* in production and value is the *only* characteristic of importance for the concepts of capital and interest.[1] But where this factor is emphasised by earlier writers—and it is, almost without exception, by the *great* economists, Ricardo, von Thünen, Senior, etc.—Böhm-Bawerk's criticism seems to go too far, and is occasionally even forced. In spite of serious efforts, in the course of several years' correspondence with Böhm-Bawerk to understand his viewpoint, I am unable to agree with his rejection of Senior's 'abstinence' theory, in modern terminology, the 'waiting' theory. Actually it seems to me that Senior's theory and his own are fundamentally identical—though this may be due to a lack of insight on my part. I also agree with Cassel (*The Nature and Necessity of Interest*) that Böhm-Bawerk scarcely does Ricardo justice. It seems to me that however incomplete Ricardo's theory of interest may be, it is quite correct so far as it goes. Its greatest defect is probably that Ricardo, like English economists in general, regards the sole function of capital to be the advancement of *wages*, whereas it is actually to almost the same extent the advancement of *rents* as well.

On the other hand, I fail to discern the 'depth' which Cassel says he has found in Turgot's reflections on interest, and which Böhm-Bawerk is said to have been incapable of grasping. It may be true that Turgot never expressed in clear language the naïve 'fructification' theory (that interest is associated with the fact that a sum of money may be used to buy, say, land which yields rent), extracted, or one might say constructed, from his writings by Böhm-Bawerk. A man such as Turgot was not so stupid that he himself could not see in the end that he argued in a circle. Nevertheless, it does seem indisputable that this was in some vague way the line of thought that he had in mind.[2] Otherwise, it is impossible to understand why Turgot should have made the purchase of land the first of all his uses of capital when it is not really a use of capital from the economic point of

---

[1] Davidson anticipated several of Böhm-Bawerk's ideas in his early publication *De ekonomiska lagarna för kapitalbildningen* (The Economic Laws of Capital Formation), Uppsala 1878. In particular, his criticism of Hermann's so-called utility theory, in spite of its brevity, coincides in its essentials with the far more detailed criticism given by Böhm-Bawerk. The similarity is partly explained by the fact that both are based on Menger's theory of value.

[2] An earlier critic of Turgot, Sivers, came to the conclusion that Turgot did not explain interest at all. So the 'depth' of his explanation does not seem to have been particularly easy to discern.

view at all, and cannot affect the magnitude of interest in the slightest degree (unless the one who sells the land dissipates the capital and thereby contributes towards a diminution of the supply of capital). When Cassel says of Turgot that he 'knows that the buyer of land does not increase the demand for capital,' it would be interesting to have some evidence for this statement. My impression of Turgot's argument is just the contrary: that it was just this that he overlooked. And when Cassel goes on to suggest that 'it was naturally impossible for Turgot (speaking of the productive aspect of capital) to omit to point out that capital cannot be used in industry if it does not give at least the same interest as the capitalist could obtain by purchasing land,' the reader is led to wonder why no later writer—least of all Cassel himself—has found it necessary to bother about this circumstance, if not for the reason that it is quite irrelevant to the theory of capital. It seems to me, therefore, that Cassel's criticism of Böhm-Bawerk on this point, notwithstanding his quoting a conversation with A. Marshall as reference, is rather abortive.

If we proceed to Böhm-Bawerk's own 'positive theory,' it is now possible, so long after its appearance, to venture the statement that it is, and will remain, one of the milestones on the road of progress in political economy. It seems difficult to say anything about the general concept of capital or its mode of operation which is not to be found completely elucidated in that excellent and thought-provoking work. One fault is its great size, and the most recent edition—only partly published at present—threatens to be of even greater dimensions. But more important is the fact that Böhm-Bawerk has not succeeded in unifying his presentation completely. *Two* or even *three* threads may be distinguished, differing from each other in some respects, and woven together in a somewhat confusing manner—almost like the ancient writings of the Pentateuch.

Already in the introduction comes the brilliant suggestion that the capitalistic process of production—'the adoption of wisely chosen roundabout methods of production'—should be regarded as the *primary* concept, and capital itself as the *secondary*: 'essentially the intermediary products brought into existence at particular stages of the time-consuming roundabout process of production.' This idea, which really renders superfluous all further discussion of the limits and extent of the concept of capital, is taken further in the masterly Book II, 'Capital as an Instrument of Production.' It is not completely rounded off, however, until the fourth and fifth sections of Book III, 'The Origin and Rate of Interest,' especially in the second main part of the latter, 'The Rate of Interest in the Market.' There,

178

for the first time in the literature of this subject, a proper analysis of the relation between wages and interest is given, an entirely rational interpretation of the varying rate of interest under free competition—although it is true that the assumptions introduce very considerable simplifications, and that *land* as a production factor is intentionally omitted.[1] These parts of his book might as a matter of fact be read by themselves, as a complete and valuable whole. But Böhm-Bawerk has not been quite consistent here either: for in his account of the basis of the quantitative determination of the rate of interest on capital, he reverts, probably for didactic reasons, to the earlier Jevonian conception that national capital is a 'Subsistence fund,' an aggregate of (potential) wages, so that capital once more becomes the primary concept and the capitalistic process of production to some extent a secondary, derived concept.[2]

The large middle section of his work, and that to which the critics have paid by far the greatest attention, is of quite a different character. After a thorough—considering its purpose even too thorough—résumé of the modern theory of value (in its 'Austrian' form),[3] he goes on, under the heading 'The Present and Future in Human Economy,' to his well-known presentation of interest in its widest sense as an exchange phenomenon (no longer as exclusively the result of production and distribution)—as the *agio* which arises

[1] Here too—I fail to understand Cassel when he says that in this part of the work Böhm-Bawerk's argument 'does not prove anything for a mathematician.' On the contrary, a mathematician is in a better position than others to appreciate the effective and generally valid features of the reasoning which the layman might perhaps suppose to be an arbitrary series of columns of figures. If Cassel thought that he saw some *error* in Böhm-Bawerk's conclusions, he should have pointed it out. For my part, I find no defect in Böhm-Bawerk's argument, except that he deals throughout with simple interest, which restricts the immediate application of his conclusions to production periods of short duration. But it is not difficult to show that they are all still valid if compound interest is considered—as it should be; especially the fundamental proposition that the production period (or the period of investment) is necessarily *lengthened* by rising wages, and *shortened* by falling wages.

[2] I have endeavoured to develop Böhm-Bawerk's original idea more directly in my published lectures, especially in the new edition of them which I hope will appear shortly.

[3] From another point of view, this résumé is on the contrary too brief. It is an extract from 'Grundzüge der Theorie des wirtschaftlichen Güterwerts' (Basic Principles of the Theory of Economic Value), published some years previously (in *Conrads Jahrbücher*, 1886) which is considerably more detailed and in several respects more valuable, though the fact that the main points of it have been included in the well-known larger work have helped to relegate the article to an undeserved oblivion.

in the exchange of present and future goods. This may be justified in so far as interest is undoubtedly a more general concept than productive capital itself; it may also appear in a direct exchange between present and future goods or services *without* any intervening production, and this, without any real accumulation or application of capital in the economic sense.

But the method of proof is not entirely satisfactory. According to Böhm-Bawerk, the difference in value between the present and future goods, which constitutes this *agio*, has its origin, like all other values, in the different *marginal utilities* of the goods, even when they are physically similar. However, Böhm-Bawerk has already defined marginal utility in the preceding part of his book as 'the importance of the least important of the concrete needs or partial needs which are satisfied by the existing stock of commodities of the sort in question'—and it might be added, in complete conformity with his reasoning, 'for a certain given consumption period.' When we attempt to apply this to present and future goods, the difficulty at once arises that both the *stock* (of the future good), and even more so the actual *consumption period*, are completely indeterminate. This difficulty is not mitigated if we do as Böhm-Bawerk sometimes does, and make the comparison instead between present and *past* goods. In such a case the supply of the latter is also given—viz. as the quantity of capital goods then in existence—but the consumption period is still just as indefinite, because it is obviously not possible for all the available past and present goods to be entirely used up, say, in the current year's consumption.

It may be that Böhm-Bawerk has not clearly recognised this obvious difficulty; at any rate he has not attacked it directly, and his procedure may perhaps best be described as an attempt to *circumvent* it. On the one hand he sets forth certain points of view from which present stocks are, or seem to be, deficient when compared with future stocks; on the other hand he claims that 'on technical grounds' the utility, simply, of present goods is in all or at any rate in the great majority of uses (in aller Regel) greater than that of future goods (and less than that of past goods) of the same kind and quantity. From this it would further follow that their *marginal* utility, and therefore their value and price, must also be greater. But this contention is obviously invalid. There are very many present needs which can only be satisfied by present goods, not by past goods (and certainly not by future goods which are not yet in existence), and there are obviously a great many future needs which can only be satisfied if future goods and productive forces come into existence spontaneously—in other words, sufficient unto the day is the evil thereof. The problem does not depend on this either, however, but on the relation between present and future goods at the boundary or margin where the question of substituting one for the other is actually relevant.

Böhm-Bawerk's reasoning is relatively most successful when applied to the *second* of the '*three main grounds*' which cause the real or apparent superiority of present over future goods: the subjective under-estimation of future needs or over-estimation of future resources, due to incorrect calculation or weakness of will. This phenomenon is undoubtedly general, although it appears to very different *degrees* in different individuals and under different social conditions, and to the extent that it is operative it obviously entails a (subjective) superiority of present over future goods.

But even the '*first* main ground'—the justified expectation of an *objectively* more abundant satisfaction of future needs—is evidently not general. It may well be true, as Böhm-Bawerk states, that those who have reason to expect a *less* abundant satisfaction of their needs in the future can always *hoard* present goods—at least in societies where durable objects such as those made of the precious metals are generally accepted as means of exchange or payment. But this cannot by itself lead to a *positive* superiority (*agio*) for the present goods; it can only ensure that the difference of value in the *negative* direction does not fall below the costs or risks of storing these objects. It is quite conceivable that those who for this reason wish to dispose of present goods (to assure themselves of the future goods) are *more numerous* than those who wish to do the opposite, and in such a case, although the latter group perhaps has on average a higher estimate of the value difference between the two 'sorts of goods,' a 'marginal pair's' estimate of this difference would in any case be near zero, possibly less. Moreover, the hoarding of precious metals does not involve any guarantee, of course, that the value of money in the future, when the accumulated wealth is dishoarded and put back into circulation, will not have fallen with respect to goods, in which case the real interest on the savings might be negative to an unlimited extent. However, as several writers, including Böhm-Bawerk himself, have pointed out, this 'main ground' does actually exert a strong influence on the *accumulation of capital*, and thereby on the rate of interest. In a rational economy there can be no question of stretching the sacrifice of present goods beyond the limit where the remaining satisfaction of present needs is equal to that expected in the future. Another circumstance involved here is that these saved-up goods themselves undergo an objective increase in quantity or quality through *production*, i.e. in accordance with the '*third* main ground.'

Böhm-Bawerk's treatment of this third ground is, however, the most unsatisfactory. The *technical* superiority of present goods (including present productive forces) over those of the future is probably the part of his reasoning which has set his readers pondering most, at least it has been so for me. I do not know how many times I have returned to this point without being clear *why* it was that Böhm-Bawerk's treatment did not satisfy me, until, particularly by reading Bortkiewicz's criticism ('Der Kardinalfehler Böhm-Bawerks,' *Schmollers Jahrbuch*, Bd XXX), I think I definitely found the solution. I do not wish to suggest by this, however, that I consider Bortkiewicz's polemic to have hit its mark, even on this point, and still less as a whole.

Proceeding from the general proposition about the profitability of the *roundabout methods* of production, Böhm-Bawerk argues, as is well known, that a certain quantity of present productive power, e.g. a labour-month, must always be more valuable for us than one which does not become available until some time in the future, say next year. For the former, he says, may be used as a *component* in a *longer production process* than the latter, and must therefore provide a relatively better yield *whatever point of time in the future the production refers to*.

This is certainly quite incorrect. The proposition about the profitability of roundabout methods of production is definitely not valid in the sense that a production process may successfully be extended for any length of time whatsoever. On the other hand it is true that the limit that is most advantageous in a technical sense *is never actually reached*, and we do not need to know more; but, as we shall see, this fact belongs to another set of considerations.

In order to avoid the absurdity that in such a case all production ought really to be extended indefinitely, Böhm-Bawerk here falls back upon the 'first and second main grounds,' to ensure that the 'economic centre of gravity' will be brought closer in time. This imparts to the whole argument something of unreality and 'intellectual exercise,' and it carries little conviction. It is quite conceivable that an extension of the production process which is advantageous in itself will not be forthcoming because the owner of the capital in question will not or cannot wait that long for his remuneration. But what restricts the length of the production process *as a rule*, however, is another thing entirely—the simple fact that technically advantageous roundabout methods of production are profitable only to a limited extent economically. If by sacrificing 50 crowns or 50 labour units now I can receive in return 100 from a one-year production process, but 150 from a two-year one, then it is obvious that I ought to choose the *one*-year alternative, even if I intend to wait two years for my returns, because by repeating the one-year production process the next year on double the scale (since I then have 100 crowns or labour units at my disposal), I will obtain 200 at the end of the second year instead of 150. In other words, if a successive lengthening of the production process is also to be economically profitable, the product must increase at a more than geometric rate of progression, as time is increasing at an arithmetic rate. In general this can only be so to a limited extent through newly occurring changes. (If the sacrifice necessary to obtain the same product had been 75 crowns instead of 50, the two-year production process would have been the more profitable, because it would have led to a doubling of the capital, whereas two successive one-year productions would have given an increase in the ratio $\frac{3}{4} \cdot \frac{3}{4} = 9 : 16$).

No one has shown all this more clearly than Böhm-Bawerk in the *subsequent* parts of his work. But in this place, where he was only concerned to explain the existence of interest, its *quale*, he evidently considered that details about its *quantum* could be disregarded, thinking to reach his immediate goal by a short-cut.

But the shortest way is not always the quickest. Here it is actually easier to arrive at the *quantum* than at the *quale*. We may either assume provisionally, as Böhm-Bawerk does, that conditions are stationary and that there is a certain social capital which is maintained from year to year without increasing or decreasing, or, what amounts to the same thing, that a certain average *time* elapses between the application of the productive forces and the appearance of the consumable products. It is then comparatively easy to show—at least now that Böhm-Bawerk has indicated the way—why and how this capital must earn interest at a certain unchanging rate under free competition. *The consumption period* and the *stock* of available present and future goods are then completely determined, since each year resembles the preceding one exactly, and every year *a whole 'year's allocation'* of labour and land, composed in a definite given way of labour and land of different 'ages' must be used. The difference in values between present and future goods (or past and present goods) which constitutes interest is therefore clearly determined by their different marginal utilities or marginal productivities—not by their total utilities, which do not enter into the comparison. The particular difficulty which Böhm-Bawerk and his readers must contend with, namely the fact that an increased *quantity* of goods does not necessarily imply increased *value*, does not exist here, because the exchange values of the different goods and services with respect to one another remain unchanged from year to year under stationary conditions.

It only remains to show that the concrete phenomena of economic life resemble this schematic picture at least to such a degree that the rate of interest constructed in an analogous manner cannot as a rule actually fall to or below zero. When we have done this we have at last established the existence of interest as a necessary element in an economic system based on free competition—and, as a matter of fact, in all systems. In this part of the discussion which clearly involves the theory of capital accumulation and its negative complement, the unproductive consumption of capital, Böhm-Bawerk's 'first and second main grounds' find their full and proper application.[1]

I think that this is the correct analysis—and, at the same time, the only defect in Böhm-Bawerk's positive exposition with which he can reasonably be charged. However, as far as I can see, none of his critics, not even Bortkiewicz, has succeeded in elucidating the matter. Walras does, in a way, put his finger on the weak spot in this part of Böhm-Bawerk's reasoning when he remarks (in the preface to the second edition of *Éléments d'économie politique pure*) that the rate of interest is determined *in the market*, and that in Böhm-Bawerk's work he 'looks for this market without finding it.' But if Walras had turned over a few more pages of the book—or rather if he had not been content with the excerpt from it which was given in the French journals—he would have come across this 'market'; though, as I have already said, the correct place for it would have been at an earlier stage of the reasoning.

The consequence of this was that Walras—and the same applies even today to his Italian disciple and successor, Pareto—considered himself justified in retaining his own theory of capital, which is practically devoid of content, since in the simplest, most fundamental case, that with stationary conditions, it gives no explanation whatsoever of the magnitude of the rate of interest—apart from the self-evident comment that if the rate were either higher or lower,

---

[1] Cassel has rendered a useful service, in his previously mentioned work, by giving new life to the question of the possible limitations to the accumulation of capital and the diminution of the rate of interest. This is not the place, however, to examine to what extent Cassel's conclusions are correct: on this point, too, I refer the reader to the new edition of my *Lectures*.

capital would begin to increase or decrease and the conditions would cease to be stationary.

However much Walras and Pareto *talk* about different kinds of capital and duly assign algebraic symbols to them in their mathematically clothed presentation, their theory of production and distribution is at bottom merely a theory of production *without capital*— or, to put it another way, of instantaneous production involving, besides labour and land, certain technical accessories called capital. This is clearly shown by the fact that none of the quantities involved are conceived of as functions of *time*.[1]

There is thus no doubt that Böhm-Bawerk's theory represents an exceptionally great scientific step forward, although it no more carries the stamp of perfection than any other human work. It is to be hoped that in the new edition of his famous work which, as already mentioned, is as yet only partly published, he will know how to remove these imperfections. His book could then without further reservations be made the basis of all future research in this field of theoretical economics.

---

[1] Even the very gifted Italian economist, Barone, who at one time seemed to be approaching Böhm-Bawerk's viewpoint, has subsequently returned to this unsatisfactory attitude to the matter, out of blind admiration for Pareto.

CARL MENGER [1]

WITH Carl Menger's death we lost the last of the three renowned economists (the other two being Jevons and Walras) who, by setting forth the concept of marginal utility or, to use a more general expression, the scarcity or marginal principle, succeeded during the 1870's in giving an impetus to economics from which it is still deriving energy. It is by no means unknown in the history of the sciences for several people, working independently, to make such epoch-making discoveries simultaneously. But usually it is a case of ideas which are 'in the air,' and which are *bound* to be brought out by the new problems with which the science in question is occupied. This was the case, for example, with differential calculus, with which the theory of marginal utility has so many points in common. As soon as Descartes' geometry began to be applied to curves of higher degree than the circle and conic sections, and as soon as people began to follow Galileo in the study of the movement of bodies whose velocities were continually changing, the use of infinitesimals was indeed unavoidable, and a calculus based on infinitesimals would surely have come into existence sooner or later, even if there had been no Newton or Leibniz.

But in this example from economics there was nothing 'in the air.' The doctrines of classical economics had begun to be criticised and to go out of favour, but nothing except pure negation had taken their place; the attempts at a rational development of theory which had been made by Cournot, Dupuit and Gossen had passed without leaving a trace; economists had instead begun to mistrust all theory turning increasingly to historical investigations. The new theory came therefore like a bolt from the blue.

As usually happens in such cases, tiresome questions of priority have not been long in presenting themselves, though not at the instigation of those most closely concerned. Jevons has pride of place so far, since he put forward his ideas in two short memoranda at conferences of the British Association as early as the 1860's, as well as in the *Journal of the Statistical Society*. His *Theory of Poli-*

[1] *Ekonomisk Tidskrift*, 1921, pp. 113–24.

tical Economy did not come out until 1871, however, the same year as Menger's *Grundsätze der Volkswirtschaftlehre* (Principles of Economics). Unfortunately, a later year of publication was given on the *cover* of Menger's book, owing to a printer's error. This caused a well-known Italian economist to make the ugly insinuation that Menger would have become acquainted with Jevons's system when he was in England and had plagiarised it, and this despite the fact that Menger did not pay his visit to England as the companion of Archduke Rudolf until 1877. The allegation is quite unfounded; there is nothing to indicate that Menger knew any more about Jevons than Jevons knew about Menger eight years afterwards when he published the second edition of his *Theory*. Walras's book did not appear until three years later, and so can have had even less effect on Menger. On the other hand, the name of *Auguste* Walras, father to Léon, is to be found among the list of authors mentioned in Menger's book, and since Léon Walras quotes his father at one of the main points of his book, it is possible that we have here a common starting-point for the works of Menger and Walras.

It is not necessary to give any account of the content of *Grundsätze*, since it has long since become common knowledge in the world of economists, particularly through the work of Menger's numerous and gifted pupils, Wieser, Sax, Böhm-Bawerk, Robert Meyer, Zuckerkandl, etc. Even writers who, like our own Cassel, always profess to 'reject' the theory of marginal utility, none the less lean heavily upon it in practice; and it is only necessary to think of the vague and meaningless definitions of concepts with which Schäffle still has to content himself—exchange value as a balance between the costs of production and the subjective use value—to realise at once the difference between the past and the present. Of especially great importance in this connection has been the brilliant and inspiring presentation given by Böhm-Bawerk.[1] This is based entirely on Menger's writings, however, as far as content is concerned, even the well-known and much-quoted example of the colonist's five sacks of wheat which have alternative uses is to be found almost word for word in Menger.

In addition to the theory of exchange proper, Menger's book also devotes a couple of (all too short) sections to the *theory of capital*, as well as to the *theory of money* in the last chapter. Menger undoubtedly influenced Böhm-Bawerk here too, by the strong emphasis he placed

---

[1] 'Grundzüge der Theorie des wirtschaftlichen Güterwerts' (Main Principles of the Theory of Economic Values), *Conrads Jahrbücher*, 1886; given in abridged form in Böhm-Bawerk's *Positive Theorie des Kapitales*.

upon capitalist production as production for the *future*, although at the same time drawing some criticism from Böhm-Bawerk by the rather unsatisfactory way he expressed himself on one point. Menger remarks that the means of production, the economic goods of 'higher order,' have a value for us only through their products, and he asks how it is that the exchange value of the former is yet regularly less than that of the latter—by the amount of the interest on the capital. His answer is that because the production takes time it is necessary to have not only the means of production themselves, but also *disposal* over them during the appropriate time, and that this disposal is itself an economic good, and that its equivalent, the interest on capital, necessarily depresses the exchange value of the means of production *below* that of the products. This reasoning is obviously unsatisfactory. Those who possess the means of production may dispose of them as they please, as Böhm-Bawerk promptly pointed out, without making any special payment for this right of disposal. But they do not have possession of the *products*, but have to *wait* for these, and it is for this waiting that they themselves stipulate or reckon on having some remuneration—one might say that the value of the means of production is equal to that of the products discounted to the present time. Menger mentioned this also in a note, but it was left to Böhm-Bawerk (and Jevons) to clear the matter up properly.

Later on Menger returned once more to the subject of capital, in an article in *Conrads Jahrbücher*, 1888, that is just before Böhm-Bawerk published his *Positive Theory*. It seems to me that the point of view he adopts there, however, is something of a step backwards from the one put forward in *Grundsätze*. One of the things he opposes is the old definition, taken from Adam Smith, of capital, as 'produced means of production,' and he maintains that resources provided spontaneously by nature must also be included in capital, as soon as they become economically significant through scarcity. The comment is quite correct, of course, but it is really only concerned with Smith's over-narrow definition of 'produced,' as if production always requires the intervention of human labour. The trunk of a tree growing wild is just as much capital as is the trunk of a planted tree, says Menger. Undoubtedly; but if there were a superabundance of natural forest, no tree trunk would have exchange value, and no tree trunk would therefore be capital. If, on the other hand, forest land is scarce, then it would call forth an annual rent, and these successive rents, together with the accrued interest, must equal the value of the natural tree trunk, in equilibrium, just as the planted tree trunk is equivalent in value to the labour used in planting together with the accrued interest thereon. It is therefore only a question of two different types of production. A more difficult question is that of those stocks of means of production, found in mines and veins of ore, which can be utilised to any desired extent. But, as I have pointed out in my review of Cassel's book,[1] it is only by a *deliberate restriction* of the annual production—that is, by monopolistic trading methods—that these can possess an economic value and furnish their owners with a yearly dividend (royalty). Otherwise they would only provide remuneration for the work put into them, and would therefore not have any exchange or capital value in themselves.

As far as the theory of money is concerned, Menger occupies himself in *Grundsätze* mainly with the question of the nature and origin of money, especially the latter. He touches only briefly upon the important question of the basic determinants of the *value* of money. It seems that his point of view is still essentially 'metallist.' For instance, he says (p. 259 *n.*) that even though 'force of habit renders the purchasing power of money secure, even where its usability as ordinary metal is not immediately noticeable,' nevertheless, 'this purchasing power together with the habits upon which it rests, would soon cease to exist if, for some reason, the currency lost its property of usability as ordinary metal. It may therefore be admitted'—he continues—'that in a highly developed economy money is for many people merely a *symbol*. But it is certain that this easily explainable illusion would soon disappear if the currency lost its property of usability as an ordinary metal.'

But Menger later had the experience of seeing inconvertible paper money in his own country actually at a *higher* value for several years than the silver into which it had previously been convertible—as he asserts himself in his later writings on money. This constitutes no decisive disproof of the metallist theory, of course, because it was *hoped* to convert the notes at a later stage into *gold*. Through the force of circumstances, however, the full free convertibility into gold was never realised for the Austrian notes, and yet up to the outbreak of the World War they kept their value with respect to gold about as well as notes of countries on the proper gold standard. These experiences could not fail to affect Menger's point of view on this question. There are certain echoes of his old point of view in his great monograph 'Das Geld' in *Conrads Handwörterbuch* (and also in an earlier

[1] *Ekonomisk Tidskrift*, 1919. [An English translation of this paper has been published as Appendix to Wicksell's *Lectures on Political Economy*, I, pp. 219–73.]

article in *Revue d'économie politique* 1892)—he says, among other things, that the significance of the question of the velocity of circulation of money had been 'over-estimated'—but on the whole he bases his point of view in these articles on the purely formal conception of the quantity theory. He gives it expressly as his opinion that it ought to be possible, by a mutual effort on the part of different states, to regulate gold production, cover requirements for paper currency, etc., to create a means of exchange whose 'internal' value could be maintained at a constant level through time.

Menger's attitude to contemporary German economics was by no means strongly polemical at the beginning. In the preface to *Grundzätze*, he says—assuredly with considerable exaggeration—that 'this attempted reform of the highest principles of our science rests on a basis of preparatory work which is almost entirely the result of diligent *German* research,'[1] and he wishes his own work—which was dedicated to Roscher—to be regarded as 'a friendly greeting from one who is working along the same lines in Austria,' and so on.

This friendly mode of address seems to have gone unnoticed in Germany, however. In his Vienna colleague, Lorenz von Stein (whose obituary he wrote in *Conrads Jahrbücher*, 1891), Menger had a representative of German Reich economics close at hand, and I have been told that he was not at all sympathetic to Menger's 'attempted reform'; and there was just as little response from Germany proper, where the historical or historico-ethical trend was beginning to dominate economic thought, and even, for a time, to displace theoretical treatment entirely. That Menger should feel offended by this lack of understanding is not surprising, although rather regrettable. His next major work (1883) was not the continuation or extension of the first that had been promised on the title page of *Grundsätze*, but instead a bulky monograph on the *method* of the social sciences. This work, too, undoubtedly contains many shrewd comments and the last section is particularly interesting. There the author gives, on the one hand, a number of quotations from Bodinus, Bacon, Macchiavelli, and others, to show that the importance of an historical treatment of the social science had been known

---

[1] It is surely unthinkable that he would have uttered such a statement if he had been acquainted with the works of Jevons—that is to say, with the two above-mentioned items. It does seem that his knowledge of English economics was somewhat deficient on the whole, for he ascribes (p. 146) to Ricardo the absurd opinion that if all the land in a country were equally good and equally well situated 'no rent whatever would arise.'

and appreciated since the earliest times (and was therefore no discovery of the historical school), and, on the other, he points out that the supposed parallelism between the historical trend in economics and so-called 'historical jurisprudence' (the Savigny School) is really founded on a misunderstanding of the significance and purpose of the latter. So far from denying that juridical phenomena conform to certain laws, this school wishes to raise them to the rank of laws of nature, independent of the conscious intervention of man; in other words, almost exactly the opposite of what the 'historical' school of economists wished to do with regard to economic laws.

In my opinion this book suffers from a tedious prolixity, however. Much easier to read is the pamphlet *Die Irrtümer des Historismus* (The Errors of the Historical School), which was published in the following year, and is an extremely well-written phillipic against Schmoller. On the whole I fear that Menger's purely methodological works, of which there was another, larger one, planned but not published, were a waste of effort which to some extent directed him from work in his proper field. The promised continuation of his first book never actually appeared, and even the new edition of it which was already printed was held back by Menger and, through a misunderstanding, finally cancelled. It looks as if Menger began to lose faith in his own ability to continue his life's work once he had let it drop for a time. It is not improbable that the very attention which was paid to 'the Austrian School'—that is to say, to ideas which were ultimately his—all over the world, excepting only Germany, in part *prevented* him from carrying on with his work, because he felt that the expectations centred upon any new work of his would be too high for him to be able to live up to them. However that may be, his remaining writings, which are mainly concerned with practical questions connected with the Austrian currency reforms, are certainly worthy of our respect, but none of them can be said to have fulfilled the promise of the brilliant first work. It is upon that work that his fame rests, and it is through that work that his name will pass on to posterity, for one can safely say that no book since Ricardo's *Principles* has had such a great influence on the development of economic theory as Menger's *Grundsätze*—not even excluding the ingenious, but too aphoristic work of Jevons, nor that of Walras, which is unfortunately extremely difficult to read. This influence has been felt not only in the field of national economy, but also in the field of state economy and the theory of public finance, a development that is certainly only in its initial stages as yet.

In his youth Menger was a journalist, and for a time he managed the business section of a Vienna newspaper. Consequently he was not, as Schmoller makes him out to be, a 'Weltflüchtiger Stuben-gelehrter' (an armchair-scholar), but, as can be seen from *Grundsätze*, had had a great deal to do with practical business. Rather is he a proof of the old tag that it is the practical men, if they apply them-selves to the matter in the proper way and have sufficient talent, who often become the most daring and abstract theoreticians, whereas those economists who have always stood beyond the pale of practical affairs do not always dare to think their thoughts out to their logical conclusion for fear of falling foul of the practical men.

THE NEW EDITION OF MENGER'S
GRUNDSÄTZE[1]

THERE is something a little tragic about the life and writings of Carl Menger. It is not a tragedy of the kind that befell Cournot, or Rae, or Gossen, whose brilliant contributions went entirely unnoticed by their contemporaries, and were not recognised until long after their deaths. Menger had no cause to complain of lack of success or recognition. After only four years' study of economics he had finished the work that made him famous, and right from the beginning it was received with such approval in his own country that he had attained a professorship at Vienna University when he was no more than thirty-three years old. He received many other distinctions, and, what was more important, he was successful in establishing a school of enthusiastic and highly talented followers, the Austrian School, whose doctrines spread over the whole world, and for a period of fifty years set the course of all work and discussion in theoretical economics, and to some extent in fiscal theory too.

The tragedy lies in the fact that Menger himself had no part in this work and discussion; neither in the positive fulfilment of his own ideas, nor even as a critic of the way in which these were developed, or opposed, by others. This latter task would have been equally important, and one for which Menger, with his logical perspicuity, would certainly have been eminently suited. Instead, he allowed the lack of understanding which he encountered from the group of economists whom he had particularly in mind, the Reich Germans— especially the Schmoller group—to beguile him into wasting years of time and energy on literary feuds about the justification of his *method*. It is true that Menger carried on this discussion in a masterly fashion, but it was a more or less fruitless one. The ultimate criterion of the value of a method is provided by the results derived from it; if one wishes to defend a method, the way to do so is to *use* it, not to

---

[1] 'Mengers Grundsätze i ny upplaga,' *Ekonomisk Tidskrift*, 1924, pp. 1–10. Review of *Grundsätze der Volkswirtschaftslehre von Carl Menger*, Zweite Auflage aus dem Nachlass herausgegeben von Karl Menger, Wien, 1923.

talk or write *about* it, or at any rate, no more than is absolutely necessary.[1]

Nor do Menger's later writings bear any close relationship to his innovatory works, however noteworthy they may be in themselves; they might just as well have been written by any gifted economist.

Besides this work, Menger's son tells us that he was still busy with plans and preliminary work both for a new and enlarged edition of his principal book, and for a sequel to it, although at the time of his death in 1921 he had not completed either of them. Now that it has been decided to publish a complete edition of his works, including those published previously, as well as those not yet available in print, it is clear that *Grundsätze* will occupy a prominent position in this new edition, but there remains the question of the form which this should take. The editor has no doubt followed the wishes of the author, his father, including in the new edition of the book all the alterations and additions which Carl Menger had put into manuscript form, as well as those left in note form, thus making the whole book very different in appearance from the first edition, particularly at the beginning and the end.

For my part—and it would surprise me if many other economists were not of the same opinion—I should greatly have preferred an entirely unchanged reprint of the original edition; the fact that Menger himself could not be induced to publish one during his lifetime is quite another matter. The alterations and additions which Menger intended to make might have been included in the form of specially indicated notes under the text, or as an appendix or special section, leaving the original text undisturbed.[2]

For it is evident that a fairly old work such as this (the first and, hitherto, the only edition appeared in 1871) is mainly of historical interest. We would have preferred to see the authentic version of a work which exercised such a decisive influence on so many aspects of research in economics. The changes which Menger thought of

[1] Not all of Menger's works on method have been printed. The rest of them are to be printed shortly.

[2] The few remarks which the editor found himself called upon to make, fully deserve the space given to them, and their number might well have been increased. For instance, it is a pity that even in the new edition (p. 163) the statement remains that 'according to Ricardo, it would not be possible for any rents to exist in a country where all land was of the same quality and equally well situated'; the unreasonable nature of this statement completely neglects Ricardo's *second reason* for the occurrence of rent, increasing capital-intensity. It is incomprehensible that through the years Menger himself did not notice this error. Concerning another obvious omission, see what follows in the text.

including in a new edition are also of great value, of course, but now, so long afterwards, are of comparatively minor interest providing that they do not involve important changes in essentials, which is not the case here. Besides, it is not so certain that Menger would ultimately have retained all these changes, if he himself had been able to issue the new edition of his book. The editor mentions that Menger sometimes tried several variations on the printed text, but eventually replaced it in its original form. Perhaps this would have been the case with more than one of the alterations now undertaken by the editor in accordance with Menger's manuscript.

I am thinking especially of one passage which will be missed in the new book, even though its content is given in the introduction. Among the somewhat too aphoristic reflections on the origin of interest on capital, although correct and thought-provoking on the whole, the original edition of *Grundsätze* also includes a reference (pp. 127 ff.) to the natural human tendency to give first place to those needs which are most immediately felt. When this applies to the maintenance of life and health, then, says Menger, it is quite reasonable, since attending to the most immediate needs is thus a necessary condition for the more remote needs to be satisfied, in so far as this takes place at all. But, he adds—though without explaining the point, —'even when the satisfaction of a need is in the nature of a pleasure, then experience teaches that we humans consider a present pleasure, or one expected in the near future, more important than one of the same intensity which is not expected to occur until some more distant time.'

There is an obvious connection between these remarks and Böhm-Bawerk's 'second main ground' for the phenomenon of interest on capital: the subjective, and often erroneous, under-estimation of future needs and over-estimation of future resources, which depends on weakness of will and judgment. Admittedly, Menger does not give this as a direct reason for the origin of interest on capital, but as 'an important restriction on economic progress.' But at bottom this is the same thing. If the psychological characteristic mentioned above had not been part of the human inheritance, capital accumulation would have been more rapid at all times, and especially so in earlier periods, and the rate of interest would, as a consequence, have been considerably lower than it has actually been.

The editor tells us, however, that Menger *deleted* the whole of this passage—for the strange reason that, since he still regarded Böhm-Bawerk's theory as 'assailable,' he thought that he ought 'to remove from his book this point of association, which seemed to him to have been misinterpreted' (by Böhm-Bawerk). Nor, as far as I can see, is any substitute provided in the new edition for the deleted section. Instead, the whole of this extremely important consideration for the understanding of the cause of interest on capital has been allowed to go to waste.

I do not believe that the presentation of the theory of capital has on the whole gained anything in its new form. It has been divided into several chapters and has grown in quantity, but I have found nothing of importance which was not in the first edition. Furthermore, it now suffers from certain contradictions, as the editor himself points out, although these are of a rather formal kind. What is lacking above all is a definite standpoint with regard to Böhm-Bawerk's criticism of the so-called use-theory, which was the corner-stone of Menger's position, although at the same time he had also certain associations with the agio-theory. It is said that there are certain passages referring to this question among Menger's unprinted manuscripts, however, which will be published later.

In my book *Value, Capital and Rent,* and on several other occasions, I have given it as my opinion that use-theory, just as any other theory that is based on the *time factor,* may be used as the *starting-point* for a rational explanation of the phenomenon of interest on capital. In my opinion, Böhm-Bawerk has neglected to apply, in his voluminous criticism of use-theory, the *experimentum crucis,* which aims at showing that the theory under criticism leads to an incorrect result, conflicting with experience, or else turns a full circle and does not explain anything. An example of the former case is the 'Ausbeutung' (sweating) theory of Rodbertus and Marx, and similarly the so-called labour theory of James Mill; of the latter, Turgot's theory of fructification; but use-theory is not an example of either case. Either it is necessary to abandon the whole concept of 'use,' or else it must be admitted that even consumable goods may be used without the whole of their value being exhausted, because use itself *consists in* replacement by an equivalent value (e.g. seed corn). It is, of course, assumed initially that capital is the *only* means of production, so that nothing has to be paid for the use of the land or even for wages, and it is also assumed that the economy is *stationary,* where all goods retain their relative values. It is obviously necessary to replace this simplifying assumption, which merely serves to bring out the actual principle of the explanation (and at the same time to break the brunt of Böhm-Bawerk's well-known objections), by more complex assumptions which are more in accord with reality.

Everything depends, then, on a consistent and fruitful *development*

196

of the principle adopted for the explanation. In this respect the new edition of *Grundsätze* can hardly be said to go farther than the old; indeed, the casual relations sometimes appear to be obscured rather than clarified, as, for instance, at the bottom of p. 151. There, Menger compares two persons, one of whom possesses a certain quantity of consumable goods, which he may use now or in the future, as he pleases, while the other is assured of having the same amount of goods only at some later point of time. Consequently, says Menger, they are both alike in the future, but the former is, in addition, able to use them during the intervening period. This is an 'explanation' which itself needs a good deal of explanation, and the reference which is given to what was said previously on pp. 100–1 about 'the productivity of capital' hardly makes the matter clearer.

It therefore seems to me that the chief interest of the book still lies in the sections which deal with the origin of *value*, and also *exchange* and (to some extent) *pricing*. As is well known, Menger regarded price as what is commonly called exchange value, be it expressed in terms of money or something else, while he preferred to use the concept of exchange value in a *subjective* sense, as the economic significance of an object for us in the light of the possibilities available of exchanging it in the market for some other object. But this terminology is not used consistently throughout, at least not in the new edition, and it is hardly to be recommended, since the 'exchange value' in this sense is really only an indirect use value, and furthermore dependent on pricing, so that it is a complex concept and not a simple one.

Standing out above everything else is the short, concise explanation of the origin of value, which, with justifiable pride, Menger printed in spaced-out type (p. 98 in the first edition, p. 127 in the new one), and which reads approximately like this:

> Of those want-satisfactions which are assured to an economic man by a certain quantity of goods at his disposal, in any actual situation only that which is *least* pressing for the person in question is dependent upon his possession of a certain fractional quantity of the goods; and the value of such a fractional quantity is for him equal to the significance of the *least* important of the want-satisfactions made possible by equal fractions of the total quantity of goods at his disposal.

In an equally simple and convincing manner, Menger settles the controversial question of the correct concept of value and the relation between utility and value, a question which has kept economists busy for more than a hundred years without their being able to get at the heart of the matter. One of the many examples given by Menger in the note on pp. 133 ff. is particularly striking: it concerns the formula for determining 'the measure of value,' as put forward about twenty years earlier by Menger's colleague in Vienna, the imaginative rather than exact Lorenz von Stein:

> The actual measure of the value of a good is to be found by dividing the quantity of other goods by the quantity of the good in question. But in order to carry out this division, it is first necessary to find a common *denominator* for the total quantity of goods. This common denominator, or what is common to the goods, is only to be found in their common *nature*; namely, in the fact that each good consists of six elements: raw materials, labour, product, need, use, and actual consumption, for if one of these elements is missing, the object ceases to be a good. These elements are contained in the good in *definite* amounts, and the measure of these elements determines the measure of each *particular* good. It follows then that the quantitative relationship between all the individual goods, or their general measure of value, is given by the relationship between the amount of these elements in the one good and the corresponding amount in the other good. The determination and calculation [*sic*] of this relationship hence constitutes the determination of the actual measure of value.

We can agree with Menger that this idea of Stein's is original; in clarity, simplicity, and therefore in usefulness, however, such a concept leaves practically everything else to be desired.

Menger then goes on to show how the use value, as defined by him, is fundamental for the phenomena of exchange and pricing, and he thus achieves a *unity* of outlook which none of the older economists (even including Marx) had, since they generally *excluded* use value from their discussion as something altogether irrelevant to exchange value. But Menger (in contrast to Walras) can hardly be said to have carried this line of reasoning to its final conclusion. He first considers pricing in the case of the *isolated* exchange of two goods, and maintains that this is a determinate problem only within more or less wide limits. He next shows how these limits converge when we consider a single possessor of one good on the one hand ('the seller'), and on the other a number of competing possessors of the other good ('the buyers'). This is done by setting up the well-known and often quoted little table with the double entries, giving each buyer's subjective valuation of both his own good and the good in demand, and thus their different buying inclinations at every conceivable price for the latter good expressed in terms of the former. If we now assume that the *supply* is fixed, or that the seller has fixed a certain *price* for his good, then in the first case the uniform price, and in the second the quantity of the goods sold, are *uniquely determined*, and at the same time, in both cases, the distribution among the buyers of the goods sold. All this is set out in an extremely clear and lucid fashion, though perhaps at a length which *now* seems to us unnecessary.

However, to proceed from this to the pricing situation in a market with *mutually* free competition between both 'sellers' and 'buyers,' the obvious thing to have done would have been to draw up a similar table for the sellers, and by considering both tables, to try to arrive at the unit price at which the buyers' demand and the sellers' supply coincide. Menger would then have come to the same result as Walras, but also to the same *complications*, in that neither the market price nor the quantity sold is necessarily uniquely determined. Menger does not take that step, however. Instead, he takes another course, and first considers the single seller as a *monopolist* who regulates his supply and his price according to the usual rules of monopolistic trade; he then tries to show how the market conditions would be changed if there were not a monopolist owner or manufacturer of the good in question, but instead several sellers competing among themselves.

However, this is a roundabout route which does not really lead to any result. It is perhaps of minor importance that the mathematical treatment of the competition between two or more monopolists—not an easy matter, it is true—was not quite correct, although one would have expected the editor, who is a mathematician, to have noticed the fault and corrected it. But Menger did not succeed in grasping the chief point of the problem in its general aspects. He states (p. 214) that the essential difference between 'monopolistic and competitive policies' is that the monopolist, unhindered by competition, is in a position to restrict his supply or manufacture as soon as he sees that his total net profit would be smaller with a larger supply than with a smaller one; while the individual seller under competitive conditions 'increases his production so long as any part of it (*das einzelne Stück*) continues to be of some use to him, however small that may be.' It seems that Menger assumes here that production is subject to rising costs of manufacture, so that the seller's profit is a sort of quasi-rent, whereas, in the case of the monopolist (p. 204), he assumed that the costs of production are constant; if this latter assumption had been made for the case of free competition, it would have meant that all real profit from production (enterprise profit) disappears.

It was really inopportune at this early stage of the theory of exchange to introduce the idea of production and production costs, which complicate the problem of pricing to an extent that cannot be foreseen. Menger ought to have allowed both the monopolist and the competing sellers to put certain given quantities of goods on the market, of which they would offer a certain amount for sale and *keep the remainder*. The use value of the goods held back in that way would be of no importance to the monopolist, and could therefore be neglected—'the Dutch in the East Indies,' for instance, did not load themselves with a lot of superfluous spices, but burned them—although, strictly speaking, the amount held in reserve would cause the most favourable price for the monopolist to be a little *higher* than the so-called monopoly price as a rule. If, on the other hand, the supply in the market is derived from a number of small, mutually competing sellers, the use value of the quantity which they may decide to hold in reserve can be an important factor, and may even have such an effect that a sharp rise in the price causes a *decrease* in the supply of the good in question, which seems to have been what happened with many of our 'self-supporters' during the war.

Thus, it cannot be said that Menger gave a complete solution of the problem he set himself: to explain the phenomenon of pricing with subjective use-value as the *only* factor involved. The first one of the Austrian School to succeed in doing this was Böhm-Bawerk, who undoubtedly gave an entirely correct treatment of the problem in his well-known example of the *horse market*, although he employed the further simplification that each seller has at his disposal only one specimen of the good which is offered for sale in the market (and likewise, each buyer wishes to buy only one). In this way, the problem is made easier by the exclusion of the paradox of a possible *decrease* in supply while the price is increasing.

Jevons's treatment of the problem was also not completely satisfactory. He places buyers and sellers into separate groups (trading bodies), whose members compete with one another, but at the same time he postulates a marginal utility valid for the whole group, this being dependent only on the total amount of the good or goods in question, without the distribution of this quantity among the members of the group being taken into consideration, either before or after the exchange. On this point also, Walras is far ahead of rival theorists, both in respect of the scope of his treatment and in the logical precision of it. He has also given a correct solution of a question which is extremely important, especially as regards monetary theory, namely, the problem of the exchange of *three* or more goods in the market. This is a problem which Jevons completely misunderstood, and which Menger on the whole did not treat.

200

The first edition of Menger's book had a final chapter on *monetary theory*. This, however, merely contained some reflections—very interesting ones as a matter of fact—about the origin and functions of money, but did not make any attempt to inquire into the circumstances which affect the *value* of money or its purchasing power. There is a footnote in the new edition (p. 335), however, which confirms what I pointed out in my memorial article on Carl Menger[1] that he was at the time in complete agreement with the so-called metallist point of view. He maintains explicitly 'that the exchangeability of money would disappear immediately if it were to cease to be usable as a metal for some reason or other.' This is hard to believe. If the demand for gold for industrial purposes were to cease altogether, all the newly produced gold, and some of the old as well, would then be available for monetary purposes, of course, and this would certainly cause the value of gold to *fall*, if other circumstances remained unchanged. It cannot very well be assumed, however, that its value would therefore disappear entirely, or that it would become unusable as a means of exchange.

In the new edition, the whole of this chapter has been omitted, except for the footnote just mentioned, and in its place is a new one, which is in the main a reprint of Menger's well-known monograph 'Das Geld' (Money) in *Conrads Handwörterbuch*. My opinion about this change is on the whole the same as for the other changes, although in this case the replacement is one which was published by Menger himself. The new version does not deal with the question of the value of money either, but several statements indicate that Menger had changed his viewpoint, and *in the main* had adopted the quantity theory, and that he believed in the possibility of stabilising the value of money by regulating the production of gold and the amount of notes in circulation. He draws a peculiar and original, though hardly satisfactory, distinction between the *external and internal exchange-value of money*. He interprets the term external exchange-value quite simply as the purchasing power of money in its ordinary sense, with respect to goods and other items in circulation. He does not give any proper definition of the *internal* value of money and usually puts the expression in inverted commas, which must be taken to imply that he does not use it as a definite concept but more as a manner of speaking. The whole problem turns upon the well-known observation that a change in the purchasing power of money may depend on circumstances affecting goods (or the other circulating

---

[1] Included in this volume, pp. 186 ff.

items) or on circumstances affecting money itself. If the latter is wholly or mainly the case, Menger calls the change 'a change in the internal exchange value of the money' (p. 305). I consider this expression to be incorrect; it should have been 'the internal change in the exchange value of money,' or something of the sort, since money has, of course, only *one* exchange value and one purchasing power, just as other goods.

I find myself still less in agreement with Menger's statement (p. 308) that 'the problem of finding a good with constant internal exchange value' is 'incomparably simpler than the analogous problem with regard to the external value.' The fact of the matter seems to be just the contrary. To reduce the amount of means of exchange when the price index shows a tendency to move upwards and to increase this amount when the index begins to move downward does not give rise to any insuperable difficulties, apart from the fact that the method must be as yet attended by certain imperfections. But how are we to go about the task of preventing all 'internal' changes in the value of money, in other words, the task of ensuring that price changes which actually take place are due to changed conditions of production and consumption of goods, etc.? The most obvious course would be to allow the amount of means of payment to move parallel to the movement of the population figures, so that the amount of means of payment per head of the population remains unchanged. But this will not suffice, for if a market economy gradually replaces a household economy, as has happened in the past, then more money per head of population is needed if the price level is not to fall, *in spite of* the fact that the relative size of production itself may remain unchanged. Then there is also the (virtual) increase in the velocity of circulation of money due to the continual development of banking and credit activity, the magnitude of which is probably more or less impossible to estimate.

Menger's line of thought on this point bears certain resemblance to the ideas on the regulation of the price level which Professor Davidson has often put forward. I do not wish to deny their justification, but I still fail to see how they are to be realised in practice. However, it might be conceded that this would to some extent happen automatically, if all excessively *drastic* measures for restoring a changed level of prices were avoided. If, for example, a rise in prices were caused by a decrease in production brought about through war or famine, this would accordingly find expression for the time being in an increased price level, and people with fixed incomes would have to share in the general misfortune, which could not be called unjust. Smaller changes in the volume of production, on the other hand, must be regarded as among the items of risk which are a necessary ingredient of business activity. Therefore, I think on the whole that one must be content with a monetary policy which aims at maintaining the exchange value of money in the 'external' sense.

The inclusion of the article on money, together with other additions and extensions, has made the book twice as long as the first edition, as the editor points out. There is no question that the new parts of the book, like everything written by Menger, deserve to be read and pondered upon, and furthermore, we must be grateful that the editor, although not an economist by profession, has given so much time and trouble to give this new edition a form in accordance with the intentions of the author. I also look forward with great interest to the publication of Menger's other, hitherto unpublished, manuscripts. What is fundamental and really original in the book, as well as in the whole of Menger's known literary production, is in my opinion to be found in the short chapters on value and exchange. If Menger had written no more than that, his name would have been assured of a place in the history of economics, just as the name of Leibniz would still have been immortal if he had written only that short treatise on the determination of the direction of a tangent at a point of a curve whose equation is known; the modest beginning of the whole of the new mathematics. Economics can certainly not boast of anything like the upward surge of mathematics during the first fifty years after Leibniz's (and Newton's) discovery. But this is due in the first place to the incredibly complicated nature of economic phenomena, for which there is nothing quite comparable in mathematics or physics. Add to this the fact that the equations of economic curves are hardly known even approximately, and are often just hypothetical. It is the task of economic statistics, which are making eager progress at the present time, to provide us with better data; but when this material is at last ready for use, I believe it will be found that the theoretical foundations laid by Jevons, Menger and Walras—and we might as well include Böhm-Bawerk for his theory of capital—are so durable and deeply penetrating that no other foundations can or need be laid.

MATHEMATICAL ECONOMICS [1]

IN the preface to the book [2] which is the immediate cause of the observations which follow, mathematical methods in economics are described as a 'very valuable aid to analysis.' These words of a prominent statistician pleased me greatly, for although the number of mathematical-economic books and journal articles has come to be quite considerable during the past fifty years, it still seems that this literature is regarded by the majority of economists more as a curiosity than as something of real practical value. In actual fact, mathematics has the same usefulness in economics as it has everywhere else—it helps us to think; that is, to the extent to which it can actually be applied, which unfortunately is not very far, on account of the lack of sufficient, or sufficiently exact, statistical data. It cannot replace actual thinking, of course—the occasional attempts which have been made in that direction have not turned out well— but it contributes a great deal to clarity and vigour of thought by *defining* inflexibly the assumptions and concepts upon which our reasoning is based, and which (otherwise) are only too liable to change their form, or even to become totally obscured, during the course of a long and complicated chain of reasoning, so that in the end there is no sure distinction between premiss and conclusion.

We may consider some examples by way of illustration. One of the first propositions we learn in mathematics is that the part is less than the whole. The truth of this would certainly not be denied in so many words by any intelligent person, but that is not to say that it is always a living truth for those who call themselves economists. On the contrary, it could probably be said that most of what has been written on economic subjects has involved a confusion of the part with the whole, or vice versa, and would have found its way into the wastepaper basket if the author had been obliged to use a diagram or a simple formula to make clear to the reader, and to himself *the order of magnitude* of the quantities with which he was dealing.

---

[1] 'Matematisk nationalekonomi,' *Ekonomisk Tidskrift*, 1925, pp. 103–25.
[2] A. L. Bowley, *The Mathematical Groundwork of Economics*, An Introductory Treatise, Oxford: Clarendon Press, 1924, pp. viii, 98.

Sometimes the whole is taken to be only a part of itself, as when 'the consumers' are treated as a part, sometimes a negligible part, of the population, instead of comprising the whole of it; even more often the part usurps the place of the whole, as when terms like 'the interests of agriculture' or 'the interests of industry,' etc., are used for what are really the interests of the landowners—and only the big ones at that—in raising rents, or the interests of the big capitalists in increased profits on capital; for the *smaller* landowners and capitalists are really only workers, and on the whole have the same interests as other workers. Compulsion to define mathematically the terms used, even if for the present this can only be done in a more or less hypothetical way, would probably be the best safeguard against such more or less involuntary mistakes.

One of the greatest advantages which mathematics can offer to the economists is, says Marshall, that with its aid he can convince himself that he has *sufficient* assumptions for the conclusions he wishes to draw, in other words, that the number of unknowns does not exceed the number of equations or logical relationships which connect them with one another or with quantities already known. This rule has always been far from clear for the majority of economists. Consider, for example, the important problem of the distribution of the products between the owners of the different productive factors, especially the three main classes of them: labour, land (natural resources) and capital. If we assume that the value of the products, P, is equal to the sum of the costs of production, we can express this in symbols by the equation

$$P = A + R + I,$$

where A denotes wages, R rent, and I profit on capital for the branch of production in question, or for the production of the whole country. As soon as this equation has been written down it is as clear as day that in order to solve it we must have three further independent relationships between the four quantities. But it is quite safe to declare that before Walras no economist had formulated this necessary condition clearly, although Ricardo and his followers came near to doing so. But there have been innumerable writers who have thought that they had contributed something to the solution merely, one might say, by moving one of the quantities from the right-hand side of the equation to the left, or vice versa. Walras himself mentions a work on the rent of land by a certain P. A. Boutron, which in his day was awarded a prize by the French academy of moral and political sciences. The author begins, says Wairas, by stating explicitly

205

that the selling price of products is determined by their cost price. He goes on to define the rent of land as 'the amount by which the selling price of the products exceed their cost price in wages of labour and profits on capital.' If it had been a question of deriving a theory of wages instead, then, says Walras, he would 'obviously define the wages as the amount by which the selling price of the products exceeds their cost price—in rent and profits.'[1] And if the Academy had chosen as the subject of the competition a theory of the profit on capital, he would undoubtedly have carried off the prize by defining profits as 'the amount by which the selling price of the products exceeds their cost price in rent and wages'!

The aid of mathematics is even more invaluable when one of the unknowns appears multiplied by itself (that is, to a higher power than one), as is the case with monopolist profit, for example. When the simplest assumption is made that the monopolist has no need to consume his own commodity, then his profit obviously increases or decreases in the combined proportion of the quantity sold and the net price he achieves per unit, and this, in its turn, depends on, or, as we say, is a function of, the amount of the goods sold. Even if the functional relationship here were merely 'linear' (i.e. as between the co-ordinates of a straight line), the desired amount sold (and with it the desired monopoly price) would be the root of an equation of (at least) the second degree; the same monopoly profit can be achieved at *two* different prices (or amounts of the goods sold, as the case may be), and between them the highest possible monopoly profit must be sought. The solution presents itself as soon as mathematical symbols are used (as they were by Cournot as long ago as 1838). How ungainly the treatment of the problem otherwise becomes may be seen from Fr. J. Neumann's well-known treatment of price (also in *Schönbergs Handbuch*). In speaking about 'Die Monopol- oder Vorzugspreise' Neumann says that the monopolist—as well as assuring his privileged position—must endeavour to choose that level of prices which will guarantee him the greatest profit, and consequently (*a*) the smallest practicable costs, and (*b*) the largest gross yield, for which it is necessary for him to make the greatest possible sales at the highest possible price. 'The latter expression may mean many things, of course,' continues Neumann; 'the highest possible price naturally does not mean the price which has risen the most on

[1] As I once pointed out in *Ekonomisk Tidskrift* (1914, p. 323), Mithoff's theory of wages in *Schönbergs Handbuch* is actually of just this type, and the same is also true to some extent of F. A. Walker's much discussed theory of wages, which was even accepted by Jevons.

the whole, but only those prices which are the highest possible, while fulfilling the other aims mentioned above, rise in sales, etc. For these aims taken by themselves the lowest possible prices would be sought,' and so on.

Because a mathematical treatment was lacking, a problem as important as the taxing of monopoly profit has been misinterpreted by many economists. When the monopolist has secured for himself 'the greatest possible profit,' it was believed that taxation of his production would not induce him to raise his selling price any higher. As Cournot had already shown, this is not correct. Only if the taxation is levied on the monopolist's net profit does it leave the price unchanged, whereas taxation levied on the commodity itself will usually lead to a more or less considerable rise in this price, so that this form of taxation is to the disadvantage of the consumers, and, strangely enough, without any accompanying advantage to the monopolist or to the State treasury.

If we now consider a still more complicated question, which is of particular practical importance in our own day, that of a price war between two or more 'monopolists' (that is, holders of privileged positions), either dealing in the same goods or in different ones, then the solution immediately becomes so complicated that it has actually got even practised mathematicians into a quandary, as we shall see in the following. It would seem to be futile to try to arrive at it by ordinary reasoning, or at least it would require a head of no mean mathematical ability, such as a Ricardo or a Böhm-Bawerk, both of whom were able to cope with quite complicated problems by the least mathematical means.

On the other hand, one must endorse Marshall's warning to mathematical economists to give the smallest possible space to mathematics in their *writings*, particularly with regard to algebraic symbols, and to keep them mainly for their own use, as Newton did at first with the differential calculus. This seems to be good practical advice. Since the data at the disposal of the economist are in the main not even statistical but merely such as may be obtained from immediate observation, the results of our investigations can at best only be extremely rudimentary; we are mostly concerned only with the question of plus *or* minus, forwards *or* backwards, upwards *or* downwards, and so on, and only very seldom with more detailed quantitative determinations, other than purely hypothetical ones. It is precisely for this reason that such a result, once found, may as a rule be derived by much simpler means than the mathematical apparatus which was used to find it. An Example: One of the most interesting results reached by research in this field is probably the one just mentioned, established by F. Y. Edgeworth, that although the taxation of a single monopoly does as a rule lead to an increase in its price, and never to a decrease, such is not the case with two or more goods handled by the same monopolist, provided only one, or not all, of them are taxed. For instance, a luxury tax levied on first and second class railway tickets (as in England) might under certain not unreasonable conditions, induce a railway company to *lower* the price of tickets for *all* classes of travel. That anyone other than a practised (and skilful) mathematician would have succeeded in arriving at this surprising conclusion is, to say the least, unlikely, but once it has been arrived at it is not difficult (as I have endeavoured to show in Vol. I of my *Lectures*) to demonstrate its truth by means of ordinary reasoning or a very simple graphical construction.

To lay down such a requirement rigorously would, however, be an over-statement—and Marshall for his part does not go so far as that—but what we have the right to demand is that the formulae or figures which a mathematical economic writer wishes to use must be fully *comprehensible* to every reader who is familiar with the language of mathematical symbols. No pains should be spared in explaining them to the full, and in clearing away every misunderstanding regarding their meaning. Unfortunately, well-nigh all mathematical economists are more or less guilty in this respect. That elegant lack of words which may be quite appropriate in purely mathematical papers, where the formulae may be left to speak for themselves without any doubt arising as to their meaning, is quite out of place when it is a matter of terms as vague and ill-defined as the basic concepts of economics; but sometimes it seems to be almost a matter of honour to allow the text to shrink to the same degree as the formulae are extended, instead of the other way about. To this it must be added that there is just as little fixed terminology available here as there is in economic theory in general, and that each writer uses his own notation, etc., so that it can unfortunately not be doubted that the mathematical economists' circle of readers is still very limited. This is a great pity, for it is only when many are working in the same field that it is possible to achieve the mutual criticism which alone can offer a guarantee against mistakes, and the cross-fertilisation of ideas which is the surest way of promoting the development and progress of theory as a whole.

Bowley's book will clear the way for such a general comprehension. It provides a coherent presentation of the most important things accomplished in mathematical economics, although mainly with reference to English research: Jevons, Edgeworth, Marshall, and among the younger ones Pigou and W. E. Johnson; the others mentioned include Cournot and Pareto, but not Walras, who was the first to give a completely mathematical treatment of free exchange. Bowley also wishes to introduce 'standardisation' of the whole doctrine by means of a uniform notation and uniform terminology, a proposal the importance of which cannot be over-estimated. Finally, in the form of an appendix, he gives demonstrations of the few theorems of so-called higher mathematics which he employs in his book. The author is of the opinion that the book is therefore useful even for readers only possessed of the most ordinary mathematical knowledge. I have my doubts about this, because Bowley belongs to those who love conciseness more than is desirable for the average reader; I am not at all sure that I, for my part, succeeded in gathering his meaning at every point, despite all my efforts to do so. In any case, it seems that the book would be better for those who are already engaged with these problems than for beginners. On the whole, however, it must be said that Bowley has carried out the task he set himself in an admirable way. Progressing from the simpler to the more complex cases, his presentation, from the nature of the matter, becomes so complicated in the end, when it is concerned with the influence of production upon the whole market that a list of the notation used occupies a whole page of the book; but this notation is so well chosen and so superbly handled that the reader runs no risk of losing the thread if he picks it up quite clearly in the beginning. If one is in any doubt as to the meaning of a certain expression, it is only necessary to turn back to this list (p. 46), as to a dictionary— an excellent arrangement.

He begins with the indifference lines (or surfaces) introduced by Edgeworth, that is combinations of quantities of two (or more) different commodities, which vary with respect to one another in such a way that together they always have the same utility, so that the consumer has no reason to prefer one of these combinations to another. If, for example, a person has to choose whether he will consume during a certain period of time, say the next month, 1 lb. of coffee and 1 lb. of sugar or $\frac{1}{2}$ lb. of coffee and 2 lb. of sugar, and he prefers the latter combination, it is clear that it must be possible to decrease the latter quantity of sugar (e.g. to $1\frac{1}{2}$ lb.) so that both combinations are of *equal* value to him. But in that case there must necessarily also be a whole series of *intermediate* combinations which

209

yield the same utility. These combinations, taken together, form an indifference line. If we begin with a combination having a higher (or lower) utility, for example, the ½ lb. of coffee and 2 lb. of sugar mentioned above, a new indifference line with a higher (or lower) index is obtained, and so on.

The advantage of this treatment is that the quantities dealt with are tangible physical ones from the beginning, instead of the more or less metaphysical concept of marginal utility: nevertheless, as can easily be seen, the two ways of regarding the matter are extremely close to one another, and can be interchanged at any time.

A simple geometrical construction takes us from the indifference curves to what Bowley calls 'offer curves,' first drawn up by Marshall, which show for each relative price quoted on the market for two goods, the quantities which a particular individual would always exchange if he possessed the one good and wished to acquire the other. The choice of name is not entirely a happy one (as Edgeworth points out in his review of the book),[1] because, *inter alia*, it is easy to confuse it with the individual's supply curve, which is something quite different. The expression 'exchange-' or 'bargaining-curve' would be better, particularly as the combination of the 'offer curves' of two individuals is called by the author himself their 'bargaining locus.'

It is not difficult to see that the 'exchange' or 'offer' curve indicates both the individual's demand for the good he wishes to acquire and his supply of his own good, at all conceivable market prices. Now, since, with *uniform pricing*, the ratio of the quantity of goods which a person disposes of to the quantity he procures is identical with the relative price of the latter expressed in terms of the former, a simple change of variables gives the customary demand and supply curves for each particular individual, as used by Walras, Marshall, and others—that is, his demand and supply expressed as functions of the market price. Now if it were the case that only two persons exchanged goods on the market with each other, then the market price would be given simply by the intersection (or intersections) of the demand curve of one of them and the supply curve of the other (and it is easy to show that this point gives the same price as the intersection of the former's supply curve and the latter's demand curve). This is not the case, however. Even if there were only two goods on the market, so that all exchange could be direct, then it would be a pure coincidence if, at the price ruling in the market, two

[1] *Economic Journal*, 1924, p. 432.

commodity owners could always satisfy each other's needs without one of them, as a rule, still having to exchange with one or more of the suppliers opposite. Not until all the demands and supplies at all conceivable market prices are brought together do we obtain a general demand curve for one party and a general supply curve for the other, whose intersection provides a theoretical determination of the market price. If there are more than two goods, then, as Walras has clearly shown, but Jevons neglected, direct exchange cannot by itself lead to price equilibrium on the market, but must to a greater or smaller extent be supplemented by an indirect exchange (where a quantity of goods is acquired, not for consumption, but for 'exchange with yet a third set of goods). This indirect exchange may ultimately become so extensive that, as under normal modern conditions, *all* exchange of goods is actually indirect—through the medium of money.

Bowley has perhaps not stated this with complete clarity. He does point out that individual exchange between two persons outside the market is, within certain limits, an indeterminate problem. Nevertheless he makes this the basis of market exchange—apparently, at least—and talks about 'any two persons' exchanging certain quantities of goods with one another on the market, the exchange being taken so far that the utility of *both* quantities 'is maximised,' which must undeniably suggest to the reader that the persons involved completely satisfy one another's needs, as in the case of individual exchange. This is merely an oversight, however; all is well if we confine our attention to person 'A,' and for the time being disregard what is said about 'B.' The final equations, corresponding to those derived by Walras, are quite correct, under the assumption that is the basis of the whole theory of perfect competition of course, that all those exchanging remain quite *passive* as far as the market price is concerned, and do not consciously attempt to influence it. This is a matter to which we will return later on.

Bowley describes as an 'important corollary' the fact that under free exchange every one of those exchanging 'can maximise the satisfaction of his needs at the same time.' This expression is also somewhat misleading. There can only be a real maximum under monopoly (proper). Under free exchange none of the participants (not even all of them together) attains a maximum in the strict sense, but what happens is that the general attempt to achieve such a maximum leads theoretically to a position of equilibrium, at which none of those exchanging goods has any incentive to increase or decrease the amount he exchanges *at the prices established on the market* under the influence of these very attempts.[1]

Up to this point the author has regarded the amount of goods on the market as given; the following sections deal with production and productive factors, with market equilibrium under the influence of production (in a stationary society), and lastly with some special questions of particular interest, such as taxation under free competition and under monopoly. This is presented in a way which is very elegant mathematically and comparatively easy to understand—at least by comparison with such considerably more difficult articles as those by Johnson, etc. The only criticism to be made is that the basic concepts are not sufficiently clarified or sharply defined. Unfortunately, as is usual among English theoreticians, *capital* in particular is treated in a rather stepmotherly fashion; actually, it is put on the same footing as natural resources, as the author himself emphasises in fact; time or waiting is not mentioned as a productive factor, and although the author specifically mentions that certain quantities of goods are required not for consumption but for 'saving,' we are not told to what use the saved goods are subsequently put.

He first assumes that all productive factors have prices determined in advance, so that it is up to an entrepreneur who wishes to produce a certain amount of a certain type of good to combine these factors in such a way that the cost for one unit of the good is as small as possible (the substitution principle). He then considers several producers of the same sort of good, and states that if equilibrium under free competition is to be possible, productivity must follow the law of diminishing returns, otherwise the most skilful of the entrepreneurs in the trade would gradually eliminate all his competitors and take sole charge of the entire output.[2]

[1] It is to some extent (although not exactly) the same as when everybody tries to decrease his cash holdings (and to increase his stockholdings) as much as possible, when faced with an expected decline in the value of money (as during the World War). This does not lead to any actual diminution of average cash holdings, nor to an increase of average holdings of stocks, since the sum of all the cash holdings is equal to the existent amount of money (as the sum of all holdings of stocks is equal to the existing amount of goods). But obviously the *endeavour* to do so must lead to a rise in prices, in relation to which the physically unchanged holdings of cash actually become less than normal.

[2] A reference to Pigou (for which the wrong page is given, if I interpret the intention rightly) is probably intended to refer to the circumstance already pointed out by Marshall, that an industry may follow the law of increasing returns in the national sense, while following the law of diminishing returns in the individual sense.

At this stage, however, we might ask the question: If it is possible to obtain all the productive factors, without exception, at a definite price, how is it possible for a law of decreasing returns to scale to be valid? A combination of factors of production which is economically advantageous for small scale production can *a fortiori* be applied also within the framework of larger scale production, although the converse is obviously not true. We must therefore suppose that the private entrepreneur is always limited in some way, either with regard to his geographical position or to his ownership of land or capital, or with respect to his skill and energy as an organiser. It seems, as a matter of fact, that the author himself tacitly assumes the latter, since he allows the productivity functions to be different for different entrepreneurs, despite the fact that the productive factors are supposed to be equally accessible to everybody.

In this connection Pigou's concept of marginal production costs (marginal supply prices) is also discussed—a concept which I think is unnecessarily muddled. By it is simply meant the increase in the total costs of production which occurs when normal production is increased by one unit. Nevertheless, Bowley states expressly (p. 35) that this is *not* the same as 'the cost of this last unit produced, but the additional cost of producing one more unit *after* adapting the organisation of the factors of production.' This is not at all easy to comprehend, and Pigou's own treatment of the matter in the first edition of *The Economics of Welfare* (1920, Appendix IV) certainly does not make it clearer. If the prices of the production factors are *given*, as Bowley and also Pigou suppose, then, assuming that production changes continuously, there will be no difference between these two concepts as far as I can see. Of course there must *always* be an 'adaptation of the organisation of the factors of production' when the volume of production is changed, although some time may be necessary for its completion.

It is quite a different matter if the prices of the production factors are *not* given, but vary with changes in production. For instance, suppose a country produces 100,000 tons of cereals, at a cost price including rent of 200 crowns per ton. If another 10,000 tons are needed, it may be that these cannot be produced cheaper than 210 crowns per ton. This would therefore be (approximately) 'the cost of the last unit.' But land rents would also rise at the same time so that the original 100,000 tons now cost 10 crowns more per ton, including rent, than they did before. So, from the point of view of the country as a whole, the increased cost involved in obtaining the extra 10,000 tons of cereals is not just 2·1 million crowns, but

213

3·1 million crowns, or 310 crowns per ton, which will give the landowners an increased income of about 1 million crowns.

Pigou's notorious 'marginal supply curve,' which he himself has now abandoned, was originally intended to show that a certain amount of control applied to free competition would contribute to an increase in 'the national dividend.' Unfortunately he seems to have got hold of the wrong end of the stick to some extent, and with him, *mirabile dictu,* Edgeworth. In order to illustrate what is involved, I give the following example, recently put forward by Edgeworth (which I have here further simplified and which is actually almost the same as my own example in *Finanztheoretische Untersuchungen,* p. 65). A population—that of Ireland, for instance—is divided between two main occupations: agriculture, in the usual sense, and the manufacture of linen goods. For the sake of simplicity we will assume that the latter requires almost only labour, and a relatively insignificant area of land. Agriculture proper, on the other hand, besides wages, pays rents which arise in the usual manner and accrue to landowners resident abroad. The selling prices of both products are taken as given throughout the world market. Under free competition the division of the population between these two branches of production, as well as the level of wages, is such that (1) the wages in both occupations are the same, (2) the price of the linen goods conforms with their labour costs and (3) the price of agricultural products conforms with their labour costs plus the rent of land. But this is not the best arrangement as far as the whole country is concerned. If the Government undertakes measures which force some of the agricultural workers, say half of them, to go over to the manufacture of linen, then, we might assume, their wage incomes are unaltered, but the workers who remain in agriculture earn more than they did before, since rents decline, even relatively, and may even disappear entirely. Thus a national *surplus* arises here which did not exist under free competition. The result would be still more marked if the extension of linen output were to lead to certain common measures which facilitated its manufacture and sale, that is, if production were governed nationally (though not individually) by the law of increasing returns.

The converse would apply, however, if the rents remained inside the country, especially if they found their way to the state or else were used in some other generally beneficial way. In this case it is easy to show that a decrease in agricultural production would lead to a *loss* for the country, and it might even be impossible to compensate for this loss by increased turnover in the linen industry. It was more or less this circumstance which was overlooked by Pigou and Edgeworth. It would involve too big a digression to go further into this matter now, but perhaps I will have the opportunity on some other occasion to return to this question, which has given rise to particularly lively discussion during recent years in English and American journals—though with misunderstandings on both sides.

Bowley also deals with the question of whether the price equilibrium is *stable* when a large number of relatively small producers offer their goods for sale on the market, answering in the affirmative on the following grounds. It is true, he says, that each individual producer might increase his profit, though only by a small amount, in cutting down his production a little, but since this would cause the price to rise throughout the market, the other producers would be induced to *increase* their production so that prices would consequently decline again and the profits of the first producer be changed into losses. I do not know whether this reasoning is correct, since the very cause which prompts *one* of the producers to decrease his output ought to lead to the same course of action where the others are concerned. Consider a small isolated district which is provided with cereals by ten producers, each of whom harvests about 1,000 decitons. Let us suppose that the cost of production—with rent *excluded*—follows the law of diminishing returns, increasing in steps of $0 \cdot 01$ crowns per deciton from 10 crowns to 20 crowns in labour and capital costs. The selling price is therefore about 20 crowns per deciton when there is free competition, and the average profit of the producers (rent) 5 crowns per deciton. If one of the producers now decreases his production of cereals by half, the total amount offered for sale decreases by 5 per cent, and for the sake of simplicity we may suppose that the demand price and the selling price also rise by 5 per cent, or 1 crown per deciton. He therefore gains 500 crowns on the quantity which he still produces, but he loses the whole of the profit on the decrease in his production, which would have been $2 \cdot 5$ crowns per deciton, or 1,250 crowns in all. So his move was not a good one. But if he decreases his production by only 20 tons, thereby decreasing total production by the same amount, and if we suppose that the selling price increases by 2 per cent in consequence, then it is easy to see that the profit becomes $800 \times 0 \cdot 4 - 200 \times 1 =$ 120 crowns, that is, an actual net profit; and this net profit increases to a maximum, 143 crowns, when the restriction of production is $\frac{1}{7}$ of the original harvest, or about 143 decitons. If the others now follow his example, the rise in the price will soon be so great that it will be profitable for those who first cut down their production to increase it once more; but it is not at all clear to me that this brings the situation back to the original equilibrium position, as Bowley says it does. If my calculation is correct, a new position of equilibrium will be established at a point where all the producers have decreased their harvest by $\frac{1}{16}$, while if all of them combined in a single monopoly the most advantageous limitation of production would be as much as $\frac{2}{3}$ of each producer's original harvest, so that only $\frac{1}{3}$ of it would be offered for sale. (If the number of producers is very large, this discussion is of no practical significance, of course, unless they combine into monopolistic groups.)

I have already touched on a question which becomes more interesting every day, namely, that of incomplete or multiple monopolies, the state of affairs which arises when certain sellers (or buyers) in the market are not content to let their supply (or demand) be determined passively by the price-situation established quite automatically on the market, but consciously seek to influence it. Strictly speaking, there can be no other monopolies, for a monopoly in the classical sense assumes complete passivity on the part of *all* the customers of the monopolist and it could therefore only really be enjoyed by one person in the whole world.

Bowley's treatment of this problem does not seem to me to be completely satisfactory, and on the whole his views with regard to this question are rather vague. This seems some justification for recapitulating somewhat its previous history. Cournot was the first to give a satisfactory mathematical treatment of pricing under monopoly, and he also considered multiple monopolies in two typical cases, which at the same time are diametrically opposed to each other, namely (1) the case where there are two (or more) monopolists dealing in groups of goods which *compete* strongly with one another —he assumes for the sake of simplicity that both monopolists put identical goods on the market—and (2) the case where the monopolised goods are necessary mutual *complements*, so that the demands for them are always in a certain proportion—as an example he takes copper and zinc for the manufacture of brass, assuming that there is only one brass alloy and that neither metal has any other use. In the first case, Cournot assumes that each of the monopolists puts a certain quantity of a good on the market, so that both quantities together make up the market supply of this good (either exclusively or almost so) for a certain consumption period. The price of the good is then determined in the usual way by the demand of the competing consumers. If the monopolists have no expenses (he first supposes that they are owners of mineral springs whose waters have exactly the same mineral content), this price gives their profit per unit of the good directly—otherwise, of course, it is necessary to subtract from the gross price the cost per unit, either constant or varying according to the quantity of the good, as the case may be. In the first case, and also when the cost per unit is constant and the same for both of them, the net profit per unit, which we will call p, is evidently a function of the total quantity of goods sold. Since we are primarily concerned here with the principle involved, we may take this relation to be as simple as we please—for example, linear; and at the same time we may choose our units in such a way that we need no coefficients. So we simply write

$$p = 1 - x,$$

where x is the total quantity of goods. If $x = 1$, $p = 0$; so the unit we have chosen for the quantity of goods is that amount which can only be sold when the net price is zero (when the monopolists make no profit); and similarly we have obviously chosen as the unit of price the net price at which there is no demand at all ($p = 1$, $x = 0$).

If we now suppose that the two monopolists combine, they will obviously find it desirable to make the largest possible combined profit which they can then divide by agreement. In other words, they must maximise the quantity $x \cdot p = x(1 - x)$ which, since the sum of both the factors is unity and thus constant, obviously occurs when they are equal and each $\frac{1}{2}$. We thus have $x = \frac{1}{2}$ and $p = \frac{1}{2}$, each of them therefore being half of the corresponding unit.[1]

Such is by no means the case, however, says Cournot, if each of the monopolists tries to get the greatest possible profit for himself, making the assumption that the other will not alter his supply. For in this case they will act *against* their common interest and force down the price for each other, although only to a certain extent. For instance, if we assume that one of the monopolists was the only seller in the beginning, he would, as has been said, have offered the quantity $x_1 = \frac{1}{2}$ at the (net) price $\frac{1}{2}$. If the other monopolist then makes his appearance in the market and introduces the quantity x_2 there, then the price will obviously fall all along the line; for in that curve we obviously get

$$p = 1 - x_1 - x_2.$$

[1] In fact, the above-mentioned linear relation need only apply to a small part of the scale of value—the part actually relevant—and the units chosen therefore need only be hypothetical or estimated, not quantities actually occurring in reality.

Assuming that x_1 remains unchanged at $\frac{1}{2}$, the second monopolist will make his greatest profit when

$$x_2 \cdot p = x_2(1 - x_1 - x_2) = x_2(\tfrac{1}{2} - x_2)$$

is a maximum, that is, when

$$x_2 = \tfrac{1}{2} - x_2 = \tfrac{1}{4}.$$

But if monopolist No. 2 accordingly now contributes $\frac{1}{4}$, it will no longer be profitable for monopolist No. 1 to offer $\frac{1}{2}$, but the quantity which gives him the greatest profit, as is easy to see, will be

$$x_1 = \frac{1 - x_2}{2} = \tfrac{3}{8}$$

whereupon the second monopolist will change his supply to

$$x_2 = \frac{1 - x_1}{2} = \tfrac{5}{16}$$

and so on. It is easy to show that the fractions of this sequence approach the value of $\frac{1}{3}$—this being actually independent of the initial quantity—so that this is the quantity which will ultimately be offered for sale by each of the monopolists. It would have been possible to arrive at the same result by postulating a position of equilibrium to begin with, a situation where each of the monopolists would make the greatest possible profit—*under the assumption* that the other will not alter his supply; we would then have obtained the simultaneous equations

$$x_1 = \frac{x_2 - 1}{2},$$

$$x_2 = \frac{x_1 - 1}{2},$$

from which $\qquad x_1 = x_2 = \tfrac{1}{3}.$

Their total supply would therefore be $\frac{2}{3}$, and the net price consequently $\frac{1}{3}$, so that the total profit would be only $\frac{2}{9}$ instead of $\frac{1}{4}$, approximately 11 per cent less than if they had combined.

Cournot also solves the problem under more general assumptions, but the main result is the same: lowered price and increased supply, to the detriment of both monopolists. If there are more than two monopolists, the result is still more marked in this respect, so that when there are a sufficient number of producers in the market they only cover their constant production costs, without making any extra profit.[1] The whole thing consequently merges into free competition.

This does not sound improbable. More surprising is the result that Cournot arrives at when he considers the *second* case, where two (or more) goods, each monopolised, are mutually *complementary* in their use. In this case the *sales* of the one monopolist are completely regulated by the other's, while, on the other hand, they can determine their *prices* freely. What happens here is that if each of the monopolists attempts to obtain the greatest possible profit under the assumption that the other will keep his price unchanged, they will force one another to set ever *higher* prices upon their goods, while disposing of *smaller* quantities than would have given them the greatest possible combined profit. Thus here too, if each of them operates independently, instead of collaborating, they will do harm to one another's interests and at the same time to those of the consumer. For example, if zinc and copper mining were in the same hands to begin with but the concern was afterwards broken up, the consumers would jump out of the frying-pan into the fire. If it were supposed, as is rather unlikely, however, that a very large number of monopolised goods were quantitatively bound up with one another in this way, be it for purposes of consumption or for the production of other goods, the endeavours of the monopolists to make a profit might simply lead to the cessation of all sales of these goods, or at least make such sales extremely uneconomical.

If there are only two goods and the functional relation between the demand and the price is here assumed to be linear too, then this relation may be written

$$x_1 = x_2 = 1 - p_1 - p_2,$$

if the units are suitably chosen, the unit for each of the goods being the amount which would be used if the total price were zero, and the unit of price being the total price of (one unit of) each good which would prevent all sales. Now, if the first commodity-owner wants a certain price p_1, then the most advantageous price for the second owner —that is, the price which makes $p_2(1 - p_1 - p_2)$ a maximum—is clearly $p_2 = (1 - p_1) : 2$, and when he adopts this price, the first seller will adjust to $(1 - p_2) : 2 = \frac{1}{4} + p_1/4$, then the second to $\frac{3}{8} - p_1/8$, then again the first to $\frac{5}{16} + p_1/16$, and so on. The second term in these expressions

---

[1] If, instead, the monopolists had had increasing (unit) costs (diminishing returns), they would have enjoyed a certain *rent* in addition—analogous to the rent on land, which should not be confused with the monopoly profit, although it is sometimes called that.

approaches zero, and can therefore be neglected; the first approaches the value $\frac{1}{3}$, as in the preceding case, a result which we could also have obtained by solving the simultaneous equations

$$p_2 = \frac{1 - p_1}{2}$$

$$p_1 = \frac{1 - p_2}{2}$$

Thus each of them will ask a price $\frac{1}{3}$—both together $\frac{2}{3}$—of the (total) price which would have prevented all sales, and they will then sell $\frac{1}{3}$ of the quantity of goods which would have been consumed at the price zero, whereas, if they had combined, both the price and the sales would have been $\frac{1}{2}$ unit.

Among these conclusions of Cournot, the first-mentioned has especially been the subject of criticism from many quarters though it is not really possible to raise any objection to its final outcome, the transition of multiple monopoly to free competition. Among the critics is the well-known French mathematician Bertrand,[1] who nevertheless seems to have misunderstood Cournot. An exhaustive and much-discussed criticism, accepted on the whole by later writers, has been produced by Edgeworth.[2] But it seems to me that Edgeworth, too, scarcely does Cournot justice. He (like Bertrand) proceeds from a premiss quite different from Cournot's, namely, that one of the monopolists attempts to cut the other out of the market by *underselling* him—in which case there cannot be any position of equilibrium unless the monopoly profits of one, or both, of them have disappeared. But this means that the first-mentioned monopolist has, or thinks he has, a production advantage which he can realise at the expense of the other; and that, of course, belongs to a quite different set of considerations. If both are monopolists in the proper sense, so that each of them can reckon on a more or less considerable margin of profit, and if their products are competitive or simply identical, then it would of course be senseless for the one monopolist to lower his price *in the expectation* that the other will maintain his.[3] A much more plausible assumption on the

[1] *Journal des Savants*, 1883.

[2] *Giornale degli Economisti*, 1897, now included in his collected papers.

[3] In his *Manuel*, Pareto has each of the monopolists set out from what is, if possible, an even more unjustifiable assumption, that the other will succeed in keeping his previously attained *net profit* unchanged. In that case, as it is easy to perceive, would equilibrium come about in *every* situation as soon as the combined profit for both of them reaches the maximum value possible if they collaborated, and this is true, contrary to what Pareto maintains, whether the goods are of the same sort or not.

220

part of the various monopolists—especially if their numbers are large—would perhaps be that the other monopolist or monopolists will keep production and supply unchanged; even if this assumption must gradually be modified, it will at any rate hold good for the attainment of Cournot's equilibrium position.

If the two goods are of different sorts, but strongly competitive with each other, then the result will be approximately the same; if, on the other hand, they are more or less rigorously complementary to each other (Cournot's second case), then the one monopolist can obviously not assume that the other will keep his *supply* unchanged when he himself changes his, but rather that the other will keep the price of his good at a certain value, although this assumption also needs to be modified by degrees and does not hold good until the equilibrium position is reached. For the general case, on the other hand, either of the assumptions, or a combination of the two, may form the foundation: a position of equilibrium is achieved thereby in each case, but the equilibrium positions will be *different*! It therefore seems best to admit that the problem of incomplete (multiple) monopolies is *to some extent* undetermined, though not to the same extent as, for example, individual exchange. I therefore consider it unjustifiable to reject Cournot's penetrating analysis, lock, stock and barrel, as Edgeworth does, the more so as multiple positions of equilibrium are by no means out of the question even with free competition.

Bowley can hardly be said to have contributed in any essential respect to the classification of the problems just mentioned. In the matter of several monopolists dealing in the same sort of goods, he seems to take up Edgeworth's standpoint, although his reasons for doing so are not at all clear. He considers that the result would be 'an oscillation in the neighbourhood of the price' at which the monopoly profit disappears for both monopolists, which is hardly conceivable except in the case when each of them tries to cut the other out of the market (see above). With regard to monopolies in several different types of goods, as far as the extremely scanty treatment allows one to judge, Bowley seems to suppose that the sales of a monopolised good depend exclusively on the price which the monopolist in question sets on his good, and not at all on the prices which the other monopolists put on their goods. This can never be more than approximately true, of course, and often does not apply at all. But even on the basis of this assumption I cannot follow his mathematics in the note on p. 26 'on universal monopoly,' where, among other things, he seems to come to the peculiar conclusion that if two goods out of four on the market are monopolised and the other two not, there may be an unambiguous, or at any rate determinate, solution to the problem of pricing, whereas this is not the case if three of the goods are monopolised and only one of them subject to free competition. I suspect that the mathematics has gone a little astray here, although I cannot go into it further, however. As I see it, the problem should be treated in the following way. Suppose that the three monopolists provisionally put certain prices on their goods, expressed, let us say, in terms of the fourth, non-monopolised good as unit. Then, in accordance with the ordinary theory of exchange, we obtain sufficient equations to express all the quantities given and taken in exchange as functions of these three prices, which we will take to be independent variables for the time being. Also, since all 'utility functions' must be regarded as given, we have at the same time an expression for each monopolist's economic situation after the exchange, and hence also for his *profit* from the latter. If it were true that this profit only depended on the price which he sets on his own good—as might approximately be the case if the monopoly in question were small compared with the market as a whole, and if, in addition, the monopolised goods were independent of each other as far as consumption (or further production) is concerned—this would show itself in negligibly small coefficients for the other two variables, and the whole problem would then resolve itself into three separate actual maximisation problems. But it is obvious that there is no proper maximum solution of the general problem—as long as the monopolists do not combine and 'share the spoils'—since each of them controls only his own price or supply and not that of the other two. But it is possible that there is an equilibrium position in Cournot's sense, that is, one where it is not profitable for any of the monopolists to change his price (or his supply, as the case may be) as long as the others do not change theirs, and it cannot be denied that there is some justification for Cournot's opinion that this equilibrium—which is, in the nature of the matter, stable—would be reached by successive shifts of the sort described above.

After a particularly elegant treatment of the general problem of production and exchange, for which the prices of production factors are no longer considered to be constant but variable, Bowley returns to the problem of monopoly and asserts that a determinate solution of the problem is still possible even if all goods are monopolised, provided that the factors of production are *not*; and conversely, if the factors of production are monopolised—for example, labour through the trade unions or capital through bank-mergers, etc.—provided the turnover of goods is free. To this it seems to me that the same objection applies as applied before: in general an equilibrium position is possible only on the lines described by Cournot.

If both the factors of production and the turnover of goods are monopolised, then, says Bowley, it is a different matter. Equilibrium then can only be brought about by collusion. For the sake of simplicity he takes as an example a single manufacturer with only one worker, though this simplification does not affect the main question, of course. (If I remember correctly, Babbage gives an example of this sort. An English toy manufacturer who had hitherto had to import *dolls' eyes*, was eventually successful after a long search in London in finding a consumptive Italian glass-blower who understood the art of making dolls' eyes, and with his help he established a flourishing trade in this article. The worker in this case was thus the manufacturing monopolist and the employer the selling monopolist.) In this case, says Bowley, the employer fixes a certain wage (piece-rate) π, and tries to arrange the selling price p and the sales x so that he obtains the greatest possible profit. This wage will induce the worker to make a certain quantity of the good, since he is also trying to obtain the greatest possible benefit for himself; but, says Bowley, this quantity will *not* in general be the same as x, and so on. This I do not understand. If the manufacturer is in a position to fix the wage, then contrary to the assumption the worker does not have a monopoly.[1] If he only works a certain amount for a certain wage, he is still not in a monopolising position. It is necessary to assume that the worker *himself* decides what wage he is to receive, and in this situation he has, within limits, a primary, real monopoly, and the employer only a secondary one. With suitably chosen units, we may suppose, as before, that sales are regulated in accordance with the equation

$$x = 1 - p$$

where p is the selling price. If π is the wage, the manufacturer's profit is

$$(p - \pi)(1 - p)$$

[1] On the contrary the manufacturer would then have a double monopoly, and would obviously arrange production and sales so that they correspond with each other, and moreover so that he would get the greatest possible profit.

which is at a maximum for each given value of π when the two factors are equal, and consequently

$$p = \frac{1 + \pi}{2}$$

at which sales become

$$x = 1 - p = \frac{1 - \pi}{2}.$$

The worker's income (per unit of time) will therefore be

$$\pi \cdot \frac{1 - \pi}{2}$$

which is at a maximum when $\pi = \frac{1}{2}$. If for the sake of simplicity we suppose that the worker only endeavours to obtain for himself the greatest possible income per unit of time, he ought to ask for a wage equal to a half of the unit we have chosen for the selling price (that which makes the sales zero); whereupon the sales price becomes $\frac{3}{4}$ of this unit; sales $\frac{1}{4}$ of the unit of quantity; and the worker's income $\frac{1}{8}$ and the manufacturer's profit $\frac{1}{16}$ of the combined unit of price and quantity, that is to say, of the sum of money determined by multiplying the quantity which would be sold per unit of time if the price were zero, by the price (of each such unit) which would make all sales impossible. (I should like to point out once again that these units need only be imagined or estimated and need not exist or be observable in reality.)

On the other hand, the employer can *not* here take the initiative by fixing a certain selling price and thereby a certain volume of sales, because in such a case it would be in the interests of the worker to demand the highest possible wage that the employer can afford to pay. The employer might possibly be able to depress the worker's wage indirectly, if, *apparently contrary to his own interest*, he fixes the selling price for each definite level of wages (in accordance with the maximising rule) as if the wage were *higher*—say twice as high—than the wage which he is actually paying. It is easy to see that in this case $p = \frac{1}{2} + \pi$, $x = \frac{1}{2} - \pi$, and the worker's total income would then be $\pi(\frac{1}{2} - \pi)$, which is a maximum when $\pi = \frac{1}{4}$. The definite selling price and the volume of sales would then be $\frac{3}{4}$ and $\frac{1}{4}$ respectively, as before, but the employer's and the worker's shares of the receipts from sales would then be the other way round, $\frac{1}{8}$ and $\frac{1}{16}$ respectively of the combined unit mentioned above. This assumes, however, that the worker allows himself to be *deceived*; but if, on the other hand, he also is fully aware of the economic situation and demands a wage of $\frac{1}{2}$, it is obvious that the employer has no alternative but to content himself with a price $\frac{1}{4}$ higher than this and the profit of $\frac{1}{16}$, which is the largest possible profit for him under these circumstances. On the other side the worker cannot get better conditions than these, as long as the employer is in a position to arrange his sales as he pleases. It may therefore be said that the worker attains a real maximum and the employer a relative maximum. The great importance and significance of the problem is easily understood if we replace the *single* worker by a strong trade union with some tens of thousands of members, and the single employer with a syndicate of employers operating in a certain branch of manufacturing.

The more doubtful points which I have criticised above constitute only a small part of the book, and I am not suggesting that my opinion is the only correct one. The greater part of the presentation is entirely correct, and many of the detailed applications are good evidence of the perspicacity of the author.

I should like to mention in passing that Bowley tries to illustrate with a simple example the question which was discussed by W. E. Johnson (*Econ. Journal*, 1913), concerning the circumstances under which a rise in the price of a good might lead to an *increase* in the demand for it. Bowley's example is quite ingenious (it concerns the purchase of a building site in certain complicated circumstances), but it is rather an analogy than a real illustration of Johnson's problem, and it further suffers from the defect that the price of a piece of land, of which *both* dimensions vary, is taken to be proportional to only one of these dimensions. Actually, the most important practical case in this connection (as I have endeavoured to show in my *Lectures*) is when two goods may entirely replace one another in the satisfaction of a *primary* need, such as food or heating, while one of them (wheat as against rye or potatoes, wood as against coke, and so on) is preferable in certain *secondary* respects, and can therefore demand a relatively higher price. A rise in the price of the cheaper good might easily lead to an increase in the demand for it—and as a consequence, to a decrease in the demand for the other good—simply because the incomes of the consumers are not sufficient to cater for their primary needs otherwise; or, more generally, because price equilibrium for the satisfaction of the secondary need could not otherwise occur.

Unfortunately, in spite of the length of this paper, I have only been able to give a very incomplete idea of the contents of Bowley's book,

225

but sufficient, I hope, to show that it is well worth while for any economist to make its acquaintance if he can spare sufficient time to work through its few but well-packed pages.[1]

[1] Editor's Note: In order to facilitate the reading of Bowley's Book, Wicksell gives at the end of the essay a long list of errata and inaccuracies, which he has found in Bowley's mathematical representation. This list has been omitted here.

IV

FOREIGN TRADE PROBLEMS

THE RIDDLE OF FOREIGN
EXCHANGES[1]

I

THE study of the rates of exchange, which at one time attracted so much practical and theoretical interest, had been almost entirely neglected by economists during the decades immediately preceding the war. We do not have to look far for the reason. As a consequence of the general adoption of the gold standard—or of the 'gold exchange standard,' which is similar in its action and effect—the rates of exchange between the different countries hardly fluctuated at all, except within the margin of the 'gold points,' and that margin was certainly becoming narrower with the easing of intercommunication. It is true that there were still matters calling for explanation in the fluctuation of rates of exchange *within* those limits: why it was, for instance, that in the case of certain countries the rate stood, on an average, rather below par, while in the case of other countries it was rather above par, and so on; but that problem was really of too little economic interest to be the object of more thorough investigation.

If such an investigation had been undertaken, however, it would certainly have revealed, among other things—as K. Helfferich pointed out several years ago—that the actual fluctuations of gold had almost completely ceased to perform the part which they formerly played, of adjusting the balance of payments and maintaining the rates of exchange. According to F. Schmidt,[2] in Germany the relation between the balance of trade and the exports and imports of gold during the years 1909–13 was as shown in the following table:

[1] 'Växelkursernas gåta,' *Ekonomisk Tidskrift*, 1919, Part I, pp. 87–103.

Translator's Note: As will become obvious from the text, the rate of exchange is here expressed as the number of units of the domestic currency needed to purchase a given unit of the foreign currency, and not vice versa as is the British custom. Thus a 'rise' in the exchange rate means that the domestic currency is falling in value relatively to the foreign currency, and conversely for a 'fall.'

[2] 'Die Beherrschung der Wechselkurse' (The Control of Exchange Rates), *Weltwirtschaftliches Archiv*, 1918, p. 543.

Millions of Marks

Year	Imports of goods	Exports of goods	Imports of gold	Exports of gold
1909	9,139	7,175	370	306
1910	9,535	8,080	555	353
1911	10,380	8,774	297	118
1912	11,572	9,684	327	143
1913	11,655	10,892	441	103

Thus, not only does the entire volume of the gold movement constitute but a small percentage of the commodity turnover, but it must further be remembered that Germany is, of course, a transit-country for gold on its way to other parts of Europe. It may therefore be asked whether this gold-movement, which closed every year with a substantial net balance in Germany's favour, was not, in the main, merely the inevitable diffusion of the metal from the gold-producing countries to the rest of the world. The casual relationship between the balance of trade, the rate of exchange and the shipments of gold had, in a way, been reversed. A country which produces gold over and above its own requirements must permanently have an adverse balance of trade or balance of payments, and an 'unfavourable' rate of exchange; for otherwise it would not be able to dispose of its gold. And the same applies, more or less, to those countries which receive the gold in the first instance, in their relation to the countries to which the gold is subsequently consigned. The natural outflow of gold from the producing centres to the rest of the world thus tends, when the gold standard is in general use, to govern the rates of exchange to a certain extent; it does not follow that a country which delivers the gold to another must necessarily find itself in a worse position economically than the other party. This fact does not seem to have been sufficiently appreciated by Heiligenstadt, who, in his well-known essays on the rates of exchange, printed in *Conrads Jahrbücher* (1892 and 1893), speaks with a certain complacency of the preponderance of the German claims upon England—being the cause of repeated gold shipments from England to Germany.[1]

The adjustment of the balance of payments between the different countries was regulated at that time by means quite different from

[1] On the other hand it is desirable for the sake of simplicity to adhere to the recognised technical terms and not exchange them for others. In Swedish language it has lately become the fashion to speak of the 'improvement' of our rates of exchange, meaning thereby that the rate on certain other countries has *risen* to par—though this is certainly an incorrect use of the word.

230

shipments of gold, and it would have been of great interest to learn more about these factors; but as the result was already known—merely that the rates of exchange were maintained in the neighbourhood of par—they were not made the subject of any closer investigation.

This neglect has now to be paid for, however. When all the exchanges were being subject to such violent disturbances during the World War, it would have been of great value to have had at our disposal a theory of foreign exchanges worked out in detail. As it is, that theory can hardly be said to have made any appreciable progress since Goschen wrote his interesting and instructive though somewhat aphoristic little book. Indeed, the theory may even be said to have retrogressed, for since the centre of interest became the tendency of the rate to move toward one gold point or the other, owing to alterations in the balance of trade or the balance of payments, there was an inclination to ascribe even the gigantic deviations of the exchange rates above or below parity which were witnessed in the World War almost exclusively to considerations of trade and credit, without bearing in mind—as Goschen had expressly pointed out—that the really large fluctuations in rates of exchange can never be attributed to such causes, but always presuppose a positive deterioration—be it actual or merely anticipated—*in the value of the country's currency*. It is well known that in Germany not only prominent bankers—I believe even the Chief Director of the Reichsbank—but also well-known political economists seriously maintained to the very last that Germany's soaring rate of exchange on neutral countries was not attributable to any actual deterioration of the currency, but wholly and solely to Germany's adverse trade balance during the war. Whether they would also apply this argument to the *Austrian* currency, which has now managed to fall to less than *one-fifth* of its nominal value and is at present excluded from our exchange market quotations, I am unable to say.

On the other hand, it is not very easy to determine what exactly is to be regarded as a deterioration in the value of money, or an inflation of the currency. To Goschen this concept was almost identical with that of the gold-agio, but nowadays, when *every* country has constrained its gold to some extent, and when a completely free movement of gold is nowhere to be found, the relation between notes and gold bullion is a somewhat obscure field for thought. Nothing would please me more than to gain a clear insight into all the complex interactions which were created in the sphere of currency by the World War. Perhaps that privilege will be vouchsafed to a future generation of economists. For my part I must content myself with examining a few typical and more or less imaginary cases, whose conditions are so simple that there seems no room for doubt as to the accuracy of the conclusions. How far such a discussion will serve to elucidate the interactions of the actually existing phenomena is of course another matter.

II

The simplest case which, in the last resort, must form the basis of any consideration of the exchange problem, however much it may be modified by circumstances, is that of a free *exchange of commodities* between two countries. If *trade in gold* is also free, so that the rate of exchange, or the relation between the two currencies, stands practically at par, it follows, if the two countries have a contiguous frontier, that the prices of all commodities which are capable of being transported will become approximately *the same* in the two countries, and that they will be exactly the same close to each side of the frontier. When a cargo can be forwarded with equal ease to Malmö or to Copenhagen, it is bound to find its way to the place where the goods can be sold to the best advantage, and on arrival there it will assist in lowering the price. If butter and eggs were 10 per cent cheaper at Elsinore than at Hälsingborg, it would follow—under a system of free trade—that baskets of eggs and tubs of butter would be ferried across to the Swedish shore, and the difference in price would very soon disappear.

Suppose, however, that the movement of gold is *not* free, and that some considerable difference has arisen between the values of the two currencies, the prices of the various commodities—still close to either side of the frontier—would now be found to adjust themselves inversely to the new ratio between the values of the two currencies (and, consequently, in direct ratio to the rates of exchange). For instance, suppose that Danish currency had risen to a value 10 per cent *higher* than that of Swedish currency; the prices of eggs and butter not only might, but must—under a free trade system—be uniformly 10 per cent higher at Hälsingborg than at Elsinore: for only if they reached a still higher level would it pay to ferry goods over to Sweden. If, on the other hand, the prices were only 5 per cent higher at Hälsingborg, it would pay the Swedish merchants to take their goods over to Elsinore, since the profit which they would make on the difference in the exchange would *more* than compensate them for their loss on the difference in the price level.

The above considerations would appear to be axiomatic. It is true that during the war Swedish currency stood higher than Danish and that, nevertheless, the prices of butter and eggs and many other necessities were substantially *lower* in Denmark than in Sweden; but this must be ascribed entirely to the fact that the trade in these goods was *not* free; had it been free such a result would have been inconceivable. It should further be remarked that this parallelism between the rates of exchange and the market prices (ignoring the small differences without which there would be nothing to stimulate mutual imports and exports between two countries so close to one another) must, under a system of free trade, be *entirely independent* of the balance of trade or the credit relations between the two countries; for the buyers and sellers on either side of the frontier are in no way influenced by such considerations. They merely inquire where the goods can be purchased most cheaply or where they can be sold most profitably, and transact their business accordingly.

Nothing has so far been said as to which of these phenomena is the cause and which is the effect. Does the difference in the level of prices cause the rate of exchange to deviate from par; or is the converse true? This question can only be answered in regard to each individual case. Either process is conceivable; and both of them are —as we shall shortly explain—quite capable of being combined with a third, which is the underlying or ultimate cause.

For instance, let us suppose that a higher level of prices obtains in one of the two countries than in the other, as a result of a scarcity of commodities or of an inflation of currency; the imports of that country will rise, while its exports will decline. Its balance of trade will suffer, and the rate of exchange[1] will rise above par, while at the same time the excessive imports will tend to *lower* the price level to a certain extent.

If, on the other hand, the rate of exchange for foreign currencies in the country has risen spontaneously—as it might occur if confidence in the country has been shaken, thus inducing foreign creditors to call in their outstanding debts, or to remove any securities of their own which they hold there, etc.—the high rate of exchange works as a premium upon exports and as an obstacle to imports, so that the internal price level tends to rise and at the same time the rate of exchange experiences a certain *improvement*. In both cases a correspondence is established between the rate of

[1] I.e. the price to be paid for a unit of the foreign currency. Cf. Translator's Note on p. 229.

exchange and the price level, a result which must always be attained in the long run, assuming that there is free trade.

The ultimate cause must again in both cases be sought in the *mismanagement of the currency* in the country in which it has deteriorated. If the banks—and more especially the central bank—of the country had reacted in good time, and to a sufficient extent, by tightening the credit conditions (raising the rates of interest given on deposits and demanded for advances), either when prices first began to rise or when the rate of exchange began to soar, neither of these phenomena would have continued, and normal conditions would have been re-established. But if they fold their arms, or if they actually stimulate the growth of the mischief by a reckless credit policy, the change may become permanent, or may even gradually be aggravated.

It should have been unnecessary to indulge in these reflections, which are in fact self-evident and have hitherto been generally considered as a part of the heritage of recognised truths—none too plentiful—in the treasure-house of economic science. Unfortunately one need only run one's eye over the countless articles on the currency question which have appeared during the war (particularly in Germany) to realise the extent to which these considerations—which, as has been said, must always form the groundwork for any discussion of the question—have been thrust on one side, or, if they have been acknowledged to possess any importance at all, have at best been accorded a place 'in the second or third rank.' People are apt to forget that international trade, however much it may be restricted or regulated, is always governed by the same principle, that of buying as cheaply and selling as profitably as possible.

III

We will now go to the opposite extreme, and suppose that a particular country has, owing to the force of circumstances, been so *absolutely and completely isolated* from foreign trade that it can neither purchase nor sell the very smallest quantity of goods. *Russia* is the country which at the present moment most nearly fulfils those conditions. We will also assume that the country in question has to effect certain annual *interest payments* to other States for the service of long-standing debts, and that the country is conscientiously striving to fulfil its obligations, or its businessmen are—at this point any parallel with present-day Russia ceases to apply. In such a case it is clear that the rate of foreign exchange should rise rapidly, till it reaches the gold point, and the export of gold should begin—if we assume, to begin with, that both the country we are considering and the rest of the world are still on the gold standard. Let us suppose that, in order to restrict the outflow of gold, the *bank rate* is raised in the usual way, and that when this has been done to a sufficient extent the *outflow of gold is stopped*, since the country's creditors prefer to carry over their claims in order to get the benefit of the high rate of interest. It is assumed, of course, that there is no serious doubt as to the country's future solvency. (We do not refer to the possibility of *securities* being exported from the country in question, because, strictly speaking, that is merely another form of the same thing.) In this case the rate of exchange will, necessarily, stand at par or thereabouts: indeed, if the rate of interest allowed on deposits and demanded for advances is fixed sufficiently high, there is no reason at all why *the rate of exchange* should not fall below par, so that the country would begin to receive gold.

Now let us suppose that the country we are considering, instead of raising its rate of interest, proceeds to *prohibit the export of gold*. Its rate of exchange with foreign countries will now necessarily rise somewhat *above* the gold point. But it will not go on rising indefinitely, without ever coming to a stop. *Where* will it stop? And *why* will it stop at that particular point? That is our problem here.

The condition to be fulfilled if the rate of exchange is to become stationary, instead of rising indefinitely, is evidently that claims for outstanding debts should be *carried over*; and this will undoubtedly occur, in one way or another, in the present case. This carrying over of debts may be regarded as voluntary, and not as compulsory, in the strict sense of the word, because an individual creditor is always able, at any given position of the exchange, to obtain payment of his claim, or at all events of a portion of it, by drawing a bill on the debtor or on the latter's bank and selling the bill in his own market at whatever price it will fetch. If the debtor has only undertaken to pay the debt in his own country and in his own national currency the creditor would have to bear the loss on the exchange. If the creditor prefers to allow the debt to remain outstanding in the country where it is owed, he does so *in the hope* that its value will appreciate later on. If he had not entertained this hope he would, as explained above, have already realised his claim, even at a loss. If, on the other hand, the debtor has undertaken to pay the creditor in the latter's currency, he would be obliged, owing to the rise in the exchange, to sacrifice a larger sum of money than that which his debt originally represented, in order to procure the necessary remittance. Instead, therefore, he persuades his creditor to allow him to re-draw the bill or bond for a rather larger amount—which from the point of view of the creditor is tantamount to receiving a higher rate of interest. The debtor does this *in the hope* that he will be able, later on, to procure the requisite sum for a smaller sacrifice. In both instances, therefore, we are dealing with a *currency speculation*, based on the assumption that the exchange will improve at a future date. The exchange must have risen—or fallen, as the case may be—sufficiently to provide the necessary *inducement* for such a speculation, but when once this has taken place the rate for the time being does not rise or fall any more.

It is, however, self-evident that a valuation of this kind, based on purely speculative considerations, will be far from stable. Anything which tends to weaken confidence in the country's future solvency will depress its rate of exchange, and anything which offers hope of an early return to normal conditions will improve it. However, as the general public has no other means of gauging these prospects than the mere fact that the exchange is rising or falling, any alteration in the rate of exchange easily tends to *intensify itself* for a time, just as an incidental alteration in the price of some commodity may, at first, have the *opposite* effect on demand and supply to that which is represented by economic theory. How far 'bull' or 'bear' speculations, in the ordinary sense, may still further accentuate this tendency is a point which I will not discuss. If they are judiciously conducted they should rather have an opposite effect.

But, in any case, the *average* estimate of the value of the country's currency must be based solely upon the prospects of the future; it is not *directly* affected by the price levels on either side of the frontier, though it may be *indirectly* affected, as for instance when a marked rise in prices or an increase in the note circulation arouses mistrust— justifiably or not—in the country's future ability to restore its currency either to par or to a substantially higher level than at present.

Some German authors, including R. Liefmann, who—unlike the great majority—see the main cause of the high rate of foreign exchange in Germany in the intrinsic depreciation of the Reichsmark, have examined this question, but, it seems to me, from an erroneous standpoint. Liefmann maintains[1] that even if Germany had no exports or imports at all, foreign claims upon Germany would never- theless stand at a low value, because of the high price level in Germany. That can scarcely be correct. If Germany pays her dividend coupons in gold or if—which comes to the same thing—she offers such high rates of interest that she can borrow money to meet them as

[1] *Weltwirtschaftliches Archiv*, 1918, p. 433.

they fall due, I fail to see why German securities should fall in value abroad, *except* of course in so far as the present high price level may give rise to a lack of confidence as to her *future* solvency.

The same thing should happen, but in the reverse order, if the country we are considering had a surplus of matured claims upon foreign countries—no matter how they came into existence. According to our first hypothesis, i.e., assuming that trade in gold is free, the country would then be liable to be inundated with gold, against which, so long as it refrained from modifying its currency legislation, it could only defend itself by *lowering* its rate of interest to such a point that creditors within the country would be inclined to carry over their foreign claims, allowing them to remain abroad. In that case the rate of exchange would remain constantly at par, or thereabouts.

However, in such circumstances it might happen that the country we are considering would prohibit the *importation* of gold—or release its central bank from the obligation to cash notes in gold in the proportion fixed by law—as was done during the war, with various degrees of purposefulness and success, by ourselves and the other Scandinavian countries, as well as by Spain (and also, I believe, in the end, by Holland and Switzerland). In such a case the country does not need to lower its rate of interest; it can allow it to remain at the same level as that of foreign countries, or even at a higher rate if it pleases. Gold will cease to come in, and instead the rate of foreign exchange will fall below par and below the lower gold point, till it reaches a figure at which it becomes advantageous for creditors in the country to let their matured claims remain outstanding abroad, even though they cannot obtain a higher rate of interest, or even in spite of the better rate offered by the country's own banks—and in so doing they will be actuated solely by the expectation of an exchange profit, and not by any other motive. (Of course in all these examples some *other* person or some finance company may be substituted for the individual creditor.)

So far we have assumed that the rest of the world was living on the full gold standard and—we might have added—was at peace, so that we have been able to talk of the country's rate of foreign exchange *in the singular*. If we change that assumption for one which more closely resembles the actual circumstances, it is evident that the country we are considering will encounter as many different rates of exchange as there are countries in the world outside its own frontier, and each of these rates will be determined independently—always on the assumption, which we made above and have not yet abandoned, that the country is completely isolated from foreign trade—with *exclusive* regard to the favourable or unfavourable prospects of a resumption of payments in gold, or speaking more generally, to the probable position of the currency, when normal conditions are eventually re-established.

IV

It was between these two extremes—of completely free trade and absolute blockade—that events actually developed during the World War, with its multifarious restrictions and obstructions of international trade. During the first half of the war, when these difficulties were still of moderate extent, the economic situation approximated to the former type. Cassel's well-known attempt to show that there is a direct parallelism between rates of exchange, price levels and note circulation might at that time, at least, have been something like to valid. During the latter half of the war, when export prohibitions, with or without licences, had become the rule, and freights had soared to the most extravagant figures, while liabilities incurred during the first stage still remained undischarged, the second type became more and more frequent, although it did not, of course, hold the field entirely. Cassel's contention (in his work on Germany's economic power of resistance) that the theory which regards the situation of the exchange rates at a given moment as the expression of the degree of *confidence* felt in the future of the exchange, is 'arbitrary and untenable' since 'transactions are concluded from day to day and from hour to hour and do not imply any speculation on the ultimate prospects of either of the currencies,' does not appear to express a very well-considered opinion. To the man who sells for cash, with a view to making fresh purchases immediately afterwards, the subsequent fluctuations of the currency are of course of no interest; but they are all the more a matter of concern for the man who sells upon *credit* and does not expect to be paid till some future date; and for this purpose, as we have already observed, it is immaterial whether some other party—e.g. a bank—is substituted for the creditor.

Cassel's statement is repeated with approval by Terhalle,[1] but it appears, strictly speaking, to be in direct conflict with the figures which Terhalle himself quotes[2] regarding the movements, for example, of the German exchange rates during the latter half of 1917 and the

---

[1] 'Wechselkurs und Goldentwertung' (Exchange Rate and Depreciation of Gold), *Zeitschrift für Sozialwissenschaft*, 1918, p. 436.
[2] See above quoted work, *passim*.

beginning of 1918. In the first part of the former year the German Reichsmark was quoted on the *Swiss* market at about 32 per cent below par; in May of the same year its 'disagio' had risen to 37 per cent and at the end of October to 49.5 per cent. After that, as is known, a violent revulsion set in. In the middle of December the 'disagio' had diminished to 38 per cent and at the beginning of January 1918 to as low as 28 per cent, after which, however, it increased again, and had reached 33 per cent at the beginning of April. It is self-evident that such fluctuations (which, as we know, found their complete counterpart in our own market) could not be regarded as connected with the internal value or purchasing power of the German mark.

Indeed, if we compare them with simultaneous alterations in the Entente currencies (on the Swiss money market) which, according to Terhalle, *declined* almost continuously in value from October till April, it seems clear that the improvement of the German mark must have been due to the important political events which were happening at that time; moreover, it was being supported by direct German exchange operations on the neutral markets, as has been explained by Swiss authorities.[1] An alteration of the rates of exchange which is brought about in this way must react in its turn upon the ratio between the *price levels* in the two countries, as we have already pointed out; but it will do so more feebly, or at any rate more slowly, than if there were free intercourse, because its influence is now confined to those commodities which continue to be more or less freely exchanged between the countries, and only affects other commodities indirectly, through the general interdependence of prices.

It would be equally erroneous, or even more so, to deny the influence which may be exercised on the rate of exchange even in this case—though in a less degree than with free trade—by spontaneous inflation in either country (through too slack a policy with regard to bank credits, the issue of paper money, etc.); or, to seek, as Professor Brisman seems to do, to transform the natural association of phenomena in this connection to its exact opposite. In various newspaper articles, and most recently in his lecture before the Economic Association (in Stockholm) on December 10th last, Brisman has advanced the remarkable theory that a country has in its power, in certain circumstances, to *improve* its exchange on the foreign markets by the process of inflation. Let us suppose, as an example, he says, that both a country's exports and its imports are restricted by a system of licences or prohibitions; if the country now forces its price level upwards by means of inflation, its imports will not be increased, but neither will

[1] See an article 'The German Money Offensive' in the English *Economist*, 1918.

239

its exports be diminished, since there is every probability that foreign countries not will have been allowed to buy so much as they would have wanted at the prices which formerly ruled; for otherwise the whole system of export restrictions would be purposeless.[1] The country would, therefore, in Brisman's view, get paid more for its exports, while the value of its imports would remain unchanged; the balance of trade would thereby turn out in the country's favour and its foreign exchange rates would *decline*.

I doubt whether Brisman has thought this example out fully—though it was no less than his duty to do so, since he advanced it a second time after it had been criticised, even though in a somewhat summary fashion. For my own part I feel perfectly sure that the result would be the opposite of what Brisman supposes. Imagine the case of two countries which are or became isolated from the rest of the world and which habitually export an equal money value of commodities to each other. Suppose that as a result of export prohibitions, the amounts of goods released for export fall to one-half of their former amount. The prices of imported goods will then rise equally, let us suppose, in each country, so that the balance of trade, or the balance of payments, will still remain in equilibrium. On the other hand the *domestic* price of goods manufactured for export will evidently *fall*, since the respective countries will now obtain a larger share of them for their own consumption. In consequence there will now exist an important difference between the price at which exporters must dispose of their wares in the home markets and those which they can obtain abroad, if they are fortunate enough to secure licences. Now suppose that one country—let us say, our own—forces up the domestic price for all its commodities by inflating the paper currency. Surely, it is clear that the exporters will remain entirely *unaffected*, because, even if they can now obtain rather higher prices in the home market, the prices abroad will continue to be higher; they have therefore no inducement to diminish their offers of goods to foreign countries, and endeavours to extort still higher prices there in other ways would have little chance of success. On the other hand our *importers*, who are now making large profits (so long as the rate of exchange does not deteriorate substantially), will begin to intensify

[1] Is there not perhaps a misunderstanding here? If the marketing facilities for a given article are artificially reduced, the *seller*—but not the buyer—is thereby prevented from 'dealing to saturation point,' in other words from continuing to deal for as long as he might do so with profit to himself, *at the price which has now come into existence*. If that were true of the buyer also the price should rise even higher.

their competition for the quantities of goods released for export by foreign countries, so that the prices of these goods will *rise*, to a greater or less extent. It is, accordingly, *we*—and not our trading partner—who acquires a more unfavourable balance of payments and a rising rate of exchange; and this rise must continue till the new rate of exchange becomes adjusted to the new and higher price level, after which economic equilibrium will be once more attained. Possibly this example might be modified so as to make Brisman's paradox rather more acceptable; but on the whole I think that it must be rejected. In any case the phenomenon which he is seeking to elucidate appears to be explicable in a much simpler and clearer fashion.

This phenomenon, which attracted so much attention during the latter part of the war, is, to put it briefly, that the price levels (and note circulation) in the different countries ceased to correspond in any degree to their mutual rates of exchange. For instance, the English price level rose far higher than that of America during the war; yet the rates of exchange between the two countries were maintained, till the very end, approximately at par. Similarly *our own* price level undoubtedly rose more than that of England or Denmark in the last eighteen months, yet our rate of exchange with these countries (i.e. the price of their currencies in Swedish money) was, throughout, distinctly *below* par.

Any mystery in this respect is, however, entirely dispelled as soon as it is made clear what is meant by an *average* price level. The goods which a country produces for export must always stand at a lower price at home than that which they command abroad—at any rate in reality, that is, making allowance for the rate of exchange—for otherwise no trade would take place; provided always that the commodity sales are not combined with a *speculation in the future rate of exchange*, an operation which, as we have already seen, is by no means without practical significance, but which we must disregard for the moment. Even when there is free trade in commodities there is—as already mentioned—no strict correspondence between the price of commodities and the rate of exchange, except just on each side of the frontier; while in the interior of the country both export and import prices deviate somewhat, in opposite directions, from the prices abroad; it could, therefore, only be a coincidence if their average prices, or the average of all the prices taken together, exhibited such parallelism precisely. And this naturally applies with even greater force to countries situated at great distances from one another. But if, in addition, foreign trade is restricted, partly by the above-mentioned export prohibitions, and partly by the complete disorganisation of *freight charges*—as occurred during the World War, and particularly during its latter period—such coincidence will become very improbable and may even be regarded as impossible.

Take, for instance, the example we have just cited of the situation between England and America. In this case, so far as I know, there were no serious *legal* obstacles to trade—except possibly in regard to the important commodity *coal*, of which the immense exports from England to South America were practically suspended during the war. But rather similar effects were brought about by wartime *demands for imports* on England's part, and on the part of the Entente countries which were under her economic leadership. This circumstance, in conjunction with the lack of bulky commodities (coal) which could be used for return cargoes, resulted in American exports to England —and to Europe as a whole—having to bear freight charges much higher than those placed on English or European cargoes shipped to America. The situation was bound to result in the average price level in England during the war standing far higher than the average price level in America—as indeed proved to be the case. But this difference in prices was in no way connected with the position of currencies; it would have arisen none the less if the movement of gold between England and America had been absolutely free, in which case the rate of exchange would have remained at or near par. But in such a case the Bank of England would soon have had to raise its discount rate to such a point that American creditors would have found it profitable to let their claims remain outstanding in England, or—what comes to the same thing in theory—to accept payment in securities as soon as these had fallen, owing to the high rates of interest ruling in England, to a figure which made them attractive to American buyers. As is well known, the English preferred to adopt a so-called state 'control' of the rate of exchange with America; the method of control was that the English Treasury, after issuing a warning as to the possibility of an appropriate tax legislation, took over American securities in English hands, and then sold them or mortgaged them in America at acceptable prices. This procedure did not, in practice, produce results very different from those which would have followed if the English rates of interest had been officially raised. In point of fact it simply meant that England allowed her American creditors a *higher* rate of interest than that which it still considered right to maintain in the home market; whether that was of any real advantage I will not discuss; but if the same procedure had been adopted towards *our own country*, our rate of exchange with England would very likely have been maintained throughout the war in the neighbourhood of par.[1]

If, however, *no* such measures had been taken, and England had simply 'protected' her gold absolutely, by prohibiting its export (*in practice*, such a prohibition may be considered as having obtained during the war), the rate of exchange with America *would* undoubtedly have moved against England to some considerable extent. This would not, however, have had any connection with the existing difference between the price levels, but it would, *pro tanto*, have caused a further accentuation of that difference. Neither would it have had any direct connection with the American export surplus. It would have been almost entirely in the nature of a *speculation in currency*; in other words, the difference in the rate would, in the last resort, have been based on American opinion as to the date at which gold payments would be resumed in England. In these circumstances, American bonds would have risen in terms of English money, but would have remained stationary in terms of American money. English bonds, on the other hand, would have remained unchanged in terms of English money, but would have fallen in terms of American money. Both kinds of bonds could therefore have been profitably imported into America, *but only as a speculation in currency*; in the former case this speculation would have been conducted by the English sellers, who would have reckoned on being able to repurchase their bonds at a lower price at some future date, and in the latter case by American buyers who would have hoped to dispose of the bonds later at a higher figure. But the American buyer would not have received a substantially higher rate of interest for his money in either case, because the interest on the English bonds—which he had thus acquired at a low price—would in the meanwhile have been paid in English currency, which, according to our assumption, would have stood at a relatively low value.

Mutatis mutandis, this is precisely what occurred in England's dealings with the *Scandinavian countries*, and especially with our own country. The pound fell during 1916 and 1917, because in the balance of payments at that time England was our debtor; but the Scandinavian creditors, unlike those of America, were *not* offered any directly higher rates of interest on their money. In place of such rates it was the difference in the level of exchange which formed the inducement

---

[1] At a chance meeting with Lord Robert Cecil in the spring of 1916 I asked him why no similar steps had been taken with regard to the Scandinavian countries. His answer was very simple; that they did not think it worth while, if only the far more important rate of exchange with America could be regulated.

to them to leave their debts outstanding in England. So long as peace seemed remote and the issue uncertain, this inducement—i.e. the hope of a possible exchange profit whenever the pound should regain its value—had to be great in order to be effective. Now that the Entente have won the war, and peace stands over the threshold, the anticipation of an exchange profit of a few per cent is quite sufficient and would indeed be more than sufficient—as in Denmark—if the Swedish *rate of interest* were not still far higher than the English rate.[1]

So long as this large exchange-differential continued, it naturally assisted, *pro tanto*, in bringing down the Swedish prices for all goods which were traded to any extent between Sweden and England (and America), and thus directly assisted in lowering somewhat our general price level, although this, for *other* reasons, stood well above, not only the American price level, but probably also above the English, Danish and others.

The cause of our (even relatively) high price level during the latter part of the war probably lay—just as in the above-mentioned instance—to no small extent in the great difference between the freight charges to and from the transoceanic countries. But to this must be added the many legal or artificial restrictions on our imports, which caused the prices of imported goods and of their home-manufactured substitutes to rise to a level far above that of the remaining 'gold countries'—if we may still use that convenient though no longer fully accurate expression—whereas our exports had to be disposed of abroad at prices which, in spite of the differences in the levels of exchange, were *comparatively* little above their prices in our own home markets. The result was a marked upward trend of our average price level in relation to the levels in foreign 'gold countries,' a trend which would undoubtedly have been even more marked if the export of gold had been free on both sides, since our rates of exchange with those countries would then have stood at par.

It would seem illogical to seek for some *other* reason for this rise in prices. Of course, the rise might have been avoided, to a certain extent, by a still more restrictive policy with regard to gold and note issue on the part of the Central Bank. We should then have acquired a substantially better *currency* than our neighbours. If the export of gold had been free in their *countries* the consequence must evidently have been that our notes would have risen far above their normal gold value, and our rate of exchange with all the gold countries would

---

[1] When the above was written the recent lowering of the Swedish rate of interest had not yet taken place.

have turned out far below par; and, as a result, our *average* price level might perhaps have fallen to the same level as theirs, or even lower, *in spite of* the relative increase in price of our imported commodities. If, on the other hand, our high price level had been caused, as Professor Cassel and others believe, by an internal inflation in the note issue, so that in the case of free gold movements abroad our notes would have depreciated *below* their gold value—I cannot see how that could have failed to produce a considerable *rise* in our rates of foreign exchange. It was only the fact that the movement of gold was nowhere entirely free that obscured a situation which would otherwise have been as clear as daylight, but that fact could not transform the entire character of the phenomenon.

Cassel asserts—not quite consistently, it seems to me, with the standpoint which he adopted previously—that it was our favourable balance of trade, i.e. our excess of exports, which raised the value of the Swedish crown on the world market, in spite of its reduced 'intrinsic value.' But an excess of exports ought not, by itself, to lower our rates of exchange with other countries if, in one way or another, we are offered sufficiently high rates of interest over there to induce us to carry over our claims for the time being. It is only if that is *not* done that the rates of exchange will fall to a point so low that the exchange profits which are anticipated whenever the foreign currencies make a complete or partial recovery will more than compensate for the absence of direct profits in the shape of interest—or, for the loss of interest, if our rate of interest is higher than that of foreign countries.[1] Once that point has been reached everything will remain in equilibrium, including the balance of payments, in spite of the

---

[1] If payment had been stipulated in Swedish currency, this does not apply; such a transaction cannot, as far as I can see, exercise any influence on the rate of exchange.

Later correction by the author: It is stated in this note, that if payment has been stipulated in *Swedish* currency such a transaction could exercise no influence on the rate of exchange. After further reflection I have come to the opinion that this is incorrect. In such a case the foreign buyer has two courses open to him: Either he obtains an advance from a bank in his own country, buys a bill on Sweden at the current price and pays for the goods with the bill; or he obtains credit from the seller or from a Swedish bank and has then to pay the higher rates of interest prevailing in Sweden (usually with the addition of a commission). It is clear that the latter method will only pay him if the exchange on Sweden has risen so high that he can reasonably hope for a fall in the rate, and consequently for an *exchange profit* when the payment is ultimately effected, i.e. after the war. The influence on the rate of exchange will therefore be the same as if the payment had been stipulated in the foreign currency, except that in the first case it is the seller while in the other case it is the buyer who engages in the exchange speculation.

continued excess of exports.[1] But if, by domestic inflation, we were to lower the internal purchasing power of the Swedish crown, this condition of equilibrium would be disturbed, and—unless one is prepared to accept Brisman's paradox—this could hardly happen in any other way than by a relative upward movement of our foreign exchange rates. It must, however, be conceded, as already remarked, that this effect will become *weaker* the more foreign trade is restricted, for prices and rates of exchange influence each other immediately only in the case of commodities which are actually the object of international exchange. If we had been absolutely isolated during the latter part of the war, both from exports and imports, but had continued to hold such floating claims on foreign countries as we had acquired in its earliest stages, it follows from what has been said that the rates of exchange and the international price level might have pursued their course almost independently of each other—very much as Cassel thinks—or that they might have been influenced by each other only in a very indirect way. In practice, neither of those developments occurred and, indeed, we were able to continue our staple exports almost as in time of peace. Accordingly, the prices both of imported and of exported commodities were inevitably affected by— or themselves affected—the rate of exchange, and as was to be expected, the movement of these prices had a certain influence on the whole general price level.

If one only considered, say, the situation between England and Sweden, it might appear that the rise in the rate of the pound sterling during the last stage of the war and after the armistice could be accounted for almost as satisfactorily by Cassel's theory, since it is true that our import difficulties had been somewhat alleviated at this time. But if one examines the situation between England and America the conclusion would have to be different; for *there* the sterling rate stood quite close to par almost all through the war, in spite of England's enormous excess of imports; yet, during the last period, when England's balance of trade, as far as one can tell, was somewhat improved, the sterling rate *went down*. The reason is, of course, that during the war the English Treasury was offering American creditors, directly or indirectly, sufficiently high *rates of interest*, and that afterwards it ceased to do so. Are we not then bound to conclude that it was the absence of such an offer to our own country, combined with

[1] Of course it is necessary, especially in the case of a small country like our own, that the inducement referred to should be proportionally greater when large credits are granted. In *that* sense the extent of our exports can undoubtedly exercise an influence on the exchange situation.

246

our refusal to admit gold, which drove the pound sterling so far down in our country, at the time when the prospects of peace and the whole outcome of the war were still wrapped in uncertainty?

V

The extreme difficulty of explaining the fluctuations of the exchange rate under a regime of paper money—to which our own country adheres, of course, so long as gold may not be freely exported—is not due so much to the fact that the notes cannot be exchanged for gold, but that, in such circumstances, the monetary unit is not clearly *defined*. It is true that, at a given moment, each individual note represents a particular fraction of the whole paper currency in circulation; but that does not carry us much farther, as we have no guarantee that the whole mass of paper currency will remain approximately constant. The paper notes are thus only definable as *certificates of indebtedness on the part of the State or the Central Bank, which will presumably be redeemed in gold to a greater or lesser extent, at some uncertain date in the future*. And how can one compare the value of a piece of paper of that kind with that of another piece of paper, defined in the same manner, in some other country! When it is added that certain countries, including our own, have reserved the power, by refusing to admit gold, to give their own paper a *higher*—though still undefined—relation to gold than the rate which ruled previously, it is clear that the difficulties are so much increased as to be practically insurmountable; for even the speculations in the rate of exchange referred to above were based on the assumption that one's own currency was, or was expected to become, of the same value as gold, or at any rate that it was going to acquire a fixed relation to gold.

I shall therefore refrain from making any prophecies about the position of our rates of exchange in the near future. I will only add this. As currency is primarily a *measure* of value, it ought to be possible, even in the most unfavourable external circumstances, for a country to maintain that standard just as constant as, for instance, its standards of length, capacity or weight. The universal means for doing this is provided by bank-rate policy. A country which maintains sufficiently high its borrower's and lender's rates of interest need never fear that its notes will depreciate. In theory, indeed, it should much rather be possible for such a country to raise its currency to any height that it chooses and to drive its price level down to any depth, irrespective of anything that is taking place abroad in the monetary sphere. Those who maintain that 'during the war' the bank rate was no longer able to exercise its normal functions—though no proof has ever been offered in support of this assertion—ought at least to admit that *now*, when peace is being re-established, it is once more able to exercise them. It would therefore be most regrettable if those who are urging that, in the present circumstances, our Riksbank ought to lower its discount rate[1] should succeed in getting their advice adopted. However much the Riksbank may feel obliged to show regard to the interests of 'business circles,' it cannot, on that account, lose sight of its principal duty, which is to maintain a sound currency within the country. If it has not been able to do so, owing to various circumstances, during the past four or five years, it should make good the damage as soon as possible. But a currency cannot be described as 'sound' unless its purchasing power in terms of commodities or services remains approximately constant. If this term has hitherto been used to denote a paper currency which can be redeemed unconditionally *in gold*, that is, of course, due to the tacit assumption that gold itself possesses this property of constancy of value—for otherwise it would be meaningless. But this property of gold was lost during the war and no one can say whether it will again be restored. The new gold-standard system, which is now being devised by the Great Powers, with the gold retained entirely in the banks and only paper in circulation, clearly offers a far feebler guarantee against future fluctuations in the value of money than was afforded under the old system; for in the great commercial countries a rise in prices immediately led to an increased demand for gold in circulation, and this involved withdrawals of gold from the central banks, thus compelling the latter to exercise a more stringent credit policy. Whether the cover requirements of the note-legislation—which are so easily evaded, and which, moreover, lose in relative efficacy as notes are replaced by cheques or transfers—can offer an adequate degree in this respect, remains to be seen. The memorandum of the latest English committee on currency,[2] whose authors almost appear to consider that everything will be satisfactory if only the English banks have a respectable quantity of gold in their vaults, is not exactly calculated to remove these misgivings. Of course it would be possible, in that way, to reach new parities of exchange between all countries and thus nominally to reach a new gold standard (perhaps after a 'clearance sale' of the currency, or after national bankruptcy had been declared,

---

[1] Since this was written the rate has been lowered, though fortunately only by $\frac{1}{2}$ per cent.

[2] *First Interim Report of the Committee on Currency and Foreign Exchanges after the War*, London, 1918.

in those countries whose money had plunged too far below its gold value);[1] but little would be gained by this if the inflation which arose during the war were, for all practical purposes, to become entrenched, thus involving a veritable revolution in all former conditions of property, while giving no adequate guarantee that the currency would remain stable in the future.

We ourselves, by gold restrictions and by adopting an entirely free monetary standard, have in my view chosen a better course, which ought logically to be completed by allowing free export of gold and by the proclamation of a rate both for the purchase and the sale of gold, which might be varied from time to time, and which ought to be progressively *lowered* so long as gold has not regained its pre-war value. The importation of gold could also be left free, but of course only for bar gold, and not for those gold coins (Danish and Norwegian) which would constitute legal tender within the country.[2] If other countries were also to follow our example in this matter a world monetary system could undoubtedly be established, which would fulfil the two desiderata: *a stable value of money in time as well as in space.* A currency conference convened for that purpose would indeed seem to be a natural part of the arrangements which are now to bring the nations closer together.

If this cannot be, I think it best that we should seek by our own endeavours to establish a really rational monetary system and a stable currency, perhaps abandoning, for the present, parity of exchange rates, an aim which, however desirable in itself, must be regarded as of *relatively* subordinate interest.

Merely for the sake of custom and tradition to allow our monetary craft to be towed in the wake of these great convoys, with no idea where they are leading us, seems a policy unworthy of a nation which surely numbers, among its older and younger economists, men with at least as great an insight into monetary questions as those which any other country can at present claim to possess.

[1] Whether such a step is really inevitable, or whether Germany, for example, should seek to bring its currency back to its full gold value (though this should in justice involve a suitable reduction of State debts and individual debts which were incurred when the currency was depreciated during the war), is a question that it would take too long to discuss here, so that its existence will therefore merely be indicated here.

[2] The monetary union between Denmark and Norway would consequently have to be dissolved, unless those countries were to unite with us in a common gold and discount policy.

PROTECTION AND FREE TRADE [1]

THE tariff report, to which we have long looked forward with interest, has appeared this summer in a rather peculiar form. It consists of a majority report of 300 pages, abundantly provided with statistical tables, which has the support of the committee's chairman and five other members. It is noteworthy that Dr. J. C. Lembke, who was a moderate protectionist in his younger days, has associated himself unreservedly with the majority view, which is inclined to free trade. The actual preparation of the report is largely due to the assiduous work of the committee's secretary, Dr. Karl Åmark, on the one hand, and on the other to Professor Heckscher, who in particular has written the separately published section on 'The Theoretical Basis of the Protective Tariff System.'

The published volume also contains a long minority report, signed by four members of the committee, which is rumoured to have been written by a well-known economist [Gustav Cassel] who was not on the committee, and who seems to have added to his other very considerable attributes that of omnipresence. It is with some surprise that we find him on the side of the declared protectionists. According to the information given by Professor Heckscher in a series of articles for *Dagens Nyheter* (now published as a pamphlet), on account of the protraction of the committee's work, which this caused, a great many of the arguments put forward in the minority report have never been considered by the committee, and therefore could not be dealt with in the report, so that the reader is sometimes left completely at a loss. Such a procedure can scarcely be said to accord with the aims of committee work. Moreover, it produces a rather peculiar impression when, in the newspaper which he has at his disposal, the economist in question writes a favourable review of his anonymous work. Such a proceeding cannot be called just.

I lack time, inclination, and capacity to examine the whole of the report in detail. I will confine myself to a few of the main points, and even these will be treated only from the theoretical angle. The statistics that appear in both the majority and minority reports I therefore leave for what they are worth. Statistics are admirable when they

[1] 'Tullskydd och frihandel,' *Ekonomisk Tidskrift*, 1924, pp. 149–64. Review of *Betänkande angående tullsystemets verkningar i Sverige före världskriget* (Report on the Effects of the Tariff System in Sweden before the War), Part I, Stockholm, 1924.

confirm a conclusion which is plausible in itself. The empirical and rational proofs then reinforce one another. But if the statistics conflict with such a conclusion, their value is of course more dubious. The inconsistency *may* be due to incorrect theory, but it may also depend on a wrongly formulated or misinterpreted statistical observation. It is obvious that the latter alternative is more probable where the *a priori* reasons are strongest: if one fine day the sun rose at some other place or time than the one determined astronomically, we may be certain that it had nothing to do with the real sun, but was a parhelion. This may perhaps call to mind the alleged statistics of trade between Norway and Sweden, which were adduced at the time as an argument for the abolition of the trade regulations in force between the two countries soon followed by union—but which were afterwards found to be monstrously out of accordance with the facts, the actual situation being just the opposite of that indicated by the statistics. But even if the statistics themselves were completely correct, the most important thing, the necessary basis of comparison, is lacking in this case. Whether for this we choose conditions in another country, or those of the same country during other periods of time, so many new elements appear, especially nowadays, that it is extremely difficult and often impossible to isolate the object of the detailed investigation properly. Reasoning from general economic considerations to the effect it may have, cannot therefore be avoided.

But economics is a difficult science, and the proper management of trade policy, especially with regard to foreign trade, is not one of its easier problems. The customary arguments for or against protection or free trade are commonly so full of dead ends and pitfalls that one sometimes despairs of ever finding a result which is certain and generally valid. Fortunately, however, there is one relatively fixed point in this chaos of conflicting opinions, interests and influences— namely, the fact that, *for the world as a whole*, general free trade must be considered to be equally and indisputably as beneficial to the whole as internal economic freedom is for each separate country. If, in the former case, each country were able to devote itself to the production which best fits its natural conditions and the creative ability of the people, as, in the latter case, with the parts of each country, then it seems beyond doubt that the result must be the greatest possible production, the greatest possible total of means of satisfying our needs. Admittedly, a certain reservation must be made even here—a reservation which applies moreover to both cases: the actual distribution of property and incomes not only has a modifying effect on the total satisfaction of subjective needs, but also imparts objectively to production, and the kinds of goods produced, characteristics different from those which would occur if there were greater social equality. It seems probable that more pairs of working boots would be manufactured in a socialist state, and fewer diamonds polished, than in the present society based on private ownership, and however equalitarian and just the distribution of diamonds is, it cannot compensate for a real scarcity of working boots. It would therefore be more correct to say that world-wide free trade, like international economic freedom, would make it *possible* to achieve the highest conceivable production, and thereby the greatest conceivable satisfaction of needs —but that this possibility could only become reality to the extent that a socially satisfactory distribution of incomes were achieved; and to all this must be added the assumption which is at the basis of all advocacy of free competition, though it is far from always fulfilled— the assumption that each individual is the best judge of what is economically advantageous for himself.

Since most countries have nevertheless erected, and now continue to erect, tariff barriers, we must conclude either that this system of tariffs is entirely irrational, and is due to misconceptions, mutual mistrust, or private interests that have been able to push themselves to the fore at the expense of the general public—or, a possibility which cannot be overlooked, that the full utilisation of the benefits of free trade perhaps requires a reformation, not only of the economic systems of the different countries, but also of their international social conditions.

With this proviso—to which we will return shortly—we have so far found the free trade argument successful; but the very next step becomes more doubtful, for what applies to the whole does not necessarily apply to every one of its parts. A country which surrounds itself with tariffs, whether on imports or on exports, behaves to some extent like a buying cartel for its import goods and at the same time a selling or production cartel for its export goods. It may be that the country in question, especially if it is backed by a monopolistic or quasi-monopolistic position in some respect, can, by a skilful use of this weapon, gain an advantage in international trade which more than compensates for the inconvenience caused by the obstructed exchange of commodities. For instance, this may easily come about if it is the chief customer for the products of another country, or the chief supplier of one of its necessities, or both, provided the other country remains passive or is for some reason unable to make reprisals. The sharp decline in the price of rye in the 1880's (see p. 171 of the Report) was probably to a great extent due to the tariff which

252

Germany put on grain; and if the Scandinavian countries were holding together, it is by no means uncertain that they could not actually profit from the very measures that were designed to *decrease* their exports. If two countries are of comparable size and dependent on one another, it is quite conceivable that the one which *first* introduced tariffs could gain a net profit for itself at the expense of the other; if the latter replies with tariffs of its own, it may perhaps *cut* its losses, although it cannot cancel them, because the final result as a rule would be that *both* would be worse off than under free trade. It is therefore not altogether correct when Heckscher (p. 51) says that the country which embarks upon counter-tariffs must inevitably injure itself and 'add more stones to its burden.' It would be better to say that its response to stones thrown at it is to throw stones itself, which may well be quite effective while international relations are conducted with such lack of decorum. Or, to continue with Heckscher's simile: the combined burden has certainly increased in weight, but the country's share of it may nevertheless have diminished compared with the period before the imposition of the counter-tariff, when, according to our assumption, it bore the whole of the burden by itself—and a little more besides.

It is not impossible that a tariff gain achieved in this way may persist despite all attempts at reprisals. Fortunately, however, such cases appear to be rare. I say fortunately, because there is something repugnant and at the same time unreasonable in the idea that a country may gain for itself a profit, which is perhaps very small, by involving its neighbours in a much larger loss—this must be what happens, since, in accordance with what has been said above, the algebraic sum of the advantages and disadvantages must always be negative.

Thus, if the whole question were merely one of maximising national gains, it is probable that tariffs would long ago have been abolished by mutual consent. But it is unfortunately much more complicated than that. The arguments set out above really constitute everything that can be said for free trade—except for one other which I will save until the end. The other thousand and one arguments which are advanced in discussing this difficult question seem to support the protectionists—at any rate to the extent that they do actually say something, and do not merely flow from a confusion of ideas. It seems doubtful, however, whether all of them together can outmatch the great free trade argument: making the national product a maximum. This seems unthinkable theoretically: if we have more to share, and if it is shared in an appropriate manner, there should be more for each recipient than if there were less to share. It remains to be seen whether practical difficulties, or non-economic considerations, will still block the way here.

As has already been stated, general free trade ought to guarantee increased benefits both for the whole of the world's population and, in the main, for the separate sections of it, but it does not guarantee that the increased benefits will be enjoyed within the boundaries of a particular country. On the contrary, the amalgamation and division of labour on an international basis, which is the very core and *raison d'être* of free trade, seems as a rule to require a concentration of labour and capital at certain points of the globe, and, if we disregard the general increase in population and capital, a consequent reduction of these productive factors at the other. Similarly, internal economic freedom and the abolition of compulsory guild membership have contributed much to population movements within individual countries. To put it another way: the establishment of free trade between two countries, e.g. Sweden and Denmark, would in all probability lead to economic advantages for both, but it cannot be assumed that these advantages would be mathematically equal. As soon as the productive capacity of the one country increases *more* than that of the other, the consequence should be a movement of capital and labour from the one country to the other unless this is prevented by special measures.

From a purely nationalistic point of view, such a movement may arouse misgivings if it assumes any considerable proportions, in whichever direction it takes place. But these misgivings should not be confused with what is economically advantageous or harmful. The minority of the committee, or their spokesman, is repeatedly guilty of this error, however. As soon as it is admitted that free trade may, in certain circumstances, cause emigration of labour and capital, they consider the argument won, for, they say, 'there would clearly never have been such an emigration if the living conditions of groups of workers within the country had not been lowered more than they would have been under a protective system' (p. 317, and several other places).

This conclusion is too hasty. We will shortly take up the case where it is justified. But it is quite obvious that the reason may also be that the country to which the emigration and export of capital takes place, just owing to the abolition of the tariff restrictions, is in a position to take more people and to pay interest on more capital than it could before, and in this case it is clear that there *need not* have been a worsening of the living conditions for any group of population in the former country. If we consider the internal movement, it is well known that since liberty to pursue a trade was introduced during the 1840's and in part certainly because of that, together with improvements in communications of course, the population of large areas of our country [i.e. Sweden], the purely agricultural districts, has *decreased*, both absolutely and relatively, while that of others, the industrial districts and the towns, has increased many times over. But it cannot be suggested that the population of those areas which people have left, lives under worse conditions than before the coming of economic liberty (and the railways), whether they be among those who have been left behind, or those who moved to other parts. Conditions are certainly better for them, and would probably be better still if the movement of population had been carried even farther. Or, if we consider the great emigration across the Atlantic during the second half of the nineteenth century, occasioned by the overpopulation of Europe, and made possible by the establishment of the great Atlantic steamship lines, as well as by easier communications in general, no one can imagine for a moment that the population of Europe, especially the working people, would have been better off if this easier intercommunication had never come about. But free trade and free choice of occupation are only one facet of general intercommunication, and every restriction of them implies, as has often been pointed out, that we must renounce some of the possibilities that the progress in the technique of communication has put at our disposal.

Besides the nationalistic misgivings about free trade, which may have their validity as long as there are no higher and more comprehensive viewpoints to replace them, there are others of a *social* kind. Free trade guarantees—with the above reservations—the largest possible social product, the largest total of incomes; but it says nothing about the distribution of these among the different social classes. Nor have we the consolation here that what is profitable for all can hardly be unprofitable or harmful for any, as was asserted in the case of the relations between different countries. For the differences between the propertyless and propertied classes in a society—including those possessing the society's capital of education and knowledge— or rather, the differences between the productive powers which these classes own or represent, are undoubtedly greater than the differences between two neighbouring countries. Unfortunately, the very concept of free trade, not least when regarded on a world-wide scale, contains certain features which might lead to a development of the total social product *opposite* to that of the part of it which provides the livelihood of the mass of the people. If the various countries each devote themselves to the production of relatively few groups of commodities, they should be able to produce on the greatest possible scale, and, at the same time, use the most rational technical methods. But most technical innovations, both in agriculture and in industry, tend to be *labour-saving*. In direct production, capital and natural power are 'substituted' for labour: wholly or partly automatic machines, draught animals or motor engines take the place of the old hand-power, and at the same time capital goods, machines and buildings are made more durable, so that less labour is required for their maintenance or successive renewal. Thus the result of general free trade might undeniably be the difficult social paradox that on the one hand the total efficiency of labour rises considerably because of technical progress, whereas the *marginal* productivity of labour and therefore the wage for unskilled work, falls very low, perhaps below the subsistence minimum. This latter result of course would be sharpened to a considerable degree by an increase in the population, but it is not altogether impossible for it to occur even with a stationary level of population.

To take an extremely simple example, we might suppose that there are two countries, of which the first possesses excellent pastures but poor land for bread grain, and the second excellent land for grain but poor (though extensive) pastures. Then, with free trade between them, the first country would produce wholly or mainly animal products, and the other vegetable products, of which part would be exchanged. We may further suppose that, with a given number of labourers in each country, wages have fallen very low, and the rent of land has consequently risen very high (for the sake of simplicity, we disregard the part played by capital in production), but without it yet being profitable to produce either country's products in the other. If, however, each country were to be cut off from the other by a tariff barrier, and each forced to produce all its needs itself, then the price of grain in the first country would rise so high compared with that of animal produce, and the price of animal produce so high with respect to that of grain in the second country, that it would be profitable in both countries to transfer some labour to the production which the tariffs had made possible. It is easy to construct the productivity functions for the two groups of products in each country in such a way that the tariff barrier would lead to a considerable decline in land rent and a raising of real wages, that is, the labourer would be able to consume both more grain and more animal produce than formerly, although the contrary would be the case for each country as a whole.

Of course, I do not suggest that there is any real situation corresponding fully to this example. Furthermore, even in the case we have been considering, if the workers in both countries consumed mainly vegetable products, only the workers in the country originally producing grain would definitely experience a gain, since grain there would be cheaper relative to animal produce because of the protective duties. In the other country, even if wages, expressed in terms of animal produce, rose, the higher price of grain would constitute such a large drawback that the gain would perhaps be changed to a loss.

A further assumption underlying all this is that in both countries rent must be high compared with wages. Otherwise, all labourers must lose by the cessation of free trade, since the increase in wages, even when expressed in the commodity or group of commodities made cheaper by the tariffs, would be quite insignificant, and probably would not outweigh the higher price of the other commodity for either country's workers.

If this were the consequence of general free trade, what could be done about it? The fixing of a minimum wage would not suffice; it would only give rise to permanent unemployment, and as a rule would diminish the total social product.[1] The making of grants from public funds to augment insufficient wages, as was practised formerly in England to a considerable extent (the allowance system, 'Gilbert's law'), has the disadvantage that the relief in practice only benefits the workers who are worst placed. There would thus be no incentive for the workers at the level immediately above this to earn a slightly better wage by a greater effort, and we might fall back into Soviet conditions. The only completely rational way to achieve the largest possible production—provided that pitfalls do not still lie concealed in the theory!—would be to allow all production factors, including labour, to find their equilibrium positions unhindered, under free competition, however low they may be, but at the same time to discard resolutely the principle that the worker's only source of income is his wages. He, like every other citizen, ought rather to be entitled to a certain share of the earnings of the society's natural resources, capital, and (where they cannot be avoided) monopolies.

[1] I say, as a rule; for it might occur in exceptional cases that the value of labour fell so much that it did not even balance the *difference* between the necessary consumption of the workers in question while working and while resting. In such a case, it would be cheaper to maintain a certain number of workers completely unemployed. As I have said, this appears to be an exception from the rule, although it may occur seasonally, as, for instance, in primitive agriculture during the winter months (Russia!). Heckscher's proposition 'that a use for labour is never lacking in a society'—which is on the whole a somewhat doubtful one—is definitely incorrect in this case, even in the improved form given by the minority report: 'if any wage whatsoever is acceptable.' It is impossible to set a wage lower than that which makes it possible to carry out a certain amount of work, but it can happen that the work in question is not worth even this wage.

It is unnecessary to point out to what extent these considerations, however just in other respects, provide grist for the mill of those who want socialisation. Karl Marx considered free trade from precisely this point of view as merely a preparatory school for socialism. On the other hand, it should be stressed that although these above-mentioned consequences are conceivable, they need not necessarily follow, especially if the tendency to a lower birth-rate, which seems general at the moment, should persist in the future. The considerable increase in real wages, particularly in hourly rates, which has occured in Sweden since the period before the war, certainly has its roots in something quite outside trade policy; but it is nevertheless strange that it began at the same time as the *decrease* in tariffs which came about automatically because of the fall in the value of money. If the development had gone the opposite way, so that the wages had fallen instead, the committee minority would presumably not have neglected to point it out when they observed the fact that real tariffs had decreased.

Even at the best, *protection* can only provide an easily applicable *substitute* for the solution which is theoretically the best, though extremely involved, as well as being new and untried. As Heckscher quite correctly points out, it subsidises a number of activities which are only slightly or not at all profitable in themselves, and it is on this artificially created basis that the internal economy is then free to operate; yet it is often possible for entrepreneurs in a protected industry to combine among themselves into trusts and cartels and to *suppress* free competition. If in this way, however, one does succeed in preventing wages from falling so much as they might have done under free trade, it could, of course, be maintained that the tariff burden is not in its entirety a burden for the country because the subsidy which it involves would also have to be paid out under free trade—though from increased total incomes—in order to keep the workers' needs above water. But when the minority, or their spokesman, goes so far as to suggest that a well-balanced protective system would maximise the national income, then they immediately put themselves in the wrong by attempting to prove too much, for the circumstances to which they refer—the different kinds of labour, women working as well as men, and so on—are not especially characteristic of Sweden. The conclusion should really have been that it is the existence of tariffs in *every* country, and consequently in the world as a whole, that brings about a maximum of goods, presumably by retaining in each individual country the labour and capital which would otherwise have emigrated—from every country to every country!

It may be objected that the minority report repeatedly describes *our* export industries unlike those of other countries, as 'exploiting industries,' which would make all the difference. Heckscher has dealt with this objection in what I consider to be such an excellent fashion in his pamphlet *Tullfrågan* (The Tariff Question), that it is unnecessary to go into it here. A rational timber industry—and there can be no question of anything else in the long run, even under free trade—is not an 'exploiting industry,' any more so than the working of a coal mine, for instance. The fact that we are at present cutting too much of our natural forests is another matter, which actually would not have injured the country at all if we had not, unhappily on the basis of this temporary natural benefit, fostered an excess of natural population that cannot be so easily eliminated. As happens so often, we find that the question of protection and free trade, however important it may be, takes us beyond itself, and must be seen against the background of the far more important questions of pressure of the population on the means of subsistence and the lack of a socially satisfactory distribution of property.

However, if we consider more closely the conditions of our own country, it is obvious that the committee minority are right when they say that the free traders ought to show *where* the workers now employed in the protected industries (and the surplus of workers in our protected agriculture) would be fitted in should the protective tariffs be removed. However, this question can only be answered by hypothesis from the theoretical viewpoint and by experiment in practice. If we had unlimited natural resources for our export industries, so that these could be extended on the same lines with the same production costs, the answer would be self-evident, and would be so attractive, even to the entrepreneurs, that any protective tariffs could scarcely have arisen or been maintained. But if the available natural resources are limited, these industries must sooner or later come under the sway of the inexorable 'law of diminishing returns'; and it seems that this happened some time ago, for the export of timber and other saw-mill products is much more profitable in itself than the export of joinery, paper pulp and paper. These industries ought nevertheless to be able to expand, and this obviously means that the export of finished goods must increasingly take the place of raw-material export. If our foreign customers oppose this with tariffs, I for my part—here perhaps contrary to Heckscher—consider that a *duty*, namely, an export duty on the raw material, would roughly restore the free trade position between us and the foreign countries (provided, of course, that the export duty were effective,

259

which would depend chiefly on the co-operation of our competitors, especially Finland and Norway) until such time that both duties were repealed by common consent. But, in any case, such a development could hardly take place without a lowering of wages in the industry. If, however, some of the more highly protected industries could be *closed down*, it is probable that a moderate decrease in wages could be outweighed by cheaper living costs, so that the real wage need *not* decrease; and likewise, the other protected industries would be better off for the same reason, so that they could manage with lower tariffs or even without tariffs. It would be a question of how far down the scale of the protected industries the line could be drawn between those from which the protecting tariffs might be removed and those still requiring tariffs, without real wages falling below their present level. If it could be drawn so low—which only experience could show—that the industries below it could all be dispensed with, through their labour being absorbed in the industries above it, that would be all well and good. Otherwise, the question of some form of subsidising labour to some extent still remains.

The protectionist minority, which in general emphasises its social sensibilities, is particularly concerned for *female* labour. It regards the highly protected textile industry as created for women, and vice versa. It maintains that it is only with the aid of this industry that female labour has been saved from economic misery. Experience from the war (and to some extent, from Finland) seems to show, however, that women are more or less equally willing to take up any of the occupations which were formerly reserved for men—and on the whole with success. They would naturally prefer those which may be carried on in the home and which fit in with management of a home, but there is now no question of that, not even in the textile industry. To stand all day long in a factory knotting yarn ends amid the deafening roar of spinning machines and looms can hardly be particularly attractive to 'female labour.' There does not appear to be any justification for the maintenance of this pleasure by means of a tariff, which, if I am not mistaken, is, or at least *was*, as much as the whole amount of the wages.

But I will not spend more time on details. On the whole, it seems to me that the majority report fulfils all reasonable requirements, in view of the difficulties of the question, although I have admittedly not been able to make a really thorough study of it. Its authors may have allowed themselves to press the free trade argument a little too forcefully at times, but in the main they have taken considerable pains to be factual and even moderate. On one point, with regard to the harmfulness of the duties on food products, I myself would like to go

260

a good deal farther than they have done, for various reasons which would take too long to explain here.[1] Anyway, they deserve the credit for having tried to estimate in a truly scientific manner all the internal relationships between all the relevant multifarious facts.

It is this coherence above all which I miss in the minority report. Brilliantly written as far as its style is concerned, its various arguments are, individually, very seductive, but they do not stand up to juxtaposition. The minority, in the good old mercantilist manner, talk about excessive imports and the consequent *indebtedness* abroad, which under free trade would be the result of our well-known and unfortunate liking for everything foreign. They are also afraid of the *export of capital* and the consequent unemployment and emigration which would arise if our export industries, under free trade, had unrestricted disposal over their capital profits—and invested them abroad. One might suppose, of course, that these two opposing movements of capital might cancel one another out to some extent, so that the net result might perhaps be that capital, and with it labour, remained quite happily in this country. But they presumably mean that the capital we receive from abroad is dissipated in riotous living, while we thoughtlessly part with capital which could have been put to good use at home. I only wonder if a people of such perversity can be saved, even by a tariff muzzle.[2]

The attitude of the committee minority (or their spokesman) to

[1] The opinion I expressed in 1903 about the agricultural tariffs, which is quoted in the appendix to the minority report, was not intended in support of those tariffs, but rather to suggest that their repeal should be followed by a balancing out of unearned profits and undeserved losses. The continuation of the quoted passage, which is not given, is as follows:
'From the logical point of view, it must always be possible to carry out a measure which is designed to be of advantage to the whole country in such a manner that it is not injurious to any individual, or, at least, so that it does not lead to anyone's ruin, and on the other hand, in such a manner that the gain expected for the society as a whole does not resolve itself into gains for those individuals who need them least.'
This is still my opinion.

[2] It seems a little too much, however, that our desire for things foreign should go so far that we even prefer foreign *rags* to our own, as the committee minority gives us to understand, on the authority of the poet von Heidenstam. For I suspect that 'Foreign Rag Market immortalised by Heidenstam' was just a place where rags were *bought for foreign firms*—what else could it have been?—and in that case it bears witness to foreigners' partiality for our rags rather than the opposite. That four accomplished businessmen, together (if the rumour has it correctly) with a Professor of Economics, should use even as a rhetorical ornament the preposterous idea that trade in rags means direct consumption of rags, is certainly amazing.

the core of the free trade arguments are rather ambiguous. They maintain (p. 321) that 'the economic doctrine that the gain to the economy as a whole is greatest under free trade merely implies of course that the sum of private profits momentarily attains a maximum.' What is meant here by 'gain'? If it is only the profits of capital or enterprise, this is not at all what the doctrine of free trade says. On the contrary, this doctrine states that the national product, the total or average income (per head of the population, of course) attains its maximum under free trade, not merely 'momentarily' but at every moment. If the committee minority wish to contest this proposition, they have every right to do so, but not on grounds which could be applied more or less to all peoples, for the proof then leads to absurdity.

Similarly with regard to monopoly and dumping. The fact that tariffs favour to a great extent the formation of monopolistic combines lies in their very nature, and, as far as I know, is completely confirmed by experience of protectionist countries as compared with non-protectionist. The minority report has not been able to contest this fact, but they have endeavoured to blunt the edge of it by reminding us of 'all those cases where monopolies have been formed in order to be able to cover the costs of production.' The correctness of this observation cannot be denied. As soon as industry comes under the influence of the so-called law of increasing returns, that is to say it prospers better the larger the scale of production, then, as most economists will admit, there is no possibility of economic equilibrium under free competition; what happens is that the one entrepreneur competes the other out of business, until the survivors are obliged to combine together in a monopolistic organisation, a trust or a cartel, to avoid a a similar fate. But it is not equally certain, and indeed it is highly improbable, that *afterwards*, when they have achieved this goal, they would be modestly content just to cover their costs. One has only to think of the rubber trust, and so many others. But '*if*,' says the minority report, 'if, with the help of both protective tariffs and his monopoly, the monopolist does not get more than the normal rate of interest on his capital,' what then? In this case it would probably be beneficial for the country as a rule if the protective tariff, the monopoly, and the industry, were allowed to go the way of all flesh—not violently, so that 'its workers are thrown on to the streets,' but gently, systematically, and purposefully.

As regards dumping (selling at cut prices on the foreign market), Heckscher has shown very clearly—as I maintained several years ago against Brock—that the opportunity of dumping cannot induce the monopolist to lower the price of his good in the home market; on the contrary, the higher the price he can obtain abroad, the higher, in his own interest, he will set the monopoly price at home— the opposite to what is often supposed.[1] This rule is quite general, and applies whether the monopoly is large or small, indeed, even if it is negative. So that the author of the minority report, still assuming that the monopolist only gets 'the usual interest on his capital,' says that 'if the foreign market pays even a small part of the fixed costs of the enterprise, and even if it gets the commodity at a lower price than the home market, it does nevertheless always contribute something, so that the home consumer buys the good more cheaply than he would otherwise have done,' his conclusion is incorrect. The contrary is true. On the other hand, it may well be that if the tariffs were removed, and with them the possibility of both monopoly and dumping, domestic production of the commodity would not pay at all. But would that be any misfortune? And would not the domestic consumer then be still more 'cheaply supplied' with the good in question? Since the minority's co-opted member was here confronted by a definite viewpoint of Heckscher's, he should not have been content to play to the gallery by putting forward a superficial argument, but should instead have carried out a proper investigation of the theoretical assumptions bearing on the phenomenon in question, which would not be so difficult in this case.

Finally, with regard to tariffs as protection against foreign dumping on our market, we should on the whole only be thankful if foreigners wish to sell us their own goods at a lower price than in their own country. The only thing which is really dangerous is destructive dumping, intended to ruin the competing domestic industry so as to be able to raise the price afterwards at will. There is no doubt that such a dumping does occur, but, as Heckscher mentions, it obviously implies the existence of an *international* foreign trust, and against such giants our tariffs are probably too weak, especially as there is nothing to prevent the erection of a foreign factory within our tariff boundaries for the purpose of

---

[1] Editor's Note: The modern theory of dumping implies that it is profitable for a monopolist to *raise* the domestic price of the product in question if the foreign price obtained is *higher* than the point of intersection between the domestic marginal revenue curve and the marginal cost curve, and to *reduce* the domestic price if the foreign price is *lower* than this point of intersection. Wicksell, writing before the invention of the fruitful 'marginal revenue' concept, has overlooked the latter case, which has a great practical bearing, and, therefore, his criticism overshoots the mark.

dumping.[1] The rapid growth of international trusts constitutes a problem for international law, as troublesome as it is important, which may soon overshadow the tariff question itself.

The other contentions of the minority report, as far as I have been able to examine them and think about them, also seem to me to be little different from the usual sophistry about tariffs. For instance, it would be difficult to deny that the great emigration of the 1880's and later had its real roots in purely demographic circumstances. For my part, as early as 1881 I was able to predict, on these grounds alone and in the main correctly, the emigration which occurred during the rest of the nineteenth century. My ability to foretell the future extended no farther, for those who were to emigrate later had, for the most part, not then been born. But even if it could be proved, as of course is conceivable, that the new protective tariffs had contributed to the diminution of emigration during the 1890's and to its slower increase in the following period, there still remain the questions: was it beneficial to the country or its population, and if it was, could not the same result have been attained by some better means than tariffs?

The minority members steadfastly refuse to go into the latter question—and, for that matter, into the one before it as well. Their social sensibilities, which I have mentioned previously, do not extend beyond the tariff boundaries, so to speak, and when they reproach the majority for having approached their task with preconceived opinions about the question at issue—what is one to say about the minority members themselves?[2]

---

[1] During one of my lecture tours in southern Sweden, I once came across a factory for the manufacture of jute fabrics, which owed its existence entirely to a paragraph in the tariff regulations, and which, if I am not mistaken, was carried on with foreign capital, foreign machines, foreign raw materials, foreign management, and even foreign workers, so that at the nearby chemists they had to learn Hungarian or Rumanian in order to make up prescriptions. I do not know whether this idyllic factory was intended for dumping, but it seems in any case to be somewhat dubious.

[2] Whether the minority report has gained in strength from the support given to it by Professor Brock in *Statsvetenskaplig Tidskrift*, I cannot say for certain, although I have several times read his somewhat obscure article. But it does seem to me that by far the greater part of his review deals with minor, not to say trifling points. Almost two pages (359–60) are taken up with a criticism which, as far as it is correct, rather seems to reinforce the main argument of his opponents. Regarding the *form* of Brock's article, I would just like to ask the author if he thinks that he gains anything by choosing a manner of writing which must make it extremely difficult, or even impossible, for his opponents to enter into the discussion. The 'floridity,' 'contortions' and 'long catechisms,' etc., which he

A few words in conclusion. The preceding discussion has not provided any real answer to the question of whether the tariff question is really an *important* problem. Even if we accept the proposition that the national income can only be fully maximised under free trade, it is nevertheless in the mathematical nature of all, or practically all maximisation, that a quantity approaching its greatest possible value increases more and more gradually, and in the end quite infinitesimally. Such may also be the case here. The computed tariff burden is a rather uncertain quantity—and in this we must acknowledge that the minority are right, though the majority have not denied it—even if it is not a mere chimera, as the minority seems to prefer to think of it. However, it may well be that it is really so small, especially nowadays, that it is not worth while, for its sake, to break with a system to which we have been accustomed for several decades, and in some cases even longer. I am not of this school of thought myself, but ever since I was able to form my own opinion on these matters I have been of the conviction that there are *other* social questions of far greater *economic* significance than trade policy.

But there is one viewpoint from which the question of protection or free trade must *always* present itself as an important problem, indeed as one of the most important of all. The constant striving to procure (mostly imagined) advantages at the expense of other countries, or, by one's own moves, to check the advantages (likewise usually imagined) which foreign countries attempt to gain at our expense, creates an atmosphere of mutual distrust and envy between nations, a continual over-estimation of the economic well-being of one's neighbours and under-estimation of one's own. Such a situation is fraught with dangers. 'Tariff wars' have only too often led to the most serious disputes between nations, and even to armed conflict. Since, as I have already pointed out, the validity of the doctrine of free trade on a world-wide scale is not really open to doubt, we all

professes to have found in the report, seem to exist only in his imagination, and another product of his free creative fantasy is his statement that Professor Heckscher has described his own contribution as 'almost unique in world literature'! Even foreign literature on the subject is far from abounding in exhaustive and systematic presentations of tariff policy, as the reviewer himself knows quite well. This is even more true, of course, of the Swedish literature. Brock's own book on tariffs has its good points (as well as not a few faults), but not even he would claim that it is exhaustive and systematic.

Brock says that he intends to continue his examination of the report in a later issue, and promises to 'try to be briefer' then. In that case, perhaps he will find no place for more 'floridities,' and, to use his own expression, 'so much the better.'

ought to try to look at it from a *world view*, setting aside our purely national interests as far as possible, even if these seem at times to call for some other approach. We may well be convinced in the long run that even these interests will be best furthered on the whole by such an attitude.

A complete abandonment of national boundaries is obviously not possible as yet. The main obstacle is the fact that the population question, that unfortunate snag in all cultural progress, has not yet found its rational solution in the majority of countries. It must be solved by each nation for itself, under the intellectual influence of the rest, but not in such a way that one country is made the dumping-ground for the other's surplus population. But, to the extent that it is solved, the natural development should be that, just as tribes in the past combined to make nations or states, the nations will gradually combine together into a single society or union of states, embracing the whole world. In the political field we now stand at last on the promising threshold of such a union for the prevention in future of all bloody conflicts between peoples. But it is obvious that this movement, while it does a great deal to facilitate a free exchange of goods between countries, itself demands and presupposes this free exchange as its necessary complement. From this point of view the endeavour to establish free trade becomes a matter concerning the whole of humanity, both materially and culturally—and it can never cease until victory has been achieved.

AN OBJECT-LESSON IN THE
TARIFF QUESTION [1]

EVEN if we attempt to liberate the question of tariffs and free trade from all the countless complications which beset it in real life, so that the relevant phenomena may be presented with the greatest possible simplicity, not a few interesting and intricate points nevertheless remain. It was not until the subjective theory of value, relating exchange value to marginal utility and the associated concept of 'consumers' rent' were put forward, that it was possible to treat the problem in an entirely scientific manner. Cournot never got as far as the former concept and under-estimated the importance of the latter. As Pareto, Edgeworth,[2] and, later, Irving Fisher[3] have pointed out, Cournot's treatment of the protective tariff question in *Recherches sur les principes mathématiques de la théorie des richesses*, published in 1838, showed a radical misunderstanding of the whole problem (besides a couple of purely mathematical mistakes), which, despite all his formal penetration, render the sections of the book dealing with the matter more or less worthless. For the same reason John Stuart Mill, whose basic appreciation of the problem was much more correct and whose presentation of it was on the whole a considerable step forward, could not always get to the bottom of the matter, regarding multiple equilibrium positions, for instance, as has also been pointed out by Edgeworth.[4] The latter's well-known series of articles in the *Economic Journal* (1894) probably represent the peak of the theoretical exposition of the subject to date for those sections of it with which he deals, but it seems to me that he has not always got down to the basic element, the dispositions of the individual consumers, and has therefore arrived at conclusions on at least one important point that I consider to be too hasty or even incorrect.

---

[1] 'Ett skolexempel i tullfrågan,' *Ekonomisk Tidskrift*, 1925, pp. 23–42.

[2] *Giornale degli Economisti*, 1892.—*Economic Journal*, 1894, pp. 625 ff.

[3] *Quarterly Journal of Economics*, 1898, pp. 119 ff.

[4] Op. cit., pp. 607 ff. Cf. also my *Lectures*, vol. I (pp. 198 ff. in the English edition).

Until further notice, I shall proceed with the assumption (which is always feasible) that there is in each case only *one* possible position of equilibrium for international prices, that is, with regard to the *relative* prices of commodities. The absolute level of prices, the money prices, will—as we shall see—nevertheless display moments of uncertainty at times, a fact which hitherto seems to have received insufficient attention.

For the sake of simplicity we will consider two countries isolated from the rest of the world, which have up to now carried on unrestricted trade with one another, yet without any transfer of capital or labour power between them. One of these countries is an *agricultural* country, possessed of fertile land in abundance (so that the law of diminishing returns has not yet made itself felt, and therefore no question of rent has arisen), but lacking the most important industrial raw materials, iron and coal. The other country has poor agricultural land but coal and iron in such quantities that it is not yet necessary for any mining royalties to be paid if the present state of free competition between the mine owners continues. The only factors of production in each country are therefore labour and capital, which are supposed to exist in approximately the same amounts in each country, and which we put together, for the sake of simplicity, in a single production element: capital-and-labour. Under such circumstances it is clear that each country will only produce *one* of the two groups of commodities, agricultural and industrial products respectively; the need for other commodities is satisfied in each case by *exchange* with the other country. We also assume something which is arbitrary and inessential, that half the produce of the agricultural country goes in exchange for half the produce of the industrial country. If, for the sake of simplicity, we disregard transport costs, trade profits, and the like, each country is able to use half of its capital and labour to obtain indirectly a quantity of agricultural or industrial products, according to the respective country, which—we will suppose—would have required twice as much capital and labour, that is, the *whole* of the available productive factors in each country, if it had been produced directly. If we take as a unit the amount of each kind of commodity which is produced by means of a given amount of capital and labour, then it is obvious that according to our assumptions two such units are exchanged one against the other; if we call the money price of such a unit 1 (or 100), the average level of prices in each country is equal to 1 (or 100).

Of course this is only *one* assumption among countless conceivable ones. Even under conditions of free trade the relative price of two such units might rise to any value, according to circumstances, up to the limit where it is profitable to produce directly in a country the products of the other country. It is obvious that this has a considerable influence on the magnitude of the figures regarding quantity and value which are given below, although it does not affect the general character of the results.

Let us now suppose that one of these countries, say the agricultural one, *closes its frontiers* to all imports from the other country by means of import restrictions or high tariffs, in order to foster an industry of its own. For a time its products will continue to be exported to the industrial country, but since payment can now only be made in money (or promissory notes, which we will not consider), prices will eventually reach a level which will make this unprofitable, and *both* countries will be obliged to produce everything they need themselves. According to our assumptions, this will lead to considerable loss for both countries, and we will now attempt to arrive at some estimate of the magnitude of this loss. It is evident that it need not be the same in each country. Considering the *industrial* country first, we see that, if it still wishes to consume as much of industrial products as it did before, it will obviously be forced to restrict its consumption of agricultural products to a half of what it previously consumed. If, on the other hand, it wishes to maintain its consumption of agricultural products, it will be obliged to use the *whole* of its resources of labour and capital to produce them, as has already been pointed out, and nothing will be left over for production of industrial goods. None of these alternatives is conceivable. It is easy to see that agricultural products in the industrial country now command prices with respect to industrial goods twice as high as those obtaining under free trade. In order that equilibrium may be possible (the consumption of industrial products being unchanged) the *marginal utility* of agricultural products (for each individual consumer) must therefore rise to double what it was before, consumption having diminished to a half; but it is certain that it will actually rise to a much greater extent when a necessity so vital as foodstuffs is concerned. It can therefore be assumed that this country will need to use two-thirds, say, or three-quarters, or even more of its productive resources for food, so that only a third, or a quarter, or even less (but always something, of course) remains for the production of industrial goods. Thus, as compared with the period of free trade, in the first case consumption is cut to two-thirds for both food and industrial goods, in the second to three-quarters for food and only one-half for industrial goods, which means that the living standards of the people fall a great deal.

The state of affairs in the *agricultural* country is somewhat different. It is quite conceivable that the consumption of foodstuffs, even after the imposition of restrictions, is maintained at the old value, or it may even *increase* somewhat. The consumption of industrial products must be limited to a half or less than a half of what it was before, but since these products have become twice as dear with respect to agricultural products, their marginal utility, compared with the latter, must have doubled itself, so that the consumption of industrial products must be cut down to a half or less than a half of what it was before. But it is also possible that even when the consumption of industrial goods has been cut by half, their marginal utility has been *more* than doubled; if this happens, it is clear that the consumption of agricultural products must also *decrease* as a consequence. In any case, the consumers here also lose. It is quite obvious in the latter case, as well as when the consumption of foodstuffs is unchanged. But the same thing applies even if the consumption of agricultural products is taken to *increase* by $\frac{1}{10}$, for example; in this case it is clear that the consumption of industrial goods is cut to $\frac{9}{20}$ of what it was during the period of free trade, and is therefore diminished by $\frac{11}{20}$. Since the extra tenth of agricultural products could be advantageously exchanged for the last tenth of the amount of industrial goods consumed during the period of free trade, it must now, *a fortiori* (because of the decreased consumption of industrial goods), be worth *less* than this quantity; the consumer's net loss must therefore be reckoned as *at least* $\frac{9}{20}$ or 45 per cent of their original consumption of industrial goods. That the loss is not felt so much as in the industrial country is due to the fact that the difficulties of direct production affect the less indispensable of the two types of goods.

It is obviously this real loss (in other words, the decrease in 'consumer's surplus') which is most important from the point of view of economics, and perhaps the only important one. The changes in the level of prices in the two countries are of secondary importance by comparison—except during the actual period of transition. Nevertheless, this question too is of no little importance, and it turns out that there are some surprising factors involved. Thus, it is apparent that, while it is (in this case) completely immaterial, as far as the real economic position of the two countries is concerned, whether the initiative for trade restrictions comes from one side or the other, and whether it takes the form of a prohibition on the import or export of commodities, these factors are of decisive importance for the way in which prices arrange themselves. If we continue with the supposition that the cause of all the change is the imposition of high import tariffs by the agricultural country, the consequences are as follows. The price of industrial products in this country will be considerably higher than in the industrial country, but it cannot exceed the price in the latter country by more than the whole amount of the duty imposed, otherwise these goods would continue to be imported (we are still disregarding transport costs, etc.). Agricultural products, on the other hand, are still subject to no restriction, so it is clear that they will command *the same price* in the industrial country as in the agricultural country; the fact that they will eventually cease to be exported depends, as has already been stated, on the fact that they eventually become so *dear*, in terms of money, and the industrial goods in the industrial country so cheap, that it is advantageous to produce the foodstuffs in the industrial country. As we have already seen, the price of agricultural products in this latter country becomes exactly twice as high as the price of industrial products if the restriction takes the form of complete *prohibition*, whereas in the agricultural country, the price of the industrial products must be twice as high as that of the agricultural products. Therefore, when the restriction is a complete one, the price of the industrial products in the agricultural country must be *four* times as high as it is in the industrial country. The imposition of a duty of 100 per cent of the value of the goods involved, which might at first sight seem to be sufficient to make industrial production profitable in the agricultural country, will prove to be insufficient, and must be continually raised until it reaches a figure of 300 per cent of the value in the industrial country in order to stop the importation completely—although it should be noticed, as we shall soon see, that this latter value has simultaneously *decreased* considerably, in terms of money.[1]

Under the given assumptions, it is easy to get an idea of both the relative and absolute levels of prices in the two countries, compared with the position under free trade. If we call the price of agricultural products after complete prohibition p, which is common to both countries, and the prices of industrial products p' in the industrial country and p'' in the agricultural country, we obtain the following

---

[1] If the foreign market were very large compared to the home market, so that the price situation in the former might be taken to remain unaltered, a duty of 100 per cent would be sufficient, of course. Cf. my article 'Tullar och arbetslöner' (Tariffs and Wages) in *Ekonomisk Tidskrift*, 1912, where this assumption is implicit.

relations:

$$p = 2p'; \; p'' = 2p,$$

so that $\qquad\qquad p'' = 4\,p',$

whereas all these prices were denoted by the figure 1 during the period of free trade. If we further suppose, in accordance with what has already been said, that the consumption of foodstuffs in the agricultural country remained unchanged at the old amount so that the consumption of industrial products therefore declined by a half, the weighted average price level in the agricultural country is obviously

$$\frac{p + \tfrac{1}{2}p''}{1 + \tfrac{1}{2}} = \tfrac{4}{3}p,$$

and in the industrial country, if we assume that the consumption of agricultural products is there restricted to three-quarters and of industrial products consequently to a half:

$$\frac{\tfrac{3}{4}p + \tfrac{1}{2}p'}{\tfrac{3}{4} + \tfrac{1}{2}} = \tfrac{4}{5}p.$$

The weighted average price level in the agricultural country is therefore to that in the industrial country as 5 : 3.

If we now assume that both countries are on the gold standard, and that in the beginning they possessed equal amounts of gold, while the velocity of circulation of money in the wide sense (physically and virtually) was and remains the same for both countries, it is then clear that if the price of agricultural products remains unchanged at 1, so that p'' rises to 2 and p' falls to $\tfrac{1}{2}$, the agricultural country (the 'protected' country) will need the *same* amount of gold for its monetary circulation as it did previously, whereas, on the other hand, the industrial country (the 'unprotected' country) will need only *half* the amount of gold it needed before.[1] Their combined total of gold, which we take to remain unchanged, will then be divided between them in the ratio 2 : 1, in other words, one-third of the gold held by the industrial country makes its way over to the agricultural country during the period of transition (causing a temporary over-consumption in the former country, and a temporary under-consumption in the latter, of course). It is easy to see that as a consequence of this the common price for agricultural products rises—compared with the

[1] The former will consume a quantity of goods 1 at the price 1, and a quantity $\tfrac{1}{2}$ at the price 2; the latter country a quantity $\tfrac{3}{4}$ at the price 1 and a quantity $\tfrac{1}{2}$ at the price $\tfrac{1}{2}$.

272

period before the restrictions—by one-third. Therefore we actually get

$$p = \tfrac{4}{3}, \text{ and consequently } p' = \tfrac{2}{3} \text{ and } p'' = \tfrac{8}{3}.$$

Accordingly, the weighted average price level, which was 1 in both countries before the change, is now $\tfrac{4}{3} \cdot \tfrac{4}{3} = \tfrac{16}{9}$ in the agricultural country, and has thus risen to nearly double what it was.

But the level of prices has also risen in the industrial country since the period of free trade, although only by $\tfrac{4}{5} \cdot \tfrac{4}{3} = \tfrac{16}{15}$.[1] (It is clear that the ratio of these two price levels is 5 : 3.)

So, neither the absolute nor the relative changes in prices can be used by themselves as a criterion of the economic effect of the cessation of free trade, which depends wholly and solely on the decrease of (production and) consumption in each country. It is true that these quantities are elements in the new price situation, but this acquires its particular character from the fact that the initiative in restricting trade was taken by one country, the other remaining passive.

If it had instead been the industrial country which had taken the initiative in restricting trade by preventing the importation of agricultural products, the agricultural country remaining passive, the position with regard to prices would have been quite different. The price of industrial goods would have been the same in both countries, while the price of agricultural products in the industrial country would rise to four times what it was in the agricultural country; gold now moves from the latter country to the former; the weighted average price level in the agricultural country would *fall* somewhat, as it is not difficult to show, namely to $\tfrac{8}{9}$ of the free trade value; on the other hand, it rises to $\tfrac{32}{15}$ of its former value in the industrial country, so that the ratio between the two is now 5 : 12—but, nevertheless, the economic position in both countries is the same as it was in the previous case.

On the other hand, had the industrial country, while not taking the initiative in restricting trade, instead *responded* to the agricultural country's duties on industrial goods by imposing its own on agricultural products, thereby obviously hastening the state of complete restriction, the relative price situation between the two countries would have been more or less counterbalanced.[2] At the same time, however, it is completely *indeterminate* theoretically—a point of great interest—since in this case the basis of comparison, the common

---

[1] It is obvious that the possibility of the level of prices rising in both countries despite the unchanged amount of money depends on the fact that the quantities of goods sold has diminished.

[2] The real position would still be the same.

price of the 'unprotected' goods in the two countries, *is lacking*. The actual state of affairs which comes about depends on the tempo and energy with which the retaliation is put into effect. If the retaliatory duties are not imposed until the complete restriction described above has come into operation, they will be just so much wasted effort, without any effect on prices, provided the conditions of production in the two countries remain the same in other respects.

It should be added that *export* duties or prohibition of exports would have the same effect on the *real* position as import duties or prohibition of imports in the same country, but for the *price* position they have the same effect as measures restricting imports imposed by the *other* country.

It is not my intention to try to deal with the countless modifications which must be applied to the above conclusions as soon as we approach the field of actual reality; I would just like to draw attention to *one* deviation, however, since it is an important one, unlike most of the others. The completely prohibitive system is diametrically opposed to free trade, but they are alike in one respect, namely, that the state receives no income from customs duties; in conformity with this is the fact that, as we have already seen, the real economic position is independent of which country it is that takes the initiative. The same thing must be true of all customs duties which have a prohibitive effect, that is, which make some domestic production profitable that would not have been carried on under free trade. On the other hand, this is not the case with duties that merely make the imported goods dearer—or to the extent they make them dearer—without bringing about the production of the goods within the country itself (financial duties, as they are called, in contrast to protective duties).

According to our assumptions, when trade is prohibited the industrial country produces three-quarters of the quantity of agricultural products and half the quantity of industrial products which it was able to consume during the period of free trade. The price ratio between the two types of goods in this country is 2 : 1. If we suppose for the moment that the agricultural country lived under a *monopolistic* regime (with no counterpart in the industrial country), then, by offering the above-mentioned quantity of agricultural products, or a little more, to the industrial country at a price a little less than that giving the price-ratio 2 : 1, the agricultural country ought to be able to induce the other country to refrain from direct production of agricultural products and to obtain them by barter instead. The economic

274

position of the industrial country would then be about the same as it was when no trade took place, or perhaps a little better. It is not difficult to see that the agricultural country, on the other hand, would find itself in the happy position of being able to consume $\frac{5}{4}$ as much agricultural products and about $1\frac{1}{2}$ times as much industrial products as during the period of free trade. But it should be noticed that this is not necessarily the greatest possible profit that the agricultural country can make from monopoly. There would certainly be nothing to be gained by putting the price of agricultural products *higher*, since the industrial country, as we shall see later, would then itself begin to produce a certain amount of its needs in foodstuffs; but there might possibly be some advantage in setting the price a little *lower*. We do not wish to dwell upon this point, however, but will assume that the procedure mentioned above is both the most profitable for the agricultural country, and, at the same time, undoubtedly does the industrial country the most *harm*.

The question now arises as to whether this great advantage for the inhabitants of the agricultural country might also be achieved, under otherwise free competition, by imposing a *duty* on the products of the industrial country, to which this latter country is still supposedly passive. Let us assume that this could be achieved by an *ad valorem* duty of, say, 100 per cent (or a little less). The condition for this is obviously that the price ratio between the two types of goods, when consumption is of the size mentioned, remains at 1 : 1 in the agricultural country, just as it was under free trade, for in such circumstances it is clear that the price ratio (between agricultural and industrial products) in the industrial country is (very nearly) 2 : 1, just as it was in the monopoly case which we have just considered or in the case of complete blocking of trade. The above condition is not unreasonable; it is true that the marginal utility of both types of goods will sink when their consumption increases, but that need not prevent the *ratio* of their marginal utilities from remaining at 1 : 1.

The apparent paradox that at this price one unit of agricultural produce is exchanged in the agricultural country's market for one unit of industrial produce, while each owner of the former, by effecting an exchange with the industrial country, would have got two units of industrial products for each unit of agricultural produce supplied by him, has its explanation in the fact that there is no question of free exchange with the other country as far as the individual is concerned. Under free exchange—that is, under free trade—if the price ratio were 1 : 1 and supposing he had, for example, 8 units of agricultural produce, he would only be prepared to obtain 4 units of the foreign goods in exchange for 4 units of his own. But if from the outset he had had *more* of his own product, say, 3 units more, he would, at the same price, have been prepared to go on exchanging longer, and demanded, say, 6 units of the foreign product for 6 units of his own. Now, this is precisely what happens. When the government imposes a tariff, from which it expects to derive a certain income, it must *ceteris paribus* remit a corresponding amount of direct taxation (which, abstracting from money, we might regard as being levied *in natura* on the products of the country) or they may even make a positive distribution; so that if the tax relief—or share-out, as the case may be—is carried out in an equitable manner, then the individual in question will receive 3 units as his share. On receiving them, he demands 6 units of the foreign goods in exchange for 6 units of his own. The government takes half of the *latter* quantity as import duty on the foreign goods and as remuneration for the amount of tax remitted—or the amount shared out, as the case may be. The other country, therefore, only gets the remaining 3 units of agricultural goods, which are exchanged for 6 units of industrial goods at the price prevailing in its market.

N.B.—This remission of taxes must have taken place, or at least be definitely expected to take place, *before* the exchange of goods with the other country, as does in fact happen when the national budget is drawn up for the fiscal year ahead. If, instead, the government promises to pay each consumer of the foreign product the amount of duty which he has paid, or which has been paid on his behalf, the result would be quite different. Such a procedure would simply restore the conditions of free trade. The price of the industrial goods in the agricultural country would rise by 'the entire amount of the duty,' that is, to twice that of the agricultural goods, but the demand for them would nevertheless be the same as it was under free trade. Consequently, the prices of the two types of goods would be equal in the industrial country, so the conditions of free trade would prevail there too.

It must, of course, be remembered that it is still a question here of the pricing process on the home (or foreign) *markets*. In order that there shall be a market, it is necessary that there be trade and sales *within* the country in question. It is therefore necessary to assume that the actual exchange of goods with the foreign country, as well as the distribution of the foreign goods, must be carried on by individual merchants who purchase the domestic products and sell the foreign ones. These traders will naturally not receive any restitution for the duties they pay, because this repayment goes to the consumers of the foreign goods after each individual's purchase (or, in the case of export duty, to the original owners of the home product—who are the general public as a whole—after each separate *sale*). Consequently, in order that this trade may be profitable, the price of the foreign goods on the home market must undoubtedly be (at least) twice as high as the price of the home product (since they are equal abroad), but this does not lead to any decrease of the demand for the foreign goods (in contrast with what happens under free trade), because, according to our last assumption, half the price is returned as a repayment of duty. A customs duty manipulated in this way would thus be a means of raising or lowering the average level of prices in the country as desired, without having any effect on the rate of exchange or the real economic position.

In this connection, it will not be out of place to refer to a peculiar statement made by Edgeworth in the first of the articles already mentioned (*Economic Journal*, 1894, p. 47). He is of the opinion that a country which raises its price level by the imposition of import duties, while the level of prices abroad has gone down to some extent, would gain some advantage from this in its foreign credit relationships, regardless of whether it is a creditor or debtor nation. He says that in the former case it would obtain *more* of the foreign country's products in the form of interest and amortisation, since the value of money is higher there, while in the latter case it would gain by having to pay *less* for its own goods. This point of view seems to me exceedingly dubious, but I must leave criticism of it to the reader.

Consequently, if the price of agricultural products, which is still the same for the two countries, is denoted by p, and the price of industrial goods in the industrial country by p' and in the agricultural one by p'', as before, then $p' = \frac{1}{2}p$ (approximately), whereas $p'' = 2p' = p$. The average level of prices in the agricultural country is therefore simply p, and in the industrial country (approximately)

$$\frac{\frac{3}{4}p + \frac{1}{2}p'}{\frac{3}{4} + \frac{1}{2}} = \frac{4}{5}p$$

and the relationship between the price levels in the two countries is therefore 5 : 4.

Regarding the absolute prices, it is obvious that if p and therefore also p'' are still 1, the agricultural country will require for its circulation an amount of gold which, compared with its original holding, has increased in the ratio $(\frac{5}{4} + \frac{3}{4}) : (1 + 1) = \frac{11}{8} : 1$, while the industrial country, since p' is now $\frac{1}{2}$, can manage with a quantity of gold which has declined in the ratio $(\frac{3}{4} + \frac{1}{4}) : (1 + 1) = \frac{1}{2} : 1$.

The gold requirements of the two countries are therefore now in the ratio 11 : 4, and the quantity of gold which must have been transferred to the agricultural country in order to reach economic equilibrium is obtained from the equations

$$\frac{1 - x}{1 + x} = \frac{4}{11}; \quad x = \frac{7}{15}.$$

277

The amount of gold held by the agricultural country therefore rises in the ratio 22 : 15, and since it would only have required $\frac{11}{8}$ as much gold as before to maintain its price level unchanged, the average price level must have risen in the ratio $\frac{22}{15} : \frac{11}{8} = \frac{16}{15}$. Thus $p = p'' = \frac{16}{15}$, and consequently $p' = \frac{8}{15}$, so that the industrial country's weighted price level is now

$$\frac{\frac{3}{4} \cdot \frac{16}{15} + \frac{1}{2} \cdot \frac{8}{15}}{\frac{3}{4} + \frac{1}{2}} = \frac{64}{75},$$

and the ratio of the two price levels is obviously 5 : 4.—It is not difficult to see that the agricultural country could achieve exactly the same advantage at the expense of the industrial country by imposing on its own *export goods* an export duty of (approximately) 100 per cent *ad valorem*. (Cf. p. 281 ff. below.) The price of agricultural products would then be (nearly) twice as high in the industrial country as in the agricultural, while the price of industrial goods would be the same in both countries, and, in accordance with our assumption, also equal to the price of the agricultural goods in the agricultural country. Analogous reasoning shows that the price level in the agricultural country would be in the ratio 5 : 8 to the price level in the industrial country. Their relative gold requirements would be in the ratio 11 : 8, and, strangely enough, the industrial country would even here have to *give up* some of its gold to the agricultural country, though only $\frac{3}{19}$ of its holdings.

According to the assumptions we have made, this is the greatest possible gain the agricultural country can obtain from a unilateral imposition of duty. If the duty (whether on exports or imports) were *lower*, the conditions would be nearer to those of free trade, to the advantage of the industrial country and the disadvantage (reduced gain) of the agricultural country. If, on the other hand, the duty were to be raised to over 100 per cent, the industrial country would not be affected since it cannot be forced further than to produce agricultural products itself; but the agricultural country gains less in this case too, since the price of industrial goods relative to that of agricultural products cannot fall lower in the industrial country and must therefore rise in the agricultural country and such a rise is inconsistent with a consumption of $\frac{5}{4}$ agricultural and $1\frac{1}{2}$ industrial products, which requires the price ratio to be 1 : 1 according to our assumptions. The only possible solution is therefore that the industrial country begins to produce *part* of its requirements of agricultural goods, and therefore disposes of a smaller quantity of industrial goods than it would have done, had the duty in the agricultural country been 100 per cent (or if there had been monopoly).

Such a partial transfer of production is actually entirely consistent too with fixed real production costs. A small rise in the price of agricultural products above the equilibrium value induces home production of them, and the price equilibrium is thereby restored; if this production is extended beyond a certain limit, however, the price falls below the equilibrium value, and so on. (The critical limit will actually be between 'better' and 'worse' land—or between better and worse *farmers*.)

If the duty is further increased, the industrial country's production of agricultural goods will also increase, and when the duty approaches its upper limit of 300 per cent, the industrial country will be producing, say, $\frac{1}{4}$ of the amount of agricultural products which it consumed under free trade, and importing $\frac{1}{2}$. Its consumptions will therefore still be $\frac{3}{4}$ of the agricultural products and $\frac{1}{2}$ of the industrial products which it consumed under free trade, and the price ratio of these two types of goods will remain at 2 : 1. The agricultural country now consumes $1\frac{1}{2}$ times as much agricultural products and the same amount of industrial products at a price ratio of (nearly) 1 : 2. It is therefore still making a gain compared with the period of free trade, although less than if the duty had its optimum value of 100 per cent, because the increased consumption of agricultural products does not compensate in subjective value for the diminished consumption of industrial goods. But if the duty exceeds 300 per cent by however little, trade ceases *at once*, and independent production begins in both countries. The industrial country does not lose anything more by this, but the agricultural country not only loses the whole of its additional gain, but also gets into a considerably worse position than it was in under free trade. Of course, there is never such a discontinuity in reality, and it appears here only because we have taken the real production costs as fixed instead of rising, as they would actually be at least in the case of agricultural production, in accordance with the law of diminishing returns. Instead of the sudden deterioration in the position of a country which imposes a unilateral duty, which we have here, when the duty oversteps a certain limit, the deterioration is actually a *gradual* one.

If the industrial country replies to the duty imposed by the agricultural country by imposing a similar duty on its own products, it would in this case be able to improve its position considerably where the duty involved is a 'financial' one. If we call the price of agricultural products in the exporting country p_1, and in the importing country

279

p_2, and retain the symbols p' and p'' for industrial products, then, when duties of (almost) 100 per cent are mutually imposed, we have (approximately) $p_2 = 2 p_1$ and $p'' = 2 p'$, so that

$$p_2 : p' = 4 \cdot p_1 : p'', \text{ or } p'' : p_1 = 4p' : p_2;$$

in other words, the price of agricultural products expressed in terms of industrial products will be four times as high in the industrial country as in the agricultural country, or, what amounts to the same thing, the price of industrial products expressed in terms of agricultural products will be four times as high in the agricultural country as in the industrial country. It now only remains to determine one of these latter ratios so that the supply of and demand for each sort of goods (and therefore of both sorts) are exactly equal to one another. If, for example, in accordance with what we have previously supposed, we suppose that the quantities now exchanged by the two countries is $\frac{7}{8}$ (or possibly less) of the quantities of goods which was formerly exchanged by them, and that $\frac{1}{8}$ less of the foreign goods is now consumed in each country, and $\frac{1}{8}$ more of home products, then this consumption is not inconsistent with the assumption that the marginal utility and price of agricultural products in the agricultural country are in the ratio 1 : 2 to those of industrial goods, the ratio being the converse in the industrial country, 2 : 1.[1] We then have the following relations:

$$p_1 = \tfrac{1}{2} p'' = p' = \tfrac{1}{2}p_2,$$

and all the conditions of the problem are thus fulfilled, since $p_1 = p'$ means that the prices of the exported goods in the respective export countries are equal, so that trade debts and claims exactly equal each other.

It is evident that both countries suffer a small *loss* in this way, since the figures of consumption under free trade show that the part of the consumption satisfied by home products is subjectively worth less than the decline in the consumption of the foreign goods. It is obviously impossible to measure the magnitude of this loss by changes in the price levels. If the free trade price is taken as 1, it is easy to show that

$$p_1 = p' = \tfrac{16}{23}; p_2 = p'' = \tfrac{32}{23}.$$

The average weighted price level is simply 1 in both countries, or exactly the same as it was under free trade. The unweighted price

[1] Of course, these figures are quite arbitrary, and are only chosen for the sake of simplicity. However, they do not imply anything unreasonable, or contra the earlier assumptions, as far as I can see.

level, given by $(p_1 + p'') : 2 = (p_2 + p') : 2$, is 24 : 23 and has there-fore risen a little. There is clearly no transference of gold under these circumstances.

If the duty in both countries is raised to 100 per cent or higher (or if there is some equivalent combination of duties), there will again be a sudden transition to a complete cessation of trade.

Finally, if the agricultural country were the passive one, the industrial country could use a monopolistic regime or customs duties to secure an advantage for itself at the expense of the other, although the advantage would not be so great. In order to force the agricultural country to the limit of cessation of trade, and thus to inflict the greatest possible damage—which, here too, we will take to coincide with the greatest possible gain for the industrial country, although, as pointed out before, this need not necessarily be so—the industrial country would need to impose import or export duties of more than 100 per cent, for example 150 per cent, since, as one can easily verify, each country's consumption, compared with the period of free trade, would then be: in the agricultural country, of agricultural products 1, of industrial $\frac{1}{2}$, with a price ratio of (approximately) 1 : 2, and in the industrial country, of agricultural products 1, of industrial products $1\frac{1}{2}$, with a price ratio of (approximately) $1\frac{1}{4}$: 1 or 5 : 4[1] (which does not seem unreasonable).

For a general treatment of the problem, a more mathematical procedure, by means of geometrical curves or algebraic formulae, is almost unavoidable. These are admittedly merely hypothetical, but do, nevertheless, have certain characteristic properties from which general conclusions may be drawn. As was mentioned earlier, Edgeworth has, in articles in the *Economic Journal* for 1894, given such a treatment, using Marshall's so-called supply-and-demand curves and the so-called indifference curves which are his own invention. His reasoning is very ingenious and instructive, but it seems to me to be unsatisfactory on one main point, which he himself regards as being of the greatest importance. He considers that he has proved the commonly held idea about the 'symmetry' (or rather real identity) of export and import duties to be *incorrect*. According to him, export duties should always lead to a more favourable result for the country imposing them than import duties of the same size; in certain cases, as when the country's demand for the foreign good is 'inelastic' (so that a rise or fall of the price does not lead to a

[1] We have $1\frac{1}{4} : \frac{1}{2} = 2\frac{1}{2} : 1 =$ the ratio between the prices of the agricultural products in the two countries after the imposition of a duty of 150 per cent.

proportional decrease or increase of the demand), their effects may even be opposite: an export duty might be useful to the country in question, whereas an import duty of the same amount might be harmful.

Because of the terseness of the presentation—the whole proof consists of a bare reference to some diagrams—it is not so easy to come to a clear idea of how Edgeworth really thought the matter out. As I understand him, he considers the business of imposing duties as if the government laid claim to a certain amount of the goods *in natura*—for import duty, of those imported; and for export duty of those exported—and later, *after* the exchange with the foreign country, refunded the whole amount of the duty in some form or other, to the inhabitants of the country. However, according to Edgeworth, this latter circumstance has *no* effect on the demand for foreign products, and therefore no effect on the supply of the home product, but only affects the final economic position after the exchange.

It must be admitted that with such premises there may be an important difference between export and import duties. This is particularly evident in an extreme case. Let us assume that the demand for foreign goods is *completely* inelastic, so that (within certain limits) each consumer demands a certain amount of these goods regardless of the price, but has no use whatsoever for a larger amount of them. An import duty imposed by the government appropriating a certain amount of the imported goods would cause everyone to demand *more* of these goods than he needs to satisfy his consumption (equivalent to Edgeworth's 'extension of the ordinates'), and thus to supply more of his own goods than would have been necessary under free trade; when he subsequently receives the amount of the goods previously appropriated by the government, it has *no value* to him (at least, for the current consumption period), and his loss is obvious. If it had been an export duty on the other hand, he would also have been forced to supply more of his own goods than was necessary in order to gain possession of the amount of the foreign goods he needs, but when the duty is subsequently repaid by the government, his position is just the same as it would have been under free trade, and he suffers no loss at all (nor does he make any gain, of course).

But the premiss itself is obviously unreasonable. The consumers can be unaware that a duty will be repaid only when it is imposed for the first time. Afterwards, they will always take the repayment into account, and *adjust* their demand for the foreign goods accordingly. Therefore, the primitive supply-and-demand curve (curve OPE, op. cit., pp. 430 and 432) which Edgeworth uses for his construction is *not* the same as under free trade, a fact which he seems to have disregarded.[1]

The correct theoretical procedure seems to be to suppose the import and export duties to be paid in the same sort of goods, and preferably in the products of the country itself. They are actually paid in *money*, but each of the subjects who pays the money must have disposed of some of his *own* goods to obtain it in the first place. Under these conditions, the imposition of an import duty or an export duty is theoretically one and the same thing, and has the same effect on both the relative prices and the real economic position of the country. It is only the money prices which are different: an import duty raises the country's average price level compared with the level abroad, and an export duty lowers it; and (as a rule) this is made possible in the former case by an intake of gold, which takes place quite automatically, and in the latter case by export of gold or by equivalent credit operations.

With these reservations, Edgeworth's curves, duly modified, provide the simplest way of solving the problem in question. The general result is that a duty imposed unilaterally, either on exports or imports, must always rebound to the advantage of the country imposing it, if it is not *too* high—in much the same way as a buying or selling cartel—whereas bilateral duties are usually to the disadvantage of *both* countries.

In the same way, it is possible to maintain that a unilateral duty is in all circumstances to the disadvantage of the *other* country. According to Edgeworth's reasoning, an import duty may, on the contrary,

---

[1] It was not until after the present article had already been set up for printing that I found Edgeworth had subsequently withdrawn his statement about the lack of symmetry between export and import duties (*Economic Journal*, 1897, p. 397, and elsewhere. Cf. Bastable, *The Theory of International Trade*, 4th ed., p. 116, note.) Unfortunately, however, this withdrawal has not taken the form of a *reconstruction* of the figures upon which he based his statement, and can scarcely be said to give enough points for such a reconstruction. It is therefore impossible to deny that there is still a suspicious loophole in his theory regarding one important point. So my criticism of his original argument seems still to have some significance.

According to his present explanation, it seems, moreover, that he had supposed that the state did not repay the amount of the duty, but *consumed* it directly. But, in the first place, this consumption must be supposed to be of the *same character* in both cases (export and import duty), otherwise it is not possible to compare them, and, in the second place, the question of duty has thus been combined with a question of increased taxation so that the free trade system and the system with tariffs are no longer comparable. Therefore, the treatment of the problem which I have advanced in this article seems to be the simplest and most natural as a first approximation.

in certain cases be to the advantage of the country whose exports are thereby hindered, which seems somewhat difficult to believe, even *a priori*.[1] As is well known, Mill expressed the same opinion[2] about an export duty, which he said could sometimes even lead to a foreign country obtaining the exported goods *cheaper* than it would otherwise have done, so that it gains thereby. But Mill's reasoning is evidently incorrect. He assumes something which seems to be quite correct, namely that an export duty will, as a rule, cause the price of the goods involved to fall in the country of *export*, while at the same time a certain quantity of gold is transferred to the country of import, causing the price of its goods to rise. If the demand in the former country for the foreign goods is *extremely inelastic*, then, says Mill, it might happen that it would have to lower the price of its own goods to such an extent that, even with the duty added, they would cost less than they did before the duty was imposed. If the goods were exchanged in more or less the same quantities as previously, the country's exports would no longer suffice to pay for its imports, and the price of the exported goods would consequently fall further, so that the foreign country would actually obtain them at a lower price than under free trade. The conclusion drawn from this peculiar syllogism is quite correct in the formal sense, but one of the premises is incorrect, because the dutiable goods *can* never fall lower in price in the foreign country than to the level of its own goods, as is the case under free trade, and when the price of these goods has risen because of the importation of gold, the price abroad of the goods subject to the export duty must have risen *by an equal amount*, so that the value of exports and the value of imports correspond exactly. If the example is constructed in accordance with our assumptions above, so that both countries export half of their production under free trade, and the export duty is supposed to be 100 per cent of the value of the goods, then it is not difficult to see that the country which imposes the export duty must pay $\frac{1}{7}$ of its gold to the other country, and prices in the latter country would then become $\frac{8}{7}$ for both the imported goods and the home-produced ones, as compared with the period of free

---

[1] An altogether different matter is when the hindrance to trade is due to a third power; for example, a transit duty levied in kind may sometimes be to the advantage of the country whose *export* is affected, in the same way as the destruction of surplus supplies of goods may be to the advantage of the sellers. As far as I can see, Edgeworth's reasoning is fully appropriate to this case, and it could also be applied with success to the problem of transport costs, if the simplest case is taken to be that where the transport costs are paid to a third power, which takes them in kind and uses the goods thus obtained in its own country.

[2] *Principles*, Bk V, Ch. IV, § 6.

trade; in the former country the price of the imported goods, free of duty, is likewise $\frac{8}{7}$, but for the goods liable to the export duty, only $\frac{4}{7}$. It is easy to see that the mutual claims and debts in the two countries now cancel one another. The fact that consumption in the country levying the duty can remain the same as it was under free trade, although the relative price of the imported goods has risen to twice what it was before, depends, of course, on the complete inelasticity of the country's demand for these goods in accordance with Mill's supposition.[1]

Thus, duties which are too high, even if they are unilaterally imposed, cause a loss for each country involved and, hence, for them both together. But this latter *need* not be the case with moderate duties. It *may* happen that the gain for one country, as judged by a disinterested third party, is greater than the loss to the other, so that both of them taken together must be considered to have made a net gain. We have assumed that both countries always produced the same quantities of their respective goods, so, taking everything as a whole, it is only a question of the best possible *distribution* of the products, as long as neither country is forced into production of the other's goods. In our original example, this distribution would be that of free trade, since both countries, which were assumed to be equal in size, would then halve their resources. But our assumptions were, as has been said, only some among many possible ones. It is naturally quite possible that pricing under free trade could be such that one country would be in a much more favourable position with regard to consumption, and might conceivably come to consume more of both agricultural products and industrial goods than the other country. It would then be possible for this other country to modify this distribution to its own advantage by imposing a suitable duty, and in this way something which is better socially for both countries might be achieved, as Edgeworth has pointed out. All this is based upon the assumption that the country which originally had the advantage is sufficiently altruistic to let the matter rest here, and does not impose any duty of its own in reply!

To conclude, just a few words about a complication which Mill, as is well known, completely misunderstood, and which even Edgeworth touches only cautiously; namely, the possible existence of *multiple* states of equilibrium. We have assumed throughout, hitherto, that in each situation only one position of equilibrium is possible, about

[1] The consequences would be the same in the case of duty repayment of the sort mentioned above.

which the actual market price oscillates, and which is therefore called *stable*. That, however, is a simplification which need not necessarily apply to reality. A short example may illustrate this. We will consider two countries, which want one another's staple products, wheat and butter, say, in such quantities and at such prices that the balance of trade between them is always even. At the same time, this demand is, in both countries, so strong—or, more precisely, so inelastic—that if the price of butter rises, for example, by 10 per cent relative to wheat, the demand for butter in the wheat country immediately falls by a little less than 5 per cent, say $\frac{3}{61}$; and if the price of wheat relative to butter rises by 10 per cent, the demand for it in the butter country immediately falls by a similar amount, $\frac{3}{61}$.[1] If the demand curves (in the ordinary sense) are taken to be linear for the sake of simplicity (so that the Marshall curves are parabolas), it is possible to give a rigorous proof that the original situation does not imply a real equilibrium of prices, but only a temporary equality between supply and demand. If this equality is disturbed by even a very small change, for example, an insignificant rise in the price of butter, the price of butter will *not* return of its own accord, but will continue to *rise* until the market attains equilibrium with the price of butter (relative to wheat) 20 per cent above the initial value. In the same way, a small rise in the price of wheat would set the price rising until the market attains equilibrium with the price of wheat (relative to butter) 20 per cent above the initial value. *Both* these positions of equilibrium are stable and are therefore not changed by temporary disturbances, but there is a difference between them of no less than 44 per cent $(\frac{6}{5} \cdot \frac{6}{5} - 1)$.[2]

It is true that we are assuming the supplies from both sides to be of given sizes for the consumption period in question, and that they cannot be increased by new production; but this is a good approximation for such articles as grain or the feeding-stuffs necessary for butter production, if, for instance, it is a question of the period of time until the next harvest. But even when the supply can be increased by new production, it is ultimately productive services (here labour and the utilisation of capital, since the use of the land is considered to be free) which are exchanged for one another on both sides, and the supply of these does not change much during a short period.

[1] It is well to notice that these two assumptions are quite independent of one another, since each country's demand for the foreign commodity at a given price depends exclusively on the amount of its own commodity which it has available.

[2] Had the decline in demand been still less, 4 per cent, say, when the price rose by 10 per cent, stable equilibrium would first have occurred when the price of butter (relative to wheat) had risen to *twice* its initial value—or when it had fallen to *half*.

Even in the case of our original example, which was arbitrarily chosen to some extent, closer examination reveals that the corresponding curves for supply and demand can only be drawn to intersect in a single point with comparative difficulty, if they are to fulfil the conditions imposed upon them. The most natural arrangement involves three intersections, one on either side of the equilibrium position assumed to begin with, so that this position cannot be stable in any case. In other words, in spite of the fact that, under free trade, halving of the resources was consistent with equality between supply and demand on both sides, this could not persist. Instead, real equilibrium could occur only when *either* the agricultural country *or* the industrial country consumed *more* than half of the supplies of both countries.

It is evident that the existence of two (or more) equally possible stable positions of equilibrium must create considerable opportunities for the formation of rings of buyers and sellers, and, in the field of international trade, for creating, through tariff manipulation, market conditions which may, for a time at least, be greatly to the advantage of a particular country. It is therefore a great pity that this phenomenon has hardly received any attention from economists. Even Walras, who was the first to enquire into the matter from a theoretical point of view, was of the opinion that the matter was really of no great practical importance, but his argument on this point does not seem very convincing to me.

If, after reading this perhaps over-long article, some practical person asks what is the good of such a 'game' with hypothetical figures, then one might reply by asking what is the good of any speculations about customs duties and their effects, as long as there is not sufficient clarity about the simplest elements of the subject. For my part, I am by no means sure that I have mastered even these properly, and I shall be glad to hear any criticism of the opinions put forward here.

INDEX

289